The Speeches of Thucydides

With a General Introduction
and Introductions for the Main
Speeches and the Military Harangues

by
H. F. Harding

Coronado Press   1973

Library of Congress Catalog Card Number: 73-85648
Standard Book Number: 87291–060–1

Published by
Coronado Press
Box 3232
Lawrence, Kansas 66044

Manufactured in the USA

Preface

1. Are intellectuals good judges of practical affairs? (III 37)
2. Does leniency or severity pay best in politics? (III 45)
3. When is war justified? (II 61)
4. Is a peace by compromise or a fight to a finish best? (IV 17)
5. Does thought impair a man's power of acting? (II 39)
6. Can citizens be trusted to serve their country without compulsion? (VI 39)
7. Do the masses or the propertied classes make better rulers? (V 89)
8. What place have religion and justice in politics? (V 105)

A recent editor of *The History of the Peloponnesian War* reminds us that these are a few of the questions which Thucydides raises in the famous speeches of his history. (The citations in parentheses provide his answers.) He discusses human nature in politics, a topic as vital in a Presidential election as it was in the Age of Pericles. Thucydides made his book "a possession forever," not just a Book of the Month because he understood far better than most men the power of the spoken word. This is why the forty-odd speeches of the *History* deserve today the careful study of speakers, students of politics and public affairs, and especially of citizens with the right to vote.

Professor J. H. Finley, Jr. in his Harry Camp lectures at Stanford said "in tracing the decisions of the war as a guide to future statesmen, . . . [Thucydides] tacitly assumes that correct judgement produces success; affairs to him are analyzable, and everything hinges on the right use of intelligence" (*Four Stages of Greek Thought,* p. 63). Is not this what the American voter hopes is true and the American political scientist believes today?

Thucydides offers us much nourishment if we would only read and re-read his speeches. This is why I have been impelled to bring out this edition based on the Crawley translation. The idea was suggested to me by Dean Acheson several years ago and I have been grateful to him ever since. For each speech I have tried to supply details which will enable the general reader to understand the setting and the effect the speech produced. I have purposely avoided an analysis of the rhetorical appeals the speakers use because I want the student to discover them for himself. His best preparation for this task is a thorough study of *The Rhetoric of Aristotle* (edited by Lane Cooper, Appleton-Century-Crofts, New York, 1932), or *A Synoptic History of Classical Rhetoric* (edited by James J. Murphy, Random House, New York, 1972).

Besides the separate Speech introductions I have written a General Introduction, an Introduction for the Military Harangues, and Some Comments on the Three Speeches by Pericles. The Appendix contains the famous essay by Sir Richard C. Jebb on "The Speeches of Thucydides," now long out of print, a chapter on the speeches from John H. Finley's *Thucydides*, and A Chronology of Main Events of the Peloponnesian War. These are intended to increase an understanding of the speeches. The reader should, of course, not neglect what Thucydides says in the *History* before and after each speech.

The List of References is not a scholar's bibliography. It is meant to assist the college student and the general reader to discover that Thucydides was himself, as H.D.F. Kitto suggests, "an enquirer," a man patiently examining facts, motives, causes and effects.

I express my gratitude to the administrators of the Excellence Fund of The University of Texas at El Paso for enabling me to carry out the research for this book.

H. F. Harding

Contents

Preface (v-vi)

Part One
The History of the Peloponnesian War

Part Two
Military Harangues

The Speeches of Thucydides

Introduction

Edith Hamilton tells us that Thucydides has composed a treatise on War, its causes and its effects. The *History* has also been called a manual for statesmen and those to whom weighty decisions are intrusted. Certainly it is the best account of the Age of Pericles (429-416 B.C.) written by a scholarly observer. For content, literary style, and historical method we have a book that has been studied for centuries and today captures a reader's attention because its incidents are so startlingly modern and applicable. Its lessons are timeless. Discovering the parallels delights the reader.

For students of writing and speaking Thucydides gives a wealth of inferred precepts and striking examples. If we learn best by models there is something in the *History* for scholars of all ages. Introductions and Conclusions, Narrations, Arguments, Ethical, Logical, and Emotional Appeals, Epigrams, Antitheses, Figures of Speech, Enthymemes and Examples, Statements and Proofs. These are but a few of the rhetorical concepts to examine.

This is why there is a need for removing the speeches from the surrounding texts and studying them one by one. In Book I, for example, the eight speeches that are paired need to be examined in relation to each other. The three speeches of Pericles (in Bks. I and II) need to be compared. The presentations of the Spartans should be set against those of the Athenians. The military harangues which are remarks of commanders to troops before going into battle may profitably be examined for the differences in their methods.

In short, the *History* offers us some 42 examples, as Jebb identifies them, of a speech-writer's art. They were all written by Thucydides but he wrote either by reproducing what he heard, or on the basis of what hearers reported to him, or as in the majority of cases, on the basis of what the speaker should have said under the circumstances. And here is where the talent of Thucydides, as rhetorician and logographer, comes into play. Herodotus, to be sure, had used speeches in his *History* but he used them as a story-teller would. Thucydides, the dramatist as well as historian, used his speeches to let the *History* speak for itself. No one since has used speeches so effectively.

What prospect does such a collection offer present-day students? First, there is the opportunity to discover the structure of each speaker's remarks. Jebb tells us that Thucydides was using the divisions of Sicilian rhetoric. Is this true? The Attic style had not been fully perfected when Thucydides wrote his speeches. What then are the features of his *style*? A good reader can discover some features used over and over and still others only sparingly. Again, the alert student will find the speeches of the *History* a gold mine for principles of *inventio* and *dispositio.* If rhetoric is the discovery (not necessarily the use) of the available means of persuasion (Aristotle, *Rhetoric* 1355^b 35), we have access to the mind of a gifted writer re-creating and re-arranging ideas that presumably have aroused Greeks, Spartans, and Sicilians, to new beliefs and new courses of action in a tragic war. Before our eyes we see a great civilization gradually brought to ruin by the persuasion of the spoken word. We see on nearly every page the raw effects that passions produce when linked with greed and ambition.

A student of rhetorical criticism can discover in Thucydides the principles of human behavior that prevailed in his day and probably still prevail. Almost every important concept of Aristotle's *Rhetoric* is exemplified somewhere in the speeches of the *History.* This is not to say that the speeches are without fault. They have bad points as well as good. But, for teaching purposes their great merit rests in the fact that all were reproduced or written by one man who was consciously pursuing what seemed to him to be the correct method.

The best known single specimen of Thucydides' *History* is the Funeral Oration attributed to Pericles. We have otherwise remaining only fragments supposedly written by Pericles. The chances are good that Thucydides heard the Funeral Oration and actually reproduced in large part what Pericles spoke.

How do the other speakers in the *History* speak? We can assume that Thucydides makes his characters speak in the ways in which he was himself trained or influenced and that he is always trying to have them say what is most appropriate for the occasion. What they ought to have said implies "what was called for" as Finley translates τὰ δέοντα and this relates to the rhetorical sense of the selection of the best lines of argument available — those fitting to the occasion, the speaker's personality, and the qualifications of the audience.

Thucydides does all this in several ways. He lets his reader perform the same function the member of the Greek Ecclesia had to perform — that is to make a selection, then a judgement and a decision, from the various arguments presented to him.

Protagoras was the first to teach the value of antithesis — of contrasting arguments or points of view. Thucydides exemplifies this method in his paired speeches; and also within paragraphs — in the same sentence or in the following sentence; and again in individual words or concepts as in the expressions *the word* and *the deed*.

There are three main types of argument that Thucydides finds useful in exemplifying his contrasts of thought. They are the argument from likelihood, Εἰκός; that from expedience, τὸ συμφέρον, and finally the most subtle and pervasive of all arguments — that from human nature, φύσις.

We also find the speakers in the *History* referring to the effect of the laws of nature.

It is obvious that an older, thinking person would readily understand the whys and why-nots of these arguments. They were based on what hearers knew — from innate common sense, from the experience of their own lives, from what they had observed in other human beings and in nature itself. All these methods are classified and explained in detail in

Aristotle's *Rhetoric* — but they had been understood and used for years by Gorgias and Antiphon and others.

The speeches of Thucydides thus provide the modern student with models of how the leaders of the Age of Pericles thought and spoke. They characteristically reveal what the "speaker" (i.e. Thucydides) believed was necessary to say to win over his audience. As Professor Finley so well states: "They are great partly because a keen observer trained himself to distill the inner meaning from the events of his age. But they are great also because they reflect the first ambitious flowering of rhetoric in a great period" (*Thucydides*, p. 65).

Much has been said about the influence of Thucydides upon later speakers and writers. Demosthenes, according to Lucian (*adv. Indoct* 102), copied out the *History* eight times. Quintilian (10.1.73) praised Thucydides in a famous line: *Densus et brevis et semper instans sibi Thucydides.* Thucydides is compact in texture, terse and ever eager to press forward.

Macaulay, John Stuart Mill, and the Earl of Chatham all gave the book high endorsements. A century ago the British statesman, Sir George Cornewall Lewis (1806-1863) wrote in *A Treatise on the Methods of Observation and Reasoning in Politics* (1852): "For close, cogent, and appropriate reasoning on political questions, the speeches of Thucydides have never been surpassed; and indeed they may be considered as having reached the highest excellence of which the human mind is capable in that department."

George Kennedy calls the last sentence of Thucydides Book II, ch. 42 "one of the most emotional and perhaps the finest sentence in Greek prose" (*The Art of Persuasion in Greece*, London, 1963, p. 156). Some idea of the difficulty of translating these forty Greek words into English can be gained by scanning the seven different translations given below. Only a Greek scholar can determine which version most accurately reproduces what Thucydides intended to mean. On the other hand it is not too difficult to decide which translation in English is most pleasing to the ear, which is most poetical in language, and which is most turgid and ordinary in diction. Multiply the problems of this one sentence in Greek many thousand times and you can understand the enormous difficulty of rendering the *History* into modern English.

From a literary point of view it is even more difficult to try to decide the stylistic and rhetorical devices that the original writer is using. Without a knowledge of fifth-century Greek (or Thracian, as some scholars insist) few readers can be sure of the subtleties of the text.

Seven translations of the last sentence of II 42.4:

1. Alfred Zimmern:

So their memory has escaped the reproaches of men's lips, but they bore instead on their bodies the marks of men's hands, and in a moment of time, at the climax of their lives, were rapt away from a world filled, for their dying eyes, not with terror but with glory.

Oxford University Press edition (World's Classics) ed. by Sir R.W. Livingstone, Oxford, 1951, p. 115. Also originally in *The Greek Commonwealth* by Alfred Zimmern, Oxford University Press, 5th ed. revised, Oxford, 1961, pp. 206-207.

2. Charles Forster Smith:

And then when the moment of combat came, thinking it better to defend themselves and suffer death rather than to yield and save their lives, they fled, indeed from the shameful word of dishonour, but with life and limb, stood stoutly to their task, and in the brief instant ordained by fate, at the crowning moment not of fear but of glory, they passed away.

Translation of *Thucydides* in Loeb Library Series, 4 vols., London, 1956 I 335.

3. Benjamin Jowett:

And when the moment came they were minded to resist and suffer rather than to fly and save their lives; they ran away from the word dishonor, but on the battlefield their feet stood fast, and in an instant, at the height of their fortune, they passed away from the scene, not of their fear, but of their glory.

Thucydides, *The Peloponnesian War*, with introductory essays by Hanson Baldwin and Moses Hadas, Bantam Books, Inc., New York, 1965, p. 119.

4. Rex Warner:

As for success or failure, they left that in the doubtful hands of Hope, and when the reality of battle was before their faces, they put their trust in their own selves. In the fighting they thought it more honorable to stand their ground and suffer death than to give in and save their lives. So they fled from the reproaches of men, abiding with life and limb the brunt of battle; and, in a small moment of time, the climax of their lives, a culmination of glory, not of fear, were swept away from us.

Thucydides: *History of the Peloponnesian War*, translated with an introduction by Rex Warner, Penguin Books, Baltimore, 1965, pp. 120-121.

5. Richard Crawley:

Thus choosing to die resisting rather than to live submitting, they fled only from dishonor, but met danger face to face, and after one brief moment, while at the summit of their fortune, escaped not from their fear, but from their glory.

The Complete Writings of Thucydides, with an introduction by John H. Finley, Jr., The Modern Library, New York, 1951, p. 107.

6. A. R. Burn:

So in the shock of battle, choosing to die rather than to save themselves by hanging back, they feared dishonour and not the physical danger, and in a moment, at the very culmination of glory, rather than of terror, passed away.

Pericles and Athens, by A.R. Burn, Collier Books, New York, 1962, p.160.

7. E. C. Marchant:

What they fled from was disgrace; but on the field they stood firm at their posts, till, in an instant, at a moment ordained by Providence, at the crisis, not of their fear, but of their glory, they passed away.

Thucydides Book II, ed. by E.C. Marchant, Macmillan & Co., London, 1961, p. 254.

Part One

The History of the Peloponnesian War

Corcyrean Envoys to the Athenian Ecclesia
Book I 32-36
433 B.C.

The *History of the Peloponnesian War* has been described as the first great analysis of power. It deals with a struggle of 27 years' length. Thucydides keeps to a strict chronology of summers and winters because the fighting took place for five months in the spring and summer and the planning and evaluating of strategy took place in the fall and winter. As Professor Finley explains the first purpose of Thucydides "is to elucidate the motives, policies, decisions, and acts of leadership which dictated the course of the war, since obviously only knowledge of these could give posterity the instruction he feels history could give."[1]

We get a revealing glimpse of the historian's method of probing the "motives, policies, decisions" and acts of the leaders early in Book I. Here we find at chs. 32-36 the first of four sets of speeches designed to reveal the causes of the war. The best explanation, Thucydides insists, was the sudden rise to power of Athens. This caused the Spartans to be afraid of Athens. Modern historians, however, attribute the real cause to the economic rivalry of Athens and Corinth.

This rivalry is portrayed first by the arguments of the Corcyrean envoys and then by those of the Corinthian envoys to the Athenian Ecclesia.

We cannot neglect the arithmetic implied in the arguments of the first two speeches. Corinth spent the years 435-433 B.C. in building a fleet of 150 ships. Corcyra's fleet was smaller — only 120 ships. This is why Corcyra was ready to abandon her habitual neutrality and request admission to the Confederacy of Athens. It was simply a case of a smaller boy seeking the protection of an older, stronger boy before a fight began.

---

1. *Thucydides,* Random House edition, Introduction by John H. Finley, Jr., p. x.

"Wealthy Corinth," to use Homer's phrase, founded three colonies — Potidaea, Corcyra (Corfu), and Syracuse. All three played large roles in the Peloponnesian War. Their positions in the conflict are presented by their envoys largely by rhetorical probabilities — often turning on the practical question "What do we have to do to survive and to win?" rather than on the idealistic question "What is the just and honorable course to take?"

In the speech by the Corcyrean envoys (at I 33) the argument depends on τὸ συμφέρον, the argument from expedience and also from the fact that natural impulses are inevitable. In the case of the Corinthian speakers (I 40-41) they rely on τὸ δίκαιον, the argument from the just. Which kind of argument won out? How was the first debate decided? The final sentences of the Corcyrean speakers convinced the Athenians. They believed that the possibility of a merger of the Corinthian and Corcyrean fleets was a dangerous probability unless quick action was taken. And so the Athenians made a defensive alliance with the Corcyreans because they thought that war with Sparta was inevitable.

Since Thucydides was in Athens at the time of the Corcyrean-Corinthian debate the chances are good that he actually heard the speakers and the debate that followed in the Ecclesia.

§

[32]. Athenians! when a people that have not rendered any important service or support to their neighbours in times past, for which they might claim to be repaid, appear before them as we now appear before you to solicit their assistance, they may fairly be required to satisfy certain preliminary conditions. They should show, first, that it is expedient or at least safe to grant their request; next, that they will retain a lasting sense of the kindness. But if they cannot clearly establish any of these points, they must not be annoyed if they meet with a rebuff. Now the Corcyraeans believe that with their petition for assistance they can also give you a satisfactory answer on these points,

and they have therefore despatched us hither. It has so happened that our policy as regards you, with respect to this request, turns out to be inconsistent, and as regards our interests, to be at the present crisis inexpedient. We say inconsistent, because a power which has never in the whole of her past history been willing to ally herself with any of her neighbours, is now found asking them to ally themselves with her. And we say inexpedient, because in our present war with Corinth it has left us in a position of entire isolation, and what once seemed the wise precaution of refusing to involve ourselves in alliances with other powers, lest we should also involve ourselves in risks of their choosing, has now proved to be folly and weakness. It is true that in the late naval engagement we drove back the Corinthians from our shores single-handed. But they have now got together a still larger armament from Peloponnese and the rest of Hellas; and we, seeing our utter inability to cope with them without foreign aid, and the magnitude of the danger which subjection to them implies, find it necessary to ask help from you and from every other power. And we hope to be excused if we forswear our old principle of complete political isolation, a principle which was not adopted with any sinister intention, but was rather the consequence of an error in judgment.

[33]. Now there are many reasons why in the event of your compliance you will congratulate yourselves on this request having been made to you. First, because your assistance will be rendered to a power which, herself inoffensive, is a victim to the injustice of others. Secondly, because all that we most value is at stake in the present contest, and your welcome of us under these circumstances will be a proof of good will which will ever keep alive the gratitude you will lay up in our hearts. Thirdly, yourselves excepted, we are the greatest naval power in Hellas. Moreover, can you conceive a stroke of good fortune more rare in itself, or more disheartening to your enemies, than that the power whose adhesion you would have valued above much material and moral strength, should present herself self-invited, should deliver herself into your hands without danger and without expense, and should lastly put you in the way of gaining a high character in the eyes of the world, the gratitude of those whom you shall assist, and a great accession of strength for yourselves? You may search all history without finding many instances of a people gaining all these advantages at once, or many instances of a power that comes in quest of assistance being in a position to give to the people whose alliance she solicits as much safety and honour as she will receive. But it will be urged that it is only in the

case of a war that we shall be found useful. To this we answer that if any of you imagine that that war is far off, he is grievously mistaken, and is blind to the fact that Lacedaemon regards you with jealousy and desires war, and that Corinth is powerful there, — the same, remember, that is your enemy, and is even now trying to subdue us as a preliminary to attacking you. And this she does to prevent our becoming united by a common enmity, and her having us both on her hands, and also to insure getting the start of you in one of two ways, either by crippling our power or by making its strength her own. Now it is our policy to be beforehand with her — that is, for Corcyra to make an offer of alliance and for you to accept it; in fact, we ought to form plans against her instead of waiting to defeat the plans she forms against us.

[34]. If she asserts that for you to receive a colony of hers into alliance is not right, let her know that every colony that is well treated honours its parent state, but becomes estranged from it by injustice. For colonists are not sent forth on the understanding that they are to be the slaves of those that remain behind, but that they are to be their equals. And that Corinth was injuring us is clear. Invited to refer the dispute about Epidamnus to arbitration, they chose to prosecute their complaints by war rather than by a fair trial. And let their conduct towards us who are their kindred be a warning to you not to be misled by their deceit, nor to yield to their direct requests; concessions to adversaries only end in self-reproach, and the more strictly they are avoided the greater will be the chance of security.

[35]. If it be urged that your reception of us will be a breach of the treaty existing between you and Lacedaemon, the answer is that we are a neutral state, and that one of the express provisions of that treaty is that it shall be competent for any Hellenic state that is neutral to join whichever side it pleases. And it is intolerable for Corinth to be allowed to obtain men for her navy not only from her allies, but also from the rest of Hellas, no small number being furnished by your own subjects; while we are to be excluded both from the alliance left open to us by treaty, and from any assistance that we might get from other quarters, and you are to be accused of political immorality if you comply with our request. On the other hand, we shall have much greater cause to complain of you, if you do not comply with it; if we, who are in peril, and are no enemies of yours, meet with a repulse at your hands, while Corinth, who is the aggressor and your enemy, not only meets with no hindrance from you, but is even allowed to draw material for war from your dependencies. This ought not to be, but you should either forbid

her enlisting men in your dominions, or you should lend us too what help you may think advisable. But your real policy is to afford us avowed countenance and support. The advantages of this course, as we premised in the beginning of our speech, are many. We mention one that is perhaps the chief. Could there be a clearer guarantee of our good faith than is offered by the fact that the power which is at enmity with you, is also at enmity with us, and that that power is fully able to punish defection. And there is a wide difference between declining the alliance of an inland and of a maritime power. For your first endeavour should be to prevent, if possible, the existence of any naval power except your own; failing this, to secure the friendship of the strongest that does exist.

[36]. And if any of you believe that what we urge is expedient, but fear to act upon this belief, lest it should lead to a breach of the treaty, you must remember that on the one hand, whatever your fears, your strength will be formidable to your antagonists; on the other, whatever the confidence you derive from refusing to receive us, your weakness will have no terrors for a strong enemy. You must also remember that your decision is for Athens no less than for Corcyra, and that you are not making the best provision for her interests, if at a time when you are anxiously scanning the horizon that you may be in readiness for the breaking out of the war which is all but upon you, you hesitate to attach to your side a place whose adhesion or estrangement is alike pregnant with the most vital consequences. For it lies conveniently for the coast-navigation in the direction of Italy and Sicily, being able to bar the passage of naval reinforcements from thence to Peloponnese, and from Peloponnese thither; and it is in other respects a most desirable station. To sum up as shortly as possible, embracing both general and particular considerations, let this show you the folly of sacrificing us. Remember that there are but three considerable naval powers in Hellas, Athens, Corcyra, and Corinth, and that if you allow two of these three to become one, and Corinth to secure us for herself, you will have to hold the sea against the united fleets of Corcyra and Peloponnese. But if you receive us, you will have our ships to reinforce you in the struggle.

§

Corinthian Envoys to the Athenian Ecclesia
Book I 37-43
433 B.C.

Here the speakers make some brief opening remarks and then proceed to attack and rebut the opposing arguments in some detail.

Corinth also had advantages as an ally if Athens went to war with Sparta. The Isthmus of Corinth was about 3½ miles across at its narrow part. The Corinthians, at the base of the isthmus, controlled the land route between Central Greece and the Peloponnese. It was the chief means of access from the Ionian Sea to the Aegean Sea. In Book VIII, ch. 7 we read about the ships of the Lacedaemonians being dragged across the land at the neck so as to avoid the long trip around the Peloponnese.

Spartan fear of Athens may have been the cause of the war, as Thucydides says. But by the historian's own account it was a reluctant Sparta that was finally pushed into the war by Corinth, rich and luxurious Corinth, the mother city of Corcyra.

The Corinthians argued on the side of justice, of their past good relations with Athens, while their colony argued on the side of expediency. Here in their arguments we have the first hint of the baser motives of the Athenians — they responded not to the reminder of past friendship with the Corinthians — who eight years before could easily have attacked Athens during the Samian revolt — but to the prospect of saving their skins with the naval force, the 120 ships and the good sailors of Corcyra. It was a clear case of doing what seemed best for winning against Sparta. This attitude is repeated and confirmed in Book III, ch. 82 where Thucydides generalizes about man's inhumanity under stress: "In peace and prosperity states and individuals have better sentiments, because they do not find themselves suddenly confronted with imperious necessities; but war takes away from the easy supply of daily wants, and so proves a rough master that brings most men's characters to a level with their fortunes." It soon came about that the Ecclesia voted to send ten ships to help Corcyra. The naval battle of Sybota followed. Just as the Corinthian ships had reformed, their commander spotted twenty more Athenian ships. He assumed it was the advance element of a larger force and he again ordered a withdrawal. The account by Thucydides of the largest sea-fight of Hellenes against Hellenes is thrilling to read (I 47-54). Each side claimed a victory. But it was not decisive at all and simply added to the rage the Corinthians had generated against their former ally. With this fight the war began in earnest. (Read I 49.1-3)

The first two speeches and the events that followed foreshadowed the contrast Thucydides repeatedly uses between words and deeds. In fact, this antithesis becomes a major feature of the *History* — one we learn to expect and reflect upon. We, the readers, become the judges of men's motives and their conduct. We study human nature at its worst. We sense that the best of human nature has been cast aside. We begin to be suspicious of the speakers, even those from that most prosperous and cultivated of city-states, Athens of the age of Pericles.

§

[37]. These Corcyraeans in the speech we have just heard do not confine themselves to the question of their reception into your alliance. They also talk of our being guilty of injustice, and their being the victims of an unjustifiable war. It becomes necessary for us to touch upon both these points before we proceed to the rest of what we have to say, that you may have a more correct idea of the grounds of our claim, and have good cause to reject their petition. According to them, their old policy of refusing all offers of alliance was a policy of moderation. It was in fact adopted for bad ends, not for good; indeed their conduct is such as to make them by no means desirous of having allies present to witness it, or of having the shame of asking their

concurrence. Besides, their geographical situation makes them independent of others, and consequently the decision in cases where they injure any lies not with judges appointed by mutual agreement, but with themselves, because while they seldom make voyages to their neighbours, they are constantly being visited by foreign vessels which are compelled to put in to Corcyra. In short, the object that they propose to themselves in their specious policy of complete isolation, is not to avoid sharing in the crimes of others, but to secure a monopoly of crime to themselves, — the license of outrage wherever they can compel, of fraud wherever they can elude, and the enjoyment of their gains without shame. And yet if they were the honest men they pretend to be, the less hold that others had upon them, the stronger would be the light in which they might have put their honesty by giving and taking what was just.

[38]. But such has not been their conduct either towards others or towards us. The attitude of our colony towards us has always been one of estrangement, and is now one of hostility; for, say they, "We were not sent out to be ill-treated." We rejoin that we did not found the colony to be insulted by them, but to be their head, and to be regarded with a proper respect. At any rate, our other colonies honour us, and we are very much beloved by our colonists; and clearly, if the majority are satisfied with us, these can have no good reason for a dissatisfaction in which they stand alone, and we are not acting improperly in making war against them, nor are we making war against them without having received signal provocation. Besides, if we were in the wrong, it would be honourable in them to give way to our wishes, and disgraceful for us to trample on their moderation; but in the pride and license of wealth they have sinned again and again against us, and never more deeply than when Epidamnus, our dependency, which they took no steps to claim in its distress, upon our coming to relieve it, was by them seized, and is now held by force of arms.

[39]. As to their allegation that they wished the question to be first submitted to arbitration, it is obvious that a challenge coming from the party who is safe in a commanding position, cannot gain the credit due only to him who, before appealing to arms, in deeds as well as words, places himself on a level with his adversary. In their case, it was not before they laid siege to the place, but after they at length understood that we should not tamely suffer it, that they thought of the specious word arbitration. And not satisfied with their own misconduct there, they appear here now requiring you to join with them not in alliance,

but in crime, and to receive them in spite of their being at enmity with us. But it was when they stood firmest, that they should have made overtures to you, and not at a time when we have been wronged, and they are in peril; nor yet at a time when you will be admitting to a share in your protection those who never admitted you to a share of their power, and will be incurring an equal amount of blame from us with those in whose offences you had no hand. No, they should have shared their power with you before they asked you to share your fortunes with them.

[40]. So then the reality of the grievances we come to complain of and the violence and rapacity of our opponents have both been proved. But that you cannot equitably receive them, this you have still to learn. It may be true that one of the provisions of the treaty is that it shall be competent for any state, whose name was not down on the list, to join whichever side it pleases. But this agreement is not meant for those whose object in joining is the injury of other powers, but for those whose need of support does not arise from the fact of defection, and whose adhesion will not bring to the power that is mad enough to receive them war instead of peace; which will be the case with you, if you refuse to listen to us. For you cannot become their auxiliary and remain our friend; if you join in their attack, you must share the punishment which the defenders inflict on them. And yet you have the best possible right to be neutral, or failing this, you should on the contrary join us against them. Corinth is at least in treaty with you; with Corcyra you were never even in truce. But do not lay down the principle that defection is to be patronised. Did we on the defection of the Samians record our vote against you, when the rest of the Peloponnesian powers were equally divided on the question whether they should assist them? No, we told them to their face that every power has a right to punish its own allies. Why, if you make it your policy to receive and assist all offenders, you will find that just as many of your dependencies will come over to us, and the principle that you establish will press less heavily on us than on yourselves.

[41]. This then is what Hellenic law entitles us to demand as a right. But we have also advice to offer and claims on your gratitude, which, since there is no danger of our injuring you, as we are not enemies, and since our friendship does not amount to very frequent intercourse, we say ought to be liquidated at the present juncture. When you were in want of ships of war for the war against the Aeginetans, before the Persian invasion, Corinth supplied you with twenty vessels. That good

turn, and the line we took on the Samian question, when we were the cause of the Peloponnesians refusing to assist them, enabled you to conquer Aegina, and to punish Samos. And we acted thus at crises when, if ever, men are wont in their efforts against their enemies to forget everything for the sake of victory, regarding him who assists them then as a friend, even if thus far he has been a foe, and him who opposes them then as a foe, even if he has thus far been a friend; indeed they allow their real interests to suffer from their absorbing preoccupation in the struggle.

[42]. Weigh well these considerations, and let your youth learn what they are from their elders, and let them determine to do unto us as we have done unto you. And let them not acknowledge the justice of what we say, but dispute its wisdom in the contingency of war. Not only is the straightest path generally speaking the wisest; but the coming of the war which the Corcyraeans have used as a bugbear to persuade you to do wrong, is still uncertain, and it is not worth while to be carried away by it into gaining the instant and declared enmity of Corinth. It were, rather, wise to try and counteract the unfavourable impression which your conduct to Megara has created. For kindness opportunely shown has a greater power of removing old grievances than the facts of the case may warrant. And do not be seduced by the prospect of a great naval alliance. Abstinence from all injustice to other first-rate powers is a greater tower of strength, than anything that can be gained by the sacrifice of permanent tranquillity for an apparent temporary advantage.

[43]. It is now our turn to benefit by the principle that we laid down at Lacedaemon, that every power has a right to punish her own allies. We now claim to receive the same from you, and protest against your rewarding us for benefiting you by our vote by injuring us by yours. On the contrary, return us like for like, remembering that this is that very crisis in which he who lends aid is most a friend, and he who opposes is most a foe. And for these Corcyraeans — neither receive them into alliance in our despite, nor be their abettors in crime. So do, and you will act as we have a right to expect of you, and at the same time best consult your own interests.

§

Corinthian Envoys to the First Congress at Sparta
Book I 68-71
432 B.C.

The eight speeches of Book I, to restate, all occur before the Peloponnesian War began. They provide the backdrops — by narrative and by debate — of the tragedy that eventually develops. Indeed it is best to think of the *History* as a kind of drama and the speeches, important as they are, not as historically accurate accounts of what was said. Rather they are carefully written accounts of what the occasion called for, a dramatic comparison of views, a characterization of the actors and the governments they represent.

Here (I 68-71) we consider what the Corinthian envoys said at the First Congress at Sparta. The chances are more than likely that Thucydides did not hear this speech or the next one. But he could have later taken good notes from those who were present.

At this point too Thucydides starts his detailed analysis of the cultures and ways of life of Sparta and Athens. It is a theme that pervades the *History* and is exploited as another of the antitheses for which the book is famous.

In this speech (I 68.2) we find described for the first time the Spartan trait of being suspicious of others. It recurs several times more in the *History* and implies what we would call today the lack of an open society.

So also the Spartans are described as slow to take action (I 70). This too is found later four or five times. And the contrast with the quick-acting Athenians is stated or implied.

Almost none of the Spartan qualities compare favorably with those of the Athenians. Was this what Thucydides intended or is this the way it was? The reader can make up his own mind long before the last chapter.

The Corinthians began their speech with a series of grievances against Sparta. It was a case of a strong-willed son telling his parents, the Spartans, that their old, conservative, authoritarian ways no longer appealed. They were outmoded against an aggressive, democratic, and dynamic Athens. It was a rhetorical feat to have a prospective enemy, Athens, praised before a prospective ally, Sparta. The arguments of the Corinthians were powerfully effective both because of their novelty and their reality. The Spartans weighed every idea. They heard by word-pictures their qualities and their defects equally set forth (I 68-72 and again at 80-85). The Athenians, on the other hand are both innovative and hardworking. "Their bodies they spend ungrudgingly in their country's cause; their intellect they jealously husband to be employed in her service. Thus they toil on in trouble and danger all the days of their life with little opportunity for enjoying, being ever engaged in getting: their only idea of a holiday is to do what the occasion demands. ... To describe their character in a word, one might truly say they were born into the world to take no rest themselves and to give none to others" (I 70).

The timing of this speech was excellent. The purpose of the congress was to review the whole Spartan problem. Corinth found sympathy from states like Megara and Aegina. Thucydides gives the details of the complaints of Megara at I 139. Aegina through other delegates laid out the details of how Athens had violated the independence gained by her treaty.

Thus, after a number of injustices had been spelled out the Corinthian delegates came forward to speak along these lines to the General Assembly of Spartan citizens.

§

[68]. Lacedaemonians! the confidence which you feel in your constitution and social order, inclines you to receive any reflexions of ours on other powers with a certain scepticism. Hence springs your moderation, but hence also the rather limited knowledge which you betray in dealing with foreign politics. Time after time was our voice raised to warn you of the blows about to be dealt us by Athens, and time after time, instead of taking the trouble to ascertain the worth of

our communications, you contented yourselves with suspecting the speakers of being inspired by private interest. And so, instead of calling these allies together before the blow fell, you have delayed to do so till we are smarting under it; allies among whom we have not the worst title to speak, as having the greatest complaints to make, complaints of Athenian outrage and Lacedaemonian neglect. Now if these assaults on the rights of Hellas had been made in the dark you might be unacquainted with the facts, and it would be our duty to enlighten you. As it is, long speeches are not needed where you see servitude accomplished for some of us, meditated for others — in particular for our allies — and prolonged preparations in the aggressor against the hour of war. Or what, pray, is the meaning of their reception of Corcyra by fraud, and their holding it against us by force? what of the siege of Potidaea? — places one of which lies most conveniently for any action against the Thracian towns; while the other would have contributed a very large navy to the Peloponnesians?

[69]. For all this you are responsible. You it was who first allowed them to fortify their city after the Median war, and afterwards to erect the long walls, — you who, then and now, are always depriving of freedom not only those whom they have enslaved, but also those who have as yet been your allies. For the true author of the subjugation of a people is not so much the immediate agent, as the power which permits it having the means to prevent it; particularly if that power aspires to the glory of being the liberator of Hellas. We are at last assembled. It has not been easy to assemble, nor even now are our objects defined. We ought not to be still inquiring into the fact of our wrongs, but into the means of our defence. For the aggressors with matured plans to oppose to our indecision have cast threats aside and betaken themselves to action. And we know what are the paths by which Athenian aggression travels, and how insidious is its progress. A degree of confidence she may feel from the idea that your bluntness of perception prevents your noticing her; but it is nothing to the impulse which her advance will receive from the knowledge that you see, but do not care to interfere. You, Lacedaemonians, of all the Hellenes are alone inactive, and defend yourselves not by doing anything but by looking as if you would do something; you alone wait till the power of an enemy is becoming twice its original size, instead of crushing it in its infancy. And yet the world used to say that you were to be depended upon; but in your case, we fear, it said more than the truth. The Mede, we ourselves know, had time to come from the ends of the earth to

Peloponnese, without any force of yours worthy of the name advancing to meet him. But this was a distant enemy. Well, Athens at all events is a near neighbour, and yet Athens you utterly disregard; against Athens you prefer to act on the defensive instead of on the offensive, and to make it an affair of chances by deferring the struggle till she has grown far stronger than at first. And yet you know that on the whole the rock on which the barbarian was wrecked was himself, and that if our present enemy Athens had not again and again annihilated us, we owe it more to her blunders than to your protection. Indeed, expectations from you have before now been the ruin of some, whose faith induced them to omit preparation.

We hope that none of you will consider these words of remonstrance to be rather words of hostility; men remonstrate with friends who are in error, accusations they reserve for enemies who have wronged them. [70]. Besides, we consider that we have as good a right as any one to point out a neighbour's faults, particularly when we contemplate the great contrast between the two national characters; a contrast of which, as far as we can see, you have little perception, having never yet considered what sort of antagonists you will encounter in the Athenians, how widely, how absolutely different from yourselves. The Athenians are addicted to innovation, and their designs are characterised by swiftness alike in conception and execution; you have a genius for keeping what you have got, accompanied by a total want of invention, and when forced to act you never go far enough. Again, they are adventurous beyond their power, and daring beyond their judgment, and in danger they are sanguine; your wont is to attempt less than is justified by your power, to mistrust even what is sanctioned by your judgment, and to fancy that from danger there is no release. Further, there is promptitude on their side against procrastination on yours; they are never at home, you are never from it: for they hope by their absence to extend their acquisitions, you fear by your advance to endanger what you have left behind. They are swift to follow up a success, and slow to recoil from a reverse. Their bodies they spend ungrudgingly in their country's cause; their intellect they jealously husband to be employed in her service. A scheme unexecuted is with them a positive loss, a successful enterprise a comparative failure. The deficiency created by the miscarriage of an undertaking is soon filled up by fresh hopes; for they alone are enabled to call a thing hoped for a thing got, by the speed with which they act upon their resolutions. Thus they toil on in trouble and danger all the days of their life, with little opportunity for enjoying, being ever engaged in getting: their only idea of a holiday is to do what the occasion demands, and to them laborious occupation is less of a misfortune than the peace of a quiet life. To describe their character in a word, one might truly say that they were born into the world to take no rest themselves and to give none to others.

[71]. Such is Athens, your antagonist. And yet, Lacedaemonians, you still delay, and fail to see that peace stays longest with those, who are not more careful to use their power justly than to show their determination not to submit to injustice. On the contrary, your ideal of fair dealing is based on the principle that if you do not injure others, you need not risk your own fortunes in preventing others from injuring you. Now you could scarcely have succeeded in such a policy even with a neighbour like yourselves; but in the present instance, as we have just shown, your habits are old-fashioned as compared with theirs. It is the law as in art, so in politics, that improvements ever prevail; and though fixed usages may be best for undisturbed communities, constant necessities of action must be accompanied by the constant improvement of methods. Thus it happens that the vast experience of Athens has carried her further than you on the path of innovation.

Here, at least, let your procrastination end. For the present, assist your allies and Potidaea in particular, as you promised, by a speedy invasion of Attica, and do not sacrifice friends and kindred to their bitterest enemies, and drive the rest of us in despair to some other alliance. Such a step would not be condemned either by the gods who received our oaths, or by the men who witnessed them. The break of a treaty cannot be laid to the people whom desertion compels to seek new relations, but to the power that fails to assist its confederate. But if you will only act, we will stand by you; it would be unnatural for us to change, and never should we meet with such a congenial ally. For these reasons choose the right course, and endeavour not to let Peloponnese under your supremacy degenerate from the prestige that it enjoyed under that of your ancestors.

§

Athenian Envoys to the First Congress at Sparta
Book I 73-78
432 B.C.

Werner Jaeger in *Paideia: The Ideals of Greek Culture* attaches great importance to the four speeches (I 68-86) outlining the arguments, pro and con, of Athens and Sparta for going to war. The number is greater "than occurs at one time anywhere else in the book." Speaking of the remarks of the Athenian envoys Jaeger explains: "The external motive given by Thucydides for the delivery of the speech is, perhaps intentionally, rather obscure. Speech and counter speech (by Pericles) are not addressed to the Spartan government but to the public, and they combine to make a powerfully effective unity. To the psychological analysis made by the Corinthians and the Atehnians (I 37-78) now add a historical analysis of the rise of Athens from the beginning to the present day. ...They analyse the internal development of the motives which impelled Athens to develop her power so fully and so logically" (*Paideia* I.398).

Here the Athenians speak "to remind the old and instruct the young " (I 72.1), a purpose still important in political speeches today.

They detail their own peculiar attributes — their high spirit (I 74.1), their patriotism (I 75.1), and the "wisdom of their counsels" (I 75.1). They remind the Spartans that it is natural to conquer those who offer no resistance (I 75-76). The arguments are not entirely idealistic and they sound like those of a superior to an inferior.

In contrast, the Spartans have a reputation for their harshness as governors (I 77.6), they have used their "supremacy to settle the states in Peloponnese as is agreeable to you" (I 76.1), and in general they have behaved as those whose might makes them think they are right.

What are the three motives which Thucydides ascribes to Athens for beginning the war? Indeed, why she was *compelled* to fight (see I 76)? Briefly, the motives were fear, ambition, and self interest. For emphasis they are stated twice (I 75.3 and I 76.2). And these motives are based on the argument of human nature in I 76.2-3: "It was not we who set the example, for it has always been the law that the weaker should be subject to the stronger. ...And praise is due to all who, if not so superior to human nature as to refuse dominion, yet respect justice more than their position compels them to do."

The Athenians are frankly hardheaded in their presentation. They act as men with weapons and strong wills have always done. The Greek word πολυπρχγμοσύνη meaning *vigor* and *assertiveness* adds up to something quite different from the Spartan term ἡσυχία meaning literally *tranquillity*. Here in two words we have a large measure of explanation for the cause of the Peloponnesian War. The epigram "where force can be used, law is not needed" is found in words here for the first time but the idea is as old as man. What is strange is to hear it from speakers representing Periclean Athens. It reappears again, however, from the lips of both Pericles (II 63, 64.4) and Alcibiades (VI 18, 87).

The hatred of imperialist Athens throughout Hellas began with the first day of the war and grew every day. Sparta was cast in the role of defender of liberty and Athens as the symbol of tyranny.

§

[73]. The object of our mission here was not to argue with your allies, but to attend to the matters on which our State despatched us. However, the vehemence of the outcry that we hear against us has prevailed on us to come forward. It is not to combat the accusations of the cities (indeed you are not the judges before whom either we or they can plead), but to prevent your taking the wrong course on matters of great importance by yielding too readily to the persuasions of your allies. We also wish to show on a review of the whole indictment that we have a fair title to our possessions, and that our country has claims

to consideration. We need not refer to remote antiquity: there we could appeal to the voice of tradition, but not to the experience of our audience. But to the Median war and contemporary history we must refer, although we are rather tired of continually bringing this subject forward. In our action during that war we ran great risk to obtain certain advantages: you had your share in the solid results, do not try to rob us of all share in the good that the glory may do us. However, the story shall be told not so much to deprecate hostility as to testify against it, and to show, if you are so ill-advised as to enter into a struggle with Athens, what sort of an antagonist she is likely to prove. We assert that at Marathon we were at the front, and faced the barbarian single-handed. That when he came the second time, unable to cope with him by land we went on board our ships with all our people, and joined in the action at Salamis. This prevented his taking the Peloponnesian states in detail, and ravaging them with his fleet; when the multitude of his vessels would have made any combination for self-defence impossible. The best proof of this was furnished by the invader himself. Defeated at sea, he considered his power to be no longer what it had been, and retired as speedily as possible with the greater part of his army.

[74]. Such, then, was the result of the matter, and it was clearly proved that it was on the fleet of Hellas that her cause depended. Well, to this result we contributed three very useful elements, viz. the largest number of ships, the ablest commander, and the most unhesitating patriotism. Our contingent of ships was little less than two-thirds of the whole four hundred; the commander was Themistocles, through whom chiefly it was that the battle took place in the straits, the acknowledged salvation of our cause. Indeed, this was the reason of your receiving him with honours such as had never been accorded to any foreign visitor. While for daring patriotism we had no competitors. Receiving no reinforcements from behind, seeing everything in front of us already subjugated, we had the spirit, after abandoning our city, after sacrificing our property (instead of deserting the remainder of the league or depriving them of our services by dispersing), to throw ourselves into our ships and meet the danger, without a thought of resenting your neglect to assist us. We assert, therefore, that we conferred on you quite as much as we received. For you had a stake to fight for; the cities which you had left were still filled with your homes, and you had the prospect of enjoying them again; and your coming was prompted quite as much by fear for yourselves as for us; at all events,

you never appeared till we had nothing left to lose. But we left behind us a city that was a city no longer, and staked our lives for a city that had an existence only in desperate hope, and so bore our full share in your deliverance and in ours. But if we had copied others, and allowed fears for our territory to make us give in our adhesion to the Mede before you came, or if we had suffered our ruin to break our spirit and prevent us embarking in our ships, your naval inferiority would have made a sea-fight unnecessary, and his objects would have been peaceably attained.

[75]. Surely, Lacedaemonians, neither by the patriotism that we displayed at that crisis, nor by the wisdom of our counsels, do we merit our extreme unpopularity with the Hellenes, not at least unpopularity for our empire. That empire we acquired by no violent means, but because you were unwilling to prosecute to its conclusion the war against the barbarian, and because the allies attached themselves to us and spontaneously asked us to assume the command. And the nature of the case first compelled us to advance our empire to its present height; fear being our principal motive, though honour and interest afterwards came in. And at last, when almost all hated us, when some had already revolted and had been subdued, when you had ceased to be the friends that you once were, and had become objects of suspicion and dislike, it appeared no longer safe to give up our empire; especially as all who left us would fall to you. And no one can quarrel with a people for making, in matters of tremendous risk, the best provision that it can for its interest.

[76]. You, at all events, Lacedaemonians, have used your supremacy to settle the states in Peloponnese as is agreeable to you. And if at the period of which we were speaking you had persevered to the end of the matter, and had incurred hatred in your command, we are sure that you would have made yourselves just as galling to the allies, and would have been forced to choose between a strong government and danger to yourselves. It follows that it was not a very wonderful action, or contrary to the common practice of mankind, if we did accept an empire that was offered to us, and refused to give it up under the pressure of three of the strongest motives, fear, honour, and interest. And it was not we who set the example, for it has always been the law that the weaker should be subject to the stronger. Besides, we believed ourselves to be worthy of our position, and so you thought us till now, when calculations of interest have made you take up the cry of justice — a consideration which no one ever yet brought forward to hinder his

ambition when he had a chance of gaining anything by might. And praise is due to all who, if not so superior to human nature as to refuse dominion, yet respect justice more than their position compels them to do.

[77]. We imagine that our moderation would be best demonstrated by the conduct of others who should be placed in our position; but even our equity has very unreasonably subjected us to condemnation instead of approval. Our abatement of our rights in the contract trials with our allies, and our causing them to be decided by impartial laws at Athens, have gained us the character of being litigious. And none care to inquire why this reproach is not brought against other imperial powers, who treat their subjects with less moderation than we do; the secret being that where force can be used, law is not needed. But our subjects are so habituated to associate with us as equals, that any defeat whatever that clashes with their notions of justice, whether it proceeds from a legal judgment or from the power which our empire gives us, makes them forget to be grateful for being allowed to retain most of their possessions, and more vexed at a part being taken, than if we had from the first cast law aside and openly gratified our covetousness. If we had done so, not even would they have disputed that the weaker must give way to the stronger. Men's indignation, it seems, is more excited by legal wrong than by violent wrong; the first looks like being cheated by an equal, the second like being compelled by a superior. At all events they contrived to put up with much worse treatment than this from the Mede, yet they think our rule severe, and this is to be expected, for the present always weighs heavy on the conquered. This at least is certain. If you were to succeed in overthrowing us and in taking our place, you would speedily lose the popularity with which fear of us has invested you, if your policy of to-day is at all to tally with the sample that you gave of it during the brief period of your command against the Mede. Not only is your life at home regulated by rules and institutions incompatible with those of others, but your citizens abroad act neither on these rules nor on those which are recognised by the rest of Hellas.

[78]. Take time then in forming your resolution, as the matter is of great importance; and do not be persuaded by the opinions and complaints of others to bring trouble on yourselves, but consider the vast influence of accident in war, before you are engaged in it. As it continues, it generally becomes an affair of chances, chances from which neither of us is exempt, and whose event we must risk in the

dark. It is a common mistake in going to war to begin at the wrong end, to act first, and wait for disaster to discuss the matter. But we are not yet by any means so misguided, nor, so far as we can see, are you; accordingly, while it is still open to us both to choose aright, we bid you not to dissolve the treaty, or to break your oaths, but to have our differences settled by arbitration according to our agreement. Or else we take the gods who heard the oaths to witness, and if you begin hostilities, whatever line of action you choose, we will try not to be behindhand in repelling you.

§

King Archidamus to the Spartan Assembly
Book I 80-85
432 B.C.

The speech of King Archidamus and the "laconic" one by the Ephor Sthenelaidas that follows represent the conservative and the war-party views, the "doves" and the "hawks," as we would say today. We should pause to explain why the speakers can disagree. Sparta was governed by two hereditary Kings, the Senate or *gerousia*, the assembly or the *apella* and five ephors. The ephors were like the Commissars of the USSR. They exercised control over the Kings. The Kings were the leaders of the army in war but they were supervised by the ephors. Since the ephors could recall generals it is obvious that they could wield great influence in the strategy of a war.

Here the Spartans acknowledge for the first of six or seven times in the *History* the great experience of the Athenians as sailors, as Crawley translates it their "extraordinary familiarity with the sea" (I 80.4).

Archidamus warns of the Athenians' strength in their allies (I 81.4), of their revenue (I 81.4) and admits that Sparta has few allies and unreliable money sources. He acknowledges that education and intelligence get in the way of action (I 84.3) but he insists that unquestioning obedience to law is vital for the state (I 84.3). Then there is that famous commonplace to the effect that men being much the same everywhere, those reared in the toughest school are the most effective (I 84.4).

Archidamus gave his name to the Archidamian War, as the period 432-422, the first ten years of the Peloponnesian War, came to be known. But he was neither a strong proponent of the war nor a forceful commander. In the speech below he gives all the traditional reasons for not going to war. Sparta was not prepared. It would be long and costly. All the Spartans could do was to lay waste the Athenian crops. Siege warfare was not enough. Athens was a naval power and land troops, no matter how brave or trained to hardship, could not subdue walled cities. Athens was a financial giant and it would be enormously difficult to subvert her allies. Archidamus was a man of caution. He urged his country to talk tough, but not to fire the first shot, so to speak.

The audience was in no mood for this advice. It was plainly the wrong time, the wrong set of arguments, and as the next speaker shows, given by the wrong man, even though he was a King.

This speech is famous for its delineation of the Spartan character. The traits which Archidamus lists should be compared with those Pericles gives for the Athenian character in the Funeral Oration (II 35-46).

Archidamus naturally takes pride in the "benefits" of the Spartan discipline. He talks about the wisdom and experience of older men, the fact that high intelligence can block action, that unquestioning obedience to law is both a military and a civil strength, and that military training develops great endurance. This is a mere beginning of the list, however.

In his essay on "The Unity of Thucydides' History," Finley devotes a long footnote, with more than thirty citations, to other Spartan traits of character which Thucydides enumerates. The more important are their severity as colonizers, their fear of the slaves (helots), their religiosity, their secrecy and suspiciousness, and of course, their love of discipline.[1]

By constantly reminding us of what Spartans were really like Thucydides subtly reminds us of what he believed were the more admirable characteristics of the Athenians. In essence he is contrasting the uneducated and the vulgar with the urbane and the cultivated. In other words the Spartans were a backward people and the Athenians were a progressive

---

1. *Three Essays on Thucydides,* Harvard University Press, Cambridge, Mass., 1967, p. 132 note 45.

people. The points offered in proof make the comparison very credible.

§

[80]. I have not lived so long, Lacedaemonians, without having had the experience of many wars, and I see those among you of the same age as myself, who will not fall into the common misfortune of longing for war from inexperience or from a belief in its advantage and its safety. This, the war on which you are now debating, would be one of the greatest magnitude, on a sober consideration of the matter. In a struggle with Peloponnesians and neighbours our strength is of the same character, and it is possible to move swiftly on the different points. But a struggle with a people who live in a distant land, who have also an extraordinary familiarity with the sea, and who are in the highest state of preparation in every other department; with wealth private and public, with ships, and horses, and heavy infantry, and a population such as no one other Hellenic place can equal, and lastly a number of tributary allies — what can justify us in rashly beginning such a struggle? wherein is our trust that we should rush on it unprepared? Is it in our money? There we have a far greater deficiency. We neither have it in our treasury, nor are we ready to contribute it from our private funds.

[81]. Confidence might possibly be felt in our superiority in heavy infantry and population, which will enable us to invade and devastate their lands. But the Athenians have plenty of other land in their empire, and can import what they want by sea. Again, if we are to attempt an insurrection of their allies, these will have to be supported with a fleet, most of them being islanders. What then is to be our war? For unless we can either beat them at sea, or deprive them of the revenues which feed their navy, we shall meet with little but disaster. Meanwhile our honour will be pledged to keeping on, particularly if it be the opinion that we began the quarrel. For let us never be elated by the fatal hope of the war being quickly ended by the devastation of their lands. I fear rather that we may leave it as a legacy to our children; so improbable is it that the Athenian spirit will be the slave of their land, or Athenian experience be cowed by war.

[82]. Not that I would bid you be so unfeeling as to suffer them to injure your allies, and to refrain from unmasking their intrigues; but I do bid you not to take up arms at once, but to send and remonstrate

with them in a tone not too suggestive of war, nor again too suggestive of submission, and to employ the interval in perfecting our own preparations. The means will be, first, the acquisition of allies, Hellenic or barbarian it matters not, so long as they are an accession to our strength naval or pecuniary — I say Hellenic or barbarian, because the odium of such an accession to all who like us are the objects of the designs of the Athenians is taken away by the law of self-preservation — and secondly the development of our home resources. If they listen to our embassy, so much the better; but if not, after the lapse of two or three years our position will have become materially strengthened, and we can then attack them if we think proper. Perhaps by that time the sight of our preparations, backed by language equally significant, will have disposed them to submission, while their land is still untouched, and while their counsels may be directed to the retention of advantages as yet undestroyed. For the only light in which you can view their land is that of a hostage in your hands, a hostage the more valuable the better it is cultivated. This you ought to spare as long as possible, and not make them desperate, and so increase the difficulty of dealing with them. For if while still unprepared, hurried away by the complaints of our allies, we are induced to lay it waste, have a care that we do not bring deep disgrace and deep perplexity upon Peloponnese. Complaints, whether of communities or individuals, it is possible to adjust; but war undertaken by a coalition for sectional interests, whose progress there is no means of foreseeing, does not easily admit of creditable settlement.

[83]. And none need think it cowardice for a number of confederates to pause before they attack a single city. The Athenians have allies as numerous as our own, and allies that pay tribute, and war is a matter not so much of arms as of money, which makes arms of use. And this is more than ever true in a struggle between a continental and a maritime power. First, then, let us provide money, and not allow ourselves to be carried away by the talk of our allies before we have done so: as we shall have the largest share of responsibility for the consequences be they good or bad, we have also a right to a tranquil inquiry respecting them.

[84]. And the slowness and procrastination, the parts of our character that are most assailed by their criticism, need not make you blush. If we undertake the war without preparation, we should by hastening its commencement only delay its conclusion: further, a free and a famous city has through all time been ours. The quality which they condemn is really nothing but a wise moderation; thanks to its

possession, we alone do not become insolent in success and give way less than others in misfortune; we are not carried away by the pleasure of hearing ourselves cheered on to risks which our judgment condemns; nor, if annoyed, are we any the more convinced by attempts to exasperate us by accusation. We are both warlike and wise, and it is our sense of order that makes us so. We are warlike, because self-control contains honour as a chief constituent, and honour bravery. And we are wise, because we are educated with too little learning to despise the laws, and with too severe a self-control to disobey them, and are brought up not to be too knowing in useless matters, — such as the knowledge which can give a specious criticism of an enemy's plans in theory, but fails to assail them with equal success in practice, — but are taught to consider that the schemes of our enemies are not dissimilar to our own, and that the freaks of chance are not determinable by calculation. In practice we always base our preparations against an enemy on the assumption that his plans are good; indeed, it is right to rest our hopes not on a belief in his blunders, but on the soundness of our provisions. Nor ought we to believe that there is much difference between man and man, but to think that the superiority lies with him who is reared in the severest school.

[85]. These practices, then, which our ancestors have delivered to us, and by whose maintenance we have always profited, must not be given up. And we must not be hurried into deciding in a day's brief space a question which concerns many lives and fortunes and many cities, and in which honour is deeply involved, — but we must decide calmly. This our strength peculiarly enables us to do. As for the Athenians, send to them on the matter of Potidaea, send on the matter of the alleged wrongs of the allies, particularly as they are prepared with legal satisfaction; and to proceed against one who offers arbitration as against a wrongdoer, law forbids. Meanwhile do not omit preparation for war. This decision will be the best for yourselves, the most terrible to your opponents.

§

The Ephor Sthenelaidas to the Spartan Assembly
Book I 86
432 B.C.

This is a hot-tempered speech appropriate for an inflamed younger man. Thucydides may have written it late, some time after 404 B.C. when he revised his views about Sparta's part in starting the war. Such is the view of the German scholar, Ed. Schwartz, in *Das Geschichtswerk des Thukydides*, Bonn, 1929.

In one sense Archidamus and Sthenelaidas are representing the views of the young and the old — those who know the ravages of war and those who don't. Later, at II 81. Thucydides cites the same division between the old and the young "both in the Peloponnesus and in Athens."

Another conflict that suggests itself is the one of power between the King and the Ephors. It is unmistakably clear here that Archidamus is a figurehead. He has his say but the Ephors and the Assembly do what they want.

Archidamus was a friend of Pericles. This may have been a small reason for his mildness, for his downright reluctance to do battle. He was a lone voice, however.

The Ephor Sthenelaidas spoke 200 words — about ten sentences. He said what was wanted. Archidamus argued that Sparta could not win. But his "superior" took his hearers back to the speech of the Athenian envoy. It was so long it was impossible to follow. This was no time for words or lawsuits.

The arguments given below are simple and clear. The Athenians praised themselves. They don't deny "they are injuring our allies and Peloponnese. We can't delay assisting our allies. True, Athens has money and ships and horses — but we have good allies who must be helped. This is to time or place to weigh alternatives. Vote, therefore, O Spartans, for war as our honor demands."

Whereas other speakers who appear in pairs frequently use

intraclausal antithesis, neither Archidamus nor Sthenelaidas are made to resort to the figure in these compositions. As chairman, the Ephor put the vote. *Viva voce* was not good enough. "Those who want war, stand up and go there. Those opposed, stand up and go over there." The hawks won by a decided majority.

And then Thucydides plainly gives his reason for the declaration of war. It was not so much because the Spartans were persuaded by the arguments of the allies, "as because they feared the growth of the power of the Athenians, seeing most of Greece already subject to them."

It seems apparent that the Athenian speaker really incited the Spartan decision. It certainly was no accident that the embassy members happened to be in Sparta. Pericles most probably sent them and told them what to say. The Spartans were thus egged on. By their enemy's words they had to make ready.

§

[86.] The long speech of the Athenians I do not pretend to understand. They said a good deal in praise of themselves, but nowhere denied that they are injuring our allies and Peloponnese. And yet if they behaved well against the Mede then, but ill towards us now, they deserve double punishment for having ceased to be good and for having become bad. We meanwhile are the same then and now, and shall not, if we are wise, disregard the wrongs of our allies, or put off till to-morrow the duty of assisting those who must suffer to-day. Others have much money and ships and horses, but we have good allies whom we must not give up to the Athenians, nor by lawsuits and words decide the matter, as it is anything but in word that we are harmed, but render instant and powerful help. And let us not be told that it is fitting for us to deliberate under injustice; long deliberation is rather fitting for those who have injustice in contemplation. Vote therefore, Lacedaemonians, for war, as the honour of Sparta demands, and neither allow the further aggrandisement of Athens, nor betray our allies to ruin, but with the gods let us advance against the aggressors.

§

The Corinthians to the Second Congress at Sparta
Book I 120-124
432 B.C.

This is a deliberative speech about the ways of conducting the war and the possibilities of winning. Thucydides almost certainly could not have heard the speakers but he must have had good notes on what they said. Pericles certainly did not hear the speech but he (through Thucydides) alludes to it and refutes it point by point in the speech that follows. The two speeches are a remarkable instance of extended antithesis in the *History.*

The plans of the Peloponnesian allies are discussed (I 120-124) at length and they are designed to rebut the objections raised by Archidamus earlier.

Four main arguments emerge: (1) Delphi and Olympia can be depended upon for financial help. (2) With this money Sparta can build a navy. The foreign sailors (slaves) now in the hire of Athens can be lured over by higher pay. (3) A revolt of the allies can be started. (4) It would be possible to build a permanent fort within the Athenian lines.

G.B. Grundy suggests that the whole of the Corinthian speech at the Second Congress at Sparta was of a later date of composition "and, if so, it is also probable that that part of Pericles' speech which has reference to it is of the same date." This is one of the several instances in the *History* where Thucydides has the advantage of writing after all the later events are known to him.

The following table of contention and refutation reveals the conflicting views of the Corinthian envoy and of Pericles on main points.

Here is the most celebrated instance in the *History* of one speaker — who did not hear his opposition — actually answering almost each point as if he had been present. Great as Pericles was as orator and statesman he could never have performed this magic without the generous assistance of Thucydides.

This speech is famous for the aphorisms that "in action men do not always carry through their well laid plans" (120.5) and "war of all things proceeds least upon definite rules but draws principally upon itself for contrivances to meet an emergency" (122.2).

The Spartans fully expected (like all poorly led countries) to win a quick victory (121.4). Courage is their chief resource and this counts (121.4). The Athenians' skill at sea was the result of a lucky break — their experience in the Persian Wars (121.4). This latter theme is echoed over and over in the *History.*

Again, three of the gravest failings of a state are "want of sense, of courage, or of vigilance" (122.4). This comes from the final paragraph of exhortation in the speech and the writer well understood the attention-value of beginnings and endings.

The author of the *Rhetorica ad Alexandrum* gives a concise account of what speakers must do to persuade and dissuade. In this speech the Corinthians exhort in the beginning and closing paragraphs (120, 124) and in the middle (121-123) they argue from topics of possibility and honor. "When we are exhorting anyone to go to war we must collect as many of these pretexts (e.g. aggression, vengeance, opportunity, actual wrong, helping allies, etc.) as possible, and afterwards show that those whom we are exhorting possess most of the advantages which bring success in warfare." (*Rhet. ad Alex.*, trans. by E.S. Forster, Oxford *Works of Aristotle*, Vol. XI, 1924).

This is the way the Corinthians make plausible the possibility of winning for the Peloponnesians and explain, on the other hand, why it would be shameful if they did not try.

The Corinthians here (I 120-124) repeat their argument that the leaders of Athens must be restrained before they swallow up the rest of Greece. "Men would say (if we did not move now) that we deserved our fate, or that we put up with it from cowardice, and were proving degenerate sons in not securing for ourselves the freedom which our fathers gave to Greece..." (I 122.3). On the other hand, the fault is not all in Athenian domination. Sparta has been asleep while Athens grew arrogant and strong. But victory will come, the Corinthians promise, because of loyal and better trained men, and this point Pericles meets head on in rebuttal.

§

[120]. Fellow allies, we can no longer accuse the Lacedaemonians of having failed in their duty: they have not only voted for war themselves, but have assembled us here for that purpose. We say their duty, for supremacy has its duties. Besides equitably administering private interests, leaders are required to show a special care for the common welfare in return for the special honours accorded to them by all in other ways. For ourselves, all who have already had dealings with the Athenians require no warning to be on their guard against them. The states more inland and out of the highway of communication should understand that if they omit to support the coast powers, the result will be to injure the transit of their produce for exportation and the reception in exchange of their imports from the sea; and they must not be careless judges of what is now said, as if it had nothing to do with them, but must expect that the sacrifice of the powers on the coast will one day be followed by the extension of the danger to the interior, and must recognise that their own interests are deeply involved in this discussion. For these reasons they should not hesitate to exchange peace for war. If wise men remain quiet, while they are not injured, brave men abandon peace for war when they are injured, returning to an understanding on a favourable opportunity: in fact, they are neither intoxicated by their success in war, nor disposed to take an injury for the sake of the delightful tranquillity of peace. Indeed, to falter for the sake of such delights is, if you remain inactive, the quickest way of losing the sweets of repose to which you cling; while to conceive extravagant pretensions from success in war is to forget how hollow is the confidence by which you are elated. For if many ill-conceived plans have succeeded through the still greater fatuity of an opponent, many more, apparently well laid, have on the contrary ended in disgrace. The confidence with which we form our schemes is never completely justified in their execution; speculation is carried on in safety, but, when it comes to action, fear causes failure.

[121]. To apply these rules to ourselves, if we are now kindling war it is under the pressure of injury, and with adequate grounds of complaint; and after we have chastised the Athenians we will in season desist. We have many reasons to expect success, — first, superiority in numbers and in military experience, and secondly our general and unvarying obedience in the execution of orders. The naval strength which they possess shall be raised by us from our respective antecedent

resources, and from the monies at Olympia and Delphi. A loan from these enables us to seduce their foreign sailors by the offer of higher pay. For the power of Athens is more mercenary than national; while ours will not be exposed to the same risk, as its strength lies more in men than in money. A single defeat at sea is in all likelihood their ruin: should they hold out, in that case there will be the more time for us to exercise ourselves in naval matters; and as soon as we have arrived at an equality in science, we need scarcely ask whether we shall be their superiors in courage. For the advantages that we have by nature they cannot acquire by education; while their superiority in science must be removed by our practice. The money required for these objects shall be provided by our contributions: nothing indeed could be more monstrous than the suggestion that, while their allies never tire of contributing for their own servitude, we should refuse to spend for vengeance and self-preservation the treasure which by such refusal we shall forfeit to Athenian rapacity, and see employed for our own ruin.

[122]. We have also other ways of carrying on the war, such as revolt of their allies, the surest method of depriving them of their revenues, which are the source of their strength, and establishment of fortified positions in their country, and various operations which cannot be foreseen at present. For war of all things proceeds least upon definite rules, but draws principally upon itself for contrivances to meet an emergency; and in such cases the party who faces the struggle and keeps his temper best meets with most security, and he who loses his temper about it with correspondent disaster. Let us also reflect that if it was merely a number of disputes of territory between rival neighbours, it might be borne; but here we have an enemy in Athens, that is a match for our whole coalition, and more than a match for any of its members; so that unless as a body and as individual nationalities and individual cities we make an unanimous stand against her, she will easily conquer us divided and in detail. That conquest, terrible as it may sound, would, it must be known, have no other end than slavery pure and simple; a word which Peloponnese cannot even hear whispered without disgrace, or without disgrace see so many states abused by one. Meanwhile the opinion would be either that we were justly so used, or that we put up with it from cowardice, and were proving degenerate sons in not even securing for ourselves the freedom which our fathers gave to Hellas; and in allowing the establishment in Hellas of a tyrant state, though in individual states we think it our duty to put down sole rulers. And we do not know how this conduct can be held free from three of the

gravest failings, want of sense, of courage, or of vigilance. For we do not suppose that you have taken refuge in that contempt of an enemy which has proved so fatal in so many instances, — a feeling which from the numbers that it has ruined has come to be called, not contemptuous but contemptible.

[123]. There is, however, no advantage in reflexions on the past further than may be of service to the present. For the future we must provide by maintaining what the present gives us and redoubling our efforts; it is hereditary to us to win virtue as the fruit of labour, and you must not change the habit, even though you should have a slight advantage in wealth and resources; for it is not right that what was won in want should be lost in plenty. No, we must boldly advance to the war for many reasons; the god has commanded it and promised to be with us, and the rest of Hellas will all join in the struggle, part from fear, part from interest. You will not be the first to break a treaty which the god, in advising us to go to war, judges to be violated already, but rather to support a treaty that has been outraged. Indeed, treaties are broken not by resistance but by aggression.

[124]. Your position, therefore, from whatever quarter you may view it, will amply justify you in going to war; and this step we recommend in the interests of all, bearing in mind that identity of interests is the surest of bonds whether between states or individuals. Delay not, therefore, to assist Potidaea, a Dorian city besieged by Ionians, which is quite a reversal of the order of things; nor to assert the freedom of the rest. It is impossible for us to wait any longer when waiting can only mean immediate disaster for some of us, and, if it comes to be known that we have conferred but do not venture to protect ourselves, like disaster in the near future for the rest. Delay not, fellow allies, but convinced of the necessity of the crisis and the wisdom of this counsel, vote for the war, undeterred by its immediate terrors, but looking beyond to the lasting peace by which it will be succeeded. Out of war peace gains fresh stability, but to refuse to abandon repose for war is not so sure a method of avoiding danger. We must believe that the tyrant city that has been established in Hellas has been established against all alike, with a programme of universal empire, part fulfilled, part in contemplation; let us then attack and reduce it, and win future security for ourselves and freedom for the Hellenes who are now enslaved.

§

Pericles to the Athenian Ecclesia
Book I 140-144
432 B.C.

Thucydides called Pericles "the foremost man of the Athenians at that time [432 B.C.], wielding greatest influence both in speech and in action" (I 132-134). We have relatively little primary source material about Pericles in spite of his influence and fame. Plutarch, writing as an essayist, deals with the last twenty years of his life. Aristotle quotes some of his sayings in the *Rhetoric*. There are references in the Greek comedies of his day — not always praiseworthy to be sure. We are thus forced to rely largely on what Thucydides tells us about the last four years of Pericles' life. The three speeches in the *History* attributed to Pericles, and perhaps by him, become in the last analysis the most detailed information we can find. Since they are so well written, so clear and free from the abruptness and obscurity for which the *History* is famous, it has become traditional to say that all three orations probably closely reproduce what Pericles actually spoke.

Plato makes Socrates say in the *Phaedrus* that he conceived "Pericles to have been the most accomplished of rhetoricians" (269e). His skill came, Socrates goes on to explain, because of his study of philosophy with Anaxagoras. The fact is that Pericles was probably the first great leader to surround himself with "intellectuals" as we call highly educated men today. His friends included Damon, the musician and rhetorician; Sophocles and Aeschylus, the playwrights; Phidias, the sculptor; and of course, Anaxagoras, the philosopher. Then there was Aspasia, the mistress of Pericles who, Plato suggests in the *Mexexenus*, may have helped in the writing of the Funeral Oration and other speeches. Plutarch tells us "she had the repute of being resorted to by many of the Athenians for instruction in the art of speaking."

Despite all the scandals and attacks on Pericles' private life there was little or no evidence to indict his public life. He regularly rendered full accounts. When it appeared that King Archidamus might even spare from devastation his family estates Pericles offered to turn them over to the Athenian treasury. A student of rhetoric would have to look long to find in the ancient world a man with greater ethical appeal. He was elected General fifteen years in succession. The law was even changed so that he could represent all of the Athenians — and not have to represent one tribe. He thus became General-in-chief. It is true that after 15 years Pericles was turned out (for a five-talent shortage) and fined 15 talents. But soon Alcibiades and others urged the old man to stand for election again and he won. And again — until the last time in 429 B.C.

On his deathbed, when his friends were praising his deeds, he cited his proudest accomplishment — "that no Athenian ever wore mourning because of me."

When Pericles spoke to the Ecclesia in 432 he repeated his arguments that Sparta had forced the war on Athens. "For all claims from an equal, urged upon a neighbor as command, before any attempt at legal settlement, be they great or small, have only one meaning and that is slavery" (I 141.1).

Pericles reminds his hearers that the people have a great way of blaming their leaders (I 140.1), that this, however, is a just war (141.2-143). It is therefore well worth the risks.

Perhaps the wisest remark of the introduction — one that voters easily overlook when the hardships of war mount — is this: "I know that the spirit which inspires men while they are being persuaded to make war, is not always retained in action; that as circumstances change, resolutions change" (I 140.1).

The Athenians had both great military strength and a unified front. Their navy, Pericles argued, was unbeatable. Sparta's demands should be ignored. True, Archidamus could invade and devastate, but that strategy did not guarantee success. Athens could free her allies if Sparta did the same. These are the major points of the speech. It was well delivered and well received.

Both in this speech and in the Funeral Oration (II 65.7) Pericles warns against trying to expand the empire (I 144.1). As we shall see later this ambition was the Athenians' tragic flaw.

The German scholar, Blass, thought that the style of Pericles' actual speeches probably did not resemble those that Thucydides gives to us. The debate about the actual and the reported will continue to go on and there is no conclusive way of proving whether Thucydides gave Pericles the best imitation of his poetic and figurative way of speaking. The fact remains that in all the 40-odd speeches of the *History* there are no others like the three ascribed to Pericles.

The speaker ends with a prophetic plea: "I have many other reasons to hope for a favorable issue, if you can consent not to combine schemes of fresh conquest with the conduct of the war, and will abstain from wilfully involving yourselves in other dangers; indeed, I am more afraid of our own blunders than of the enemy's devices" (I 144.1).

Some scholars consider this first speech by Pericles to be the least impressive of the three. But Dionysius of Halicarnassus considers it among the best in the *History*. In any event it was effective. The Ecclesia voted for war by a large majority. The age-old problem of all wars loomed — "Who started it?" The evidence seems to show that if Pericles didn't actually promote the war by his manipulations he did little to prevent it. By his words and deeds it was a Periclean war.

Thucydides has now laid the ground for the actual fighting. It required eight speaking occasions, two years of debate, and great play on emotions by both sides. The speakers displayed great skill and great *ethos* — but as we view it all now — little *logos*. On balance, is there ever any logic to starting a war?

§

[140]. There is one principle, Athenians, which I hold to through everything, and that is the principle of no concession to the Peloponnesians. I know that the spirit which inspires men while they are being persuaded to make war, is not always retained in action; that as circumstances change, resolutions change. Yet I see that now as before the same, almost literally the same, counsel is demanded of me; and I put it to those of you, who are allowing yourselves to be persuaded, to support the national resolves even in the case of reverses, or to forfeit all credit for their wisdom in the event of success. For sometimes the course of things is as arbitrary as the plans of man; indeed this is why we usually blame chance for whatever does not happen as we expected. Now it was clear before, that Lacedaemon entertained designs against us; it is still more clear now. The treaty provides that we shall mutually submit our differences to legal settlement, and that we shall meanwhile each keep what we have. Yet the Lacedaemonians never yet made us any such offer, never yet would accept from us any such offer; on the contrary, they wish complaints to be settled by war instead of by negotiation; and in the end we find them here dropping the tone of expostulation and adopting that of command. They order us to raise the siege of Potidaea, to let Aegina be independent, to revoke the Megara decree; and they conclude with an ultimatum warning us to leave the Hellenes independent. I hope that you will none of you think that we shall be going to war for a trifle if we refuse to revoke the Megara decree, which appears in front of their complaints, and the revocation of which is to save us from war, or let any feeling of self-reproach linger in your minds, as if you went to war for slight cause. Why, this trifle contains the whole seal and trial of your resolution. If you give way, you will instantly have to meet some greater demand, as having been frightened into obedience in the first instance; while a firm refusal will make them clearly understand that they must treat you more as equals.

[141]. Make your decision therefore at once, either to submit before you are harmed, or if we are to go to war, as I for one think we ought, to do so without caring whether the ostensible cause be great or small, resolved against making concessions or consenting to a precarious tenure of our possessions. For all claims from an equal, urged upon a neighbour as commands, before any attempt at legal settlement, be they great or be they small, have only one meaning, and that is slavery.

As to the war and the resources of either party, a detailed comparison will not show you the inferiority of Athens. Personally engaged in the cultivation of their land, without funds either private or public, the Peloponnesians are also without experience in long wars across sea, from the strict limit which poverty imposes on their attacks upon each other. Powers of this description are quite incapable of often manning a fleet or often sending out an army: they cannot afford the absence from their homes, the expenditure from their own funds; and besides, they have not command of the sea. Capital, it must be remembered, maintains a war more than forced contributions. Farmers are a class of men that are always more ready to serve in person than in purse. Confident that the former will survive the dangers, they are by no means so sure that the latter will not be prematurely exhausted, especially if the war last longer than they expect, which it very likely will. In a single battle the Peloponnesians and their allies may be able to defy all Hellas, but they are incapacitated from carrying on a war against a power different in character from their own, by the want of the single council-chamber requisite to prompt and vigorous action, and the substitution of a diet composed of various races, in which every state possesses an equal vote, and each presses its own ends, a condition of things which generally results in no action at all. The great wish of some is to avenge themselves on some particular enemy, the great wish of others to save their own pocket. Slow in assembling, they devote a very small fraction of the time to the consideration of any public object, most of it to the prosecution of their own objects. Meanwhile each fancies that no harm will come of his neglect, that it is the business of somebody else to look after this or that for him; and so, by the same notion being entertained by all separately, the common cause imperceptibly decays.

[142]. But the principal point is the hindrance that they will experience from want of money. The slowness with which it comes in will cause delay; but the opportunities of war wait for no man. Again, we need not be alarmed either at the possibility of their raising fortifications in Attica, or at their navy. It would be difficult for any system of fortifications to establish a rival city, even in time of peace, much more, surely, in an enemy's country, with Athens just as much fortified against it, as it against Athens; while a mere post might be able to do some harm to the country by incursions and by the facilities which it would afford for desertion, but can never prevent our sailing into their country and raising fortifications there, and making reprisals

with our powerful fleet. For our naval skill is of more use to us for service on land, than their military skill for service at sea. Familiarity with the sea they will not find an easy acquisition. If you who have been practising at it ever since the Median invasion have not yet brought it to perfection, is there any chance of anything considerable being effected by an agricultural, unseafaring population, who will besides be prevented from practising by the constant presence of strong squadrons of observation from Athens? With a small squadron they might hazard an engagement, encouraging their ignorance by numbers; but the restraint of a strong force will prevent their moving, and through want of practice they will grow more clumsy, and consequently more timid. It must be kept in mind that seamanship, just like anything else, is a matter of art, and will not admit of being taken up occasionally as an occupation for times of leisure; on the contrary, it is so exacting as to leave leisure for nothing else.

[143]. Even if they were to touch the moneys at Olympia or Delphi, and try to seduce our foreign sailors by the temptation of higher pay, that would only be a serious danger if we could not still be a match for them, by embarking our own citizens and the aliens resident among us. But in fact by this means we are always a match for them; and, best of all, we have a larger and higher class of native coxswains and sailors among our own citizens than all the rest of Hellas. And to say nothing of the danger of such a step, none of our foreign sailors would consent to become an outlaw from his country, and to take service with them and their hopes, for the sake of a few days' high pay.

This, I think, is a tolerably fair account of the position of the Peloponnesians; that of Athens is free from the defects that I have criticised in them, and has other advantages of its own, which they can show nothing to equal. If they march against our country we will sail against theirs, and it will then be found that the desolation of the whole of Attica is not the same as that of even a fraction of Peloponnese; for they will not be able to supply the deficiency except by a battle, while we have plenty of land both on the islands and the continent. The rule of the sea is indeed a great matter. Consider for a moment. Suppose that we were islanders: can you conceive a more impregnable position? Well, this in future should, as far as possible, be our conception of our position. Dismissing all thought of our land and houses, we must vigilantly guard the sea and the city. No irritation that we may feel for the former must provoke us to a battle with the numerical superiority of the Peloponnesians. A victory would only be succeeded by another battle against the same superiority: a reverse involves the loss of our allies, the source of our strength, who will not remain quiet a day after we become unable to march against them. We must cry not over the loss of houses and land but of men's lives; since houses and land do not gain men, but men them. And if I had thought that I could persuade you, I would have bid you go out and lay them waste with your own hands, and show the Peloponnesians that this at any rate will not make you submit.

[144]. I have many other reasons to hope for a favourable issue, if you can consent not to combine schemes of fresh conquest with the conduct of the war, and will abstain from wilfully involving yourselves in other dangers; indeed, I am more afraid of our own blunders than of the enemy's devices. But these matters shall be explained in another speech, as events require; for the present dismiss these men with the answer that we will allow Megara the use of our market and harbours, when the Lacedaemonians suspend their alien acts in favour of us and our allies, there being nothing in the treaty to prevent either one or the other: that we will leave the cities independent, if independent we found them when we made the treaty, and when the Lacedaemonians grant to their cities an independence not involving subservience to Lacedaemonian interest, but such as each severally may desire: that we are willing to give the legal satisfaction which our agreements specify, and that we shall not commence hostilities, but shall resist those who do commence them. This is an answer agreeable at once to the rights and the dignity of Athens. It must be thoroughly understood that war is a necessity; but that the more readily we accept it, the less will be the ardour of our opponents, and that out of the greatest dangers communities and individuals acquire the greatest glory. Did not our fathers resist the Medes not only with resources far different from ours, but even when those resources had been abandoned; and more by wisdom than by fortune, more by daring than by strength, did not they beat off the barbarian and advance their affairs to their present height? We must not fall behind them, but must resist our enemies in any way and in every way, and attempt to hand down our power to our posterity unimpaired.

§

The Funeral Oration of Pericles
Book II 35-46
431 B.C.

In any collection of the world's great orations the "Funeral Oration" of Pericles would rank just above or co-equal with Demosthenes' "On the Crown" and Cicero's "Philippics." This is true whether Pericles really wrote the words that Thucydides published or not. History now attaches the name of Pericles to the oration even though we cannot be sure that Thucydides actually heard its delivery. He may have been present. But again, the style is so unlike the rest of the speeches in Thucydides that we assume it bears the stamp of Pericles. Those who admire the speech consider it the greatest of its kind in literature. It is analyzed in detail in chapter 5 (pp. 151-174) of *Interpreting Literature*, by Knox C. Hill, Chicago, 1966.

Of all the speeches in the *History* the Funeral Oration deserves the closest study — if only for the reason that its subtleties so easily escape the reader's notice. Its art conceals its method.

The speech is full of noble sentiments about democracy, the duties of citizens, the qualities of leaders, the values of open and free discussion, and the responsibilities of women in the state. Pericles deals with the Athenian way of life in its broadest sense and he assumes we will bear in mind, as Pericles perhaps assumed his hearers would bear in mind, the main features of the Spartan way of life.

What were the circumstances? In accordance with ancient Greek custom it was spoken for Athenians who had first fallen in the Peloponnesian War. Pericles seized the opportunity, much as Lincoln did at Gettysburg in 1863, to give an ideal picture of the Athenian state. As Werner Jaeger says: "No translation can rival Thucydides' masterly ease in coping with the difficult task; abandoning all the trivialities of formal oratory, he describes the contemporary city-state, with the superb practical energy of its imperialist policy and the indescribable variety of its spiritual and vital force so as to weld it all into one great unity" (*Paideia* I 408).

A recent writer has called the Funeral Oration "the greatest statement of democratic theory in our possession." It is the one and only example in the *History* of an epideictic oration. It is worth re-reading today as a reminder of our blessings.

The feature of the Funeral Oration that will most repay study is the variety of antitheses that are developed. These include: Words against deeds. Change against status quo. Ideas of leaders of Athens and of Sparta. Idealism against practicality. Written versus unwritten laws. Truth against lies. Honesty against dishonesty. Integrity and character against their lack. What is stated against what is implied. The short range view against the long range view. What is planned and foreseen against what is unplanned and unforeseen. The Good Life against the Life for the State. Pericles against his successors. This last contrast becomes more apparent in each Book of the *History* until the final disaster in Sicily.

Mid-twentieth century readers will appreciate the importance Pericles attaches to variety and change of pace in daily life. He extols the value of recreation, of allowing foreigners to the city, of freely carrying on trade, of encouraging free speech. All these attributes and more Athens possessed and, the implication is clear, Sparta did not.

The fact that Thucydides puts all the values of Athenian citizenship and residence into words expressed by Pericles simply reinforces his admiration for that leader. Why? Because many of these virtues came directly from the administration and policies of Pericles.

One of the striking contrasts of the Funeral Oration is found in the exposition of ἀρετή, excellence or goodness, by Pericles in II 40.4-5 and Cleon's defense of power at III 37.2 and III 40.2-3. Again, Thucydides expects us to keep Pericles in mind when we hear Cleon. The two speaking situations comprise a classic example of the intellectual's view against the non-intellectual's.

In our day ceremonial oratory is less frequent and certainly less well done than in ancient Athens. Audiences and speakers understood and appreciated the funeral oration far better than we do. For this reason it may help to select from some dozen references in Aristotle's *Rhetoric* a few of the requirements or the essential features of the epideictic speech. These are quotations or brief paraphrases:

1. Narration in ceremonial oratory is not continuous but intermittent. The speech is a composition containing (1) The actions themselves and (2) the proof, their quality or extent. (16^b 15ff.).

2. "In ceremonial oratory intersperse your speech with bits of episodic eulogy." (18^a 33).

3. "In ceremonial speeches you will develop your case mainly by arguing what has been done is, e.g., noble and useful. The facts themselves are to be taken on trust; proof of them is only submitted when they are not easily credible or when they have been set down to someone else." (17^b 31).

4. "In speeches of display we must make the hearer feel that the eulogy includes either himself or his family or his way of life or something or other of the kind." (15^b 28).

5. "So in speeches of display the writer should proceed in the same way (with a musical prelude as flute players do). The usual subject for introductions to speeches of display is some piece of praise or censure." (14^b 22ff.).

6. "It is only natural that methods of 'heightening the effect' should be attached particularly to speeches of praise; they aim at proving superiority over others, and any such superiority is a form of nobleness." (68^a 23).

7. "The noble is that which is both desirable for its own sake and also worthy of praise; or that which is both good and also pleasant because good. ...Courage is the virtue that disposes men to noble deeds in situations of danger in

accordance with the law and in obedience to its commands; cowardice is the opposite." (66ª 33ff.).

Aristotle does cite the "Funeral Oration" by Pericles in his *Rhetoric* and he surely must have had a speech like it in mind when he discussed the typical speech of praise and blame. Many of the qualities given above are illustrated in the Funeral Oration. And yet it departs from the traditional formula in several ways.

Instead of centering at length on the deeds of the heroic dead, Pericles went to higher ground. He sketched with discrimination the attributes of Athens — a democracy *par excellence*. It calls to mind some parts of Plato and the author of *The Athenian Commonwealth* whom Gilbert Murray called the Old Oligarch.

The reader should compare the ideas of Athenian life expressed in II 39-40 with those of Spartan life as expressed by Archidamus in I 83-84. So tightly is the *History* written that Thucydides assumes his reader will keep Sparta's characteristics in mind when he "listens" to Pericles discuss those of Athens. There are many instances in the *History* like this to prove its unity, as Professor Finley has so painstakingly detailed.

It is impossible to paraphrase the speech, but here are some of the points which Pericles sketches as qualities of Athenian democracy:

1. Unlike Sparta we live under an original and model form of government.
2. All men are equal for the settlement of their private disputes.
3. Our practices are distinctive: majority rule, freedom of speech, equality of opportunity, tolerance of others, private life without restriction, and respect for authority and law.
4. Public encouragement of culture and relaxation.
5. A high standard of living.

6. Athens welcomes foreigners.

7. We foster courage by taking our loss and by our manner of life rather than by military compulsion.

8. We are lovers of beauty with simplicity and lovers of wisdom but without softness.

9. We alone regard the man who takes no part in public affairs, not as one who minds his own business, but as a good-for-nothing.

10. We make the most important decisions — (unlike the Spartans who have decisions made for them).

11. Unlike others we are superior and most daring in action and yet we are most willing to discuss and reflect on our courses of action.

12. Athens is not provincial — we are admired both by subjects and enemies and our power extends to "every sea and every land."

With this kind of exposition of what Athens stands for, Pericles sums up: "Such then is the city for which these men nobly fought and died, deeming it their duty not to let her be taken from them; and it is fitting that every man who is left behind should suffer willingly for her sake."

This is how Thucydides and Pericles and — if we can believe Plato — Aspasia achieved the heightening effect that gives the Funeral Oration its austere, sublime beauty. It was conceived and spoken too, by the right man, the Olympian.

The traditional parts — a lament and consolation — conclude the address.

Perhaps the one sentence that stands above the others is this: "In a word, I say that our city is the school of Hellas and that Athenians as individuals would seem to me supremely fitted to meet the varied circumstances of life with grace and self-reliance" (II 41.1).

§

[35]. Most of my predecessors in this place have commended him who made this speech part of the law, telling us that it is well that it should be delivered at the burial of those who fall in battle. For myself, I should have thought that the worth which had displayed itself in deeds, would be sufficiently rewarded by honours also shown by deeds; such as you now see in this funeral prepared at the people's cost. And I could have wished that the reputations of many brave men were not to be imperilled in the mouth of a single individual, to stand or fall according as he spoke well or ill. For it is hard to speak properly upon a subject where it is even difficult to convince your hearers that you are speaking the truth. On the one hand, the friend who is familiar with every fact of the story, may think that some point has not been set forth with that fulness which he wishes and knows it to deserve; on the other, he who is a stranger to the matter may be led by envy to suspect exaggeration if he hears anything above his own nature. For men can endure to hear others praised only so long as they can severally persuade themselves of their own ability to equal the actions recounted: when this point is passed, envy comes in and with it incredulity. However, since our ancestors have stamped this custom with their approval, it becomes my duty to obey the law and to try to satisfy your several wishes and opinions as best I may.

[36]. I shall begin with our ancestors: it is both just and proper that they should have the honour of the first mention on an occasion like the present. They dwelt in the country without break in the succession from generation to generation, and handed it down free to the present time by their valour. And if our more remote ancestors deserve praise, much more do our own fathers, who added to their inheritance the empire which we now possess, and spared no pains to be able to leave their acquisitions to us of the present generation. Lastly, there are few parts of our dominions that have not been augmented by those of us here, who are still more or less in the vigour of life; while the mother country has been furnished by us with everything that can enable her to depend on her own resources whether for war or for peace. That part of our history which tells of the military achievements which gave us our several possessions, or of the ready valour with which either we or our fathers stemmed the tide of Hellenic or foreign aggression, is a theme too familiar to my hearers for me to dilate on, and I shall therefore pass it by. But what was the road by which we reached our position, what

the form of government under which our greatness grew, what the national habits out of which it sprang; these are questions which I may try to solve before I proceed to my panegyric upon these men; since I think this to be a subject upon which on the present occasion a speaker may properly dwell, and to which the whole assemblage, whether citizens or foreigners, may listen with advantage.

[37]. Our constitution does not copy the laws of neighbouring states; we are rather a pattern to others than imitators ourselves. Its administration favours the many instead of the few; this is why it is called a democracy. If we look to the laws, they afford equal justice to all in their private differences; if to social standing, advancement in public life falls to reputation for capacity, class considerations not being allowed to interfere with merit; nor again does poverty bar the way, if a man is able to serve the state, he is not hindered by the obscurity of his condition. The freedom which we enjoy in our government extends also to our ordinary life. There, far from exercising a jealous surveillance over each other, we do not feel called upon to be angry with our neighbour for doing what he likes, or even to indulge in those injurious looks which cannot fail to be offensive, although they inflict no positive penalty. But all this ease in our private relations does not make us lawless as citizens. Against this fear is our chief safeguard, teaching us to obey the magistrates and the laws, particularly such as regard the protection of the injured, whether they are actually on the statute book, or belong to that code which, although unwritten, yet cannot be broken without acknowledged disgrace.

[38]. Further, we provide plenty of means for the mind to refresh itself from business. We celebrate games and sacrifices all the year round, and the elegance of our private establishments forms a daily source of pleasure and helps to banish the spleen; while the magnitude of our city draws the produce of the world into our harbour, so that to the Athenian the fruits of other countries are as familiar a luxury as those of his own.

[39]. If we turn to our military policy, there also we differ from our antagonists. We throw open our city to the world, and never by alien acts exclude foreigners from any opportunity of learning or observing, although the eyes of an enemy may occasionally profit by our liberality; trusting less in system and policy than to the native spirit of our citizens; while in education, where our rivals from their very cradles by a painful discipline seek after manliness, at Athens we live exactly as we please, and yet are just as ready to encounter every legitimate

danger. In proof of this it may be noticed that the Lacedaemonians do not invade our country alone, but bring with them all their confederates; while we Athenians advance unsupported into the territory of a neighbour, and fighting upon a foreign soil usually vanquish with ease men who are defending their homes. Our united force was never yet encountered by any enemy, because we have at once to attend to our marine and to despatch our citizens by land upon a hundred different services; so that, wherever they engage with some such fraction of our strength, a success against a detachment is magnified into a victory over the nation, and a defeat into a reverse suffered at the hands of our entire people. And yet if with habits not of labour but of ease, and courage not of art but of nature, we are still willing to encounter danger, we have the double advantage of escaping the experience of hardships in anticipation and of facing them in the hour of need as fearlessly as those who are never free from them.

[40]. Nor are these the only points in which our city is worthy of admiration. We cultivate refinement without extravagance and knowledge without effeminacy; wealth we employ more for use than for show, and place the real disgrace of poverty not in owning to the fact but in declining the struggle against it. Our public men have, besides politics, their private affairs to attend to, and our ordinary citizens, though occupied with the pursuits of industry, are still fair judges of public matters; for, unlike any other nation, regarding him who takes no part in these duties not as unambitious but as useless, we Athenians are able to judge at all events if we cannot originate, and instead of looking on discussion as a stumbling-block in the way of action, we think it an indispensable preliminary to any wise action at all. Again, in our enterprises we present the singular spectacle of daring and deliberation, each carried to its highest point, and both united in the same persons; although usually decision is the fruit of ignorance, hesitation of reflexion. But the palm of courage will surely be adjudged most justly to those, who best know the difference between hardship and pleasure and yet are never tempted to shrink from danger. In generosity we are equally singular, acquiring our friends by conferring not by receiving favours. Yet, of course, the doer of the favour is the firmer friend of the two, in order by continued kindness to keep the recipient in his debt; while the debtor feels less keenly from the very consciousness that the return he makes will be a payment, not a free gift. And it is only the Athenians who, fearless of consequences, confer their benefits not from calculations of expediency, but in the confidence of liberality.

[41]. In short, I say that as a city we are the school of Hellas; while I doubt if the world can produce a man, who where he has only himself to depend upon, is equal to so many emergencies, and graced by so happy a versatility as the Athenian. And that this is no mere boast thrown out for the occasion, but plain matter of fact, the power of the state acquired by these habits proves. For Athens alone of her contemporaries is found when tested to be greater than her reputation, and alone gives no occasion to her assailants to blush at the antagonist by whom they have been worsted, or to her subjects to question her title by merit to rule. Rather, the admiration of the present and succeeding ages will be ours, since we have not left our power without witness, but have shown it by mighty proofs; and far from needing a Homer for our panegyrist, or other of his craft whose verses might charm for the moment only for the impression which they gave to melt at the touch of fact, we have forced every sea and land to be the highway of our daring, and everywhere, whether for evil or for good, have left imperishable monuments behind us.

[42]. Such is the Athens for which these men, in the assertion of their resolve not to lose her, nobly fought and died; and well may every one of their survivors be ready to suffer in her cause.

Indeed if I have dwelt at some length upon the character of our country, it has been to show that our stake in the struggle is not the same as theirs who have no such blessings to lose, and also that the panegyric of the men over whom I am now speaking might be by definite proofs established. That panegyric is now in a great measure complete; for the Athens that I have celebrated is only what the heroism of these and their like have made her, men whose fame, unlike that of most Hellenes, will be found to be only commensurate with the deserts. And if a test of worth be wanted, it is to be found in their closing scene, and this not only in the cases in which it set the final seal upon their merit, but also in those in which it gave the first intimation of their having any. For there is justice in the claim that steadfastness in his country's battles should be as a cloak to cover a man's other imperfections; since the good action has blotted out the bad, and his merit as a citizen more than outweighed his demerits as an individual. But none of these allowed either wealth with its prospect of future enjoyment to unnerve his spirit, or poverty with its hope of a day of freedom and riches to tempt him to shrink from danger. No, holding that vengeance upon their enemies was more to be desired than any personal blessings, and reckoning this to be the most glorious of hazards, they joyfully determined to accept the risk, to make sure of their vengeance and to let their wishes wait; and while committing to hope the uncertainty of final success, in the business before them they thought fit to act boldly and trust in themselves. Thus choosing to die resisting, rather than to live submitting, they fled only from dishonour, but met danger face to face, and after one brief moment, while at the summit of their fortune, escaped, not from their fear, but from their glory.

[43]. So died these men as became Athenians. You, their survivors, must determine to have as unaltering a resolution in the field, though you may pray that it may have a happier issue. And not contented with ideas derived only from words of the advantages which are bound up with the defence of your country, though these would furnish a valuable text to a speaker even before an audience so alive to them as the present, you must yourselves realise the power of Athens, and feed your eyes upon her from day to day, till love of her fills your hearts; and then when all her greatness shall break upon you, you must reflect that it was by courage, sense of duty, and a keen feeling of honour in action that men were enabled to win all this, and that no personal failure in an enterprise could make them consent to deprive their country of their valour, but they laid it at her feet as the most glorious contribution that they could offer. For this offering of their lives made in common by them all they each of them individually received that renown which never grows old, and for a sepulchre, not so much that in which their bones have been deposited, but that noblest of shrines wherein their glory is laid up to be eternally remembered upon every occasion on which deed or story shall fall for its commemoration. For heroes have the whole earth for their tomb; and in lands far from their own, where the column with its epitaph declares it, there is enshrined in every breast a record unwritten with no tablet to preserve it, except that of the heart. These take as your model, and judging happiness to be the fruit of freedom and freedom of valour, never decline the dangers of war. For it is not the miserable that would most justly be unsparing of their lives; these have nothing to hope for: it is rather they to whom continued life may bring reverses as yet unknown, and to whom a fall, if it came, would be most tremendous in its consequences. And surely, to a man of spirit, the degradation of cowardice must be immeasurably more grievous than the unfelt death which strikes him in the midst of his strength and patriotism!

[44]. Comfort, therefore, not condolence, is what I have to offer to the parents of the dead who may be here. Numberless are the chances

to which, as they know, the life of man is subject; but fortunate indeed are they who draw for their lot a death so glorious as that which has caused your mourning, and to whom life has been so exactly measured as to terminate in the happiness in which it has been passed. Still I know that this is a hard saying, especially when those are in question of whom you will constantly be reminded by seeing in the homes of others blessings of which once you also boasted: for grief is felt not so much for the want of what we have never known, as for the loss of that to which we have been long accustomed. Yet you who are still of an age to beget children must bear up in the hope of having others in their stead; not only will they help you to forget those whom you have lost, but will be to the state at once a reinforcement and a security; for never can a fair or just policy be expected of the citizen who does not, like his fellows, bring to the decision the interests and apprehensions of a father. While those of you who have passed your prime must congratulate yourselves with the thought that the best part of your life was fortunate, and that the brief span that remains will be cheered by the fame of the departed. For it is only the love of honour that never grows old; and honour it is, not gain, as some would have it, that rejoices the heart of age and helplessness.

[45]. Turning to the sons or brothers of the dead, I see an arduous struggle before you. When a man is gone, all are wont to praise him, and should your merit be ever so transcendent, you will still find it difficult not merely to overtake, but even to approach their renown. The living have envy to contend with, while those who are no longer in our path are honoured with a goodwill into which rivalry does not enter. On the other hand, if I must say anything on the subject of female excellence to those of you who will now be in widowhood, it will be all comprised in this brief exhortation. Great will be your glory in not falling short of your natural character; and greatest will be hers who is least talked of among the men whether for good or for bad.

[46]. My task is now finished. I have performed it to the best of my ability, and in words, at least, the requirements of the law are now satisfied. If deeds be in question, those who are here interred have received part of their honours already, and for the rest, their children will be brought up till manhood at the public expense: the state thus offers a valuable prize, as the garland of victory in this race of valour, for the reward both of those who have fallen and their survivors. And where the rewards for merit are greatest, there are found the best citizens.

And now that you have brought to a close your lamentations for your relatives, you may depart.

§

Pericles to the Athenian Ecclesia
Book II 60-64
430 B.C.

Before reading Pericles' third speech or rather, *after* reading the Funeral Oration, the reader should study that famous section of the *History* on The Plague in Book II 47-59. It stands out in sharp relief from the model Athens Pericles praised in the *Epitaphios* and, as scholars have long pointed out, is deliberately designed to make the reader aware of one extreme with another — in this case of an ideal view of Athens with the stark reality of a city suffering great disaster.

It is this very disaster that compelled Pericles as a *Strategos* to call the Assembly together so he could re-state his position on the war and revive flagging spirits.

"Sometimes in my arrogant way I think that no one should deal with present-day international politics who has not studied Thucydides, and when I say 'studied' I include every detail of language and history; sometimes in reverse I think that the gods arranged the flow of events in the first half of this 20th century expressly so that we may understand Thucydides and the ancient Greek world."[1] The speaker is A.W. Gomme and the occasion — the Sather Classical Lecture at Berkeley in 1952. Now, twenty years later, with the United States concluding a bitter, indecisive war against the Viet Cong in Viet Nam the wisdom of Gomme's words is even more obvious.

Of all the speeches in the *History* that clearly portray the qualities of the statesman — and have most to offer to us today — none is more useful than Pericles to the Ecclesia in 430 B.C. — just after the plague had struck Athens. Morale in Athens was low, the people were tired of the war, the will to fight was gone, the Athenians wanted peace.

---

1. A.W. Gomme, *The Greek Attitude to Poetry and History*, Berkeley and Los Angeles, 1954, p. 156.

Pericles makes no concessions about the necessity of the war (II 61.1-2). He admits that reverses are highly discouraging but like a good field commander he urges the Athenians to "be ready to face the greatest disasters and still to keep unimpaired the lustre of your name" (II 61.3-4).

Pericles faced a hostile audience. He was sick himself, he had lost two sons stricken by the plague, and he faced his own political ruin. Since he was still general he called the Assembly for two purposes — to restore confidence and "of leading them from these angry feelings to a calmer and more hopeful state of mind."

The three main points of the speech are: (1) an appeal to renewed patriotism and the will to fight, (2) the incomparable value of the Athenian navy, and (3) a new evaluation of Athenian imperialism. In chapter 60 Pericles justifies the war a second time and in the process sketches the attributes of the ideal politician. This was Pericles' way of introducing his own *ethos* and very effective it was because the Assembly voted to give up "all idea of sending (heralds) to Lacedaemon, and applied themselves with increased energy to the war." But the result was temporary. Pericles was later fined when his accounts were slightly out of order and his policies were renounced. "Not long afterwards, however, according to the way of the masses, they again elected him general and entrusted all their affairs to his hands, having now become less sensitive to their private and domestic afflictions, and understanding that he was the best man of all for the public necessities."

Was the speech a success? Yes, in that the audience did what the speaker wanted. No, in the sense that the same audience soon changed its mind.

The speech contains some notable passages that should be discussed. The first (II 62.3-5) expresses a view that proud or arrogant leaders have echoed many times since:

go to meet your enemies not only with pride in your heart, but despising them. Not boasting; that is for the fool in a time of prosperity or even for the coward. But to despise is the privilege of those whose *judgement* reveals that they are stronger, which is our case now. Intelligence, based on a feeling of superiority which gives strength to daring; it does not rely on hope, which is the resort of the desperate, but on judgement based on true facts.[2]

The important point for us, as Gomme points out is that Thucydides uses the very same Greek words as translated by "judgement based on the facts" in another situation to denote a different interpretation. The Spartans, for example, found that "judgement based on the facts" failed them at Sphacteria (IV 18.2).

The part about the great strategic value of the Athenian navy (II 62.1-2) is Pericles' trump card. He has not mentioned it before but the occasion demands it now. Athens operates on both land and sea. "In the whole of one of these [the sea] you are completely supreme, not merely as far as you use it at present, but also to any further extent you may think fit; in fine, your naval resources are such that your vessels may go where they please, without the King or any other nation on earth being able to stop them." Perhaps it was this very argument that made the Athenians violate the injunction of Pericles about expansion of empire and rush into the conquest of Sicily.

Another famous passage is at II 63.2-3. It deals with the benefits of an empire and sketches out the duties and the responsibilities of the citizens:

The issue is not only slavery or independence, but also loss of empire and dangers from the animosities to which it has exposed you. Besides, to recede is no longer possible, if indeed any of you in the alarm of the moment has become enamoured of the honesty of such an unambitious part. What you hold is, to speak frankly, a

---

2. *Ibid.*, p. 153.

despotism; perhaps it was wrong to take it, but to let it go is
unsafe. Men of these retiring views, making converts of others,
could quickly ruin a state; indeed the result would be the same if
they could live independent by themselves; for the retiring and
unambitious are never secure without vigourous protectors at their
side; in fine, such qualities are useless to an imperial city, though
they may help a dependency to an unmolested servitude. (Crawley
translation)

An orator soothes, warns, arouses, and inspires. Pericles
was adept at all of these. At II 64.3 he discusses the glories of
empire. He holds out the rewards of great riches and the life
of luxury that empire is supposed to give. Even so, all things
change and even empires fade. But "even if now, in
obedience to the general law of decay, we should ever be
freed to yield, still it will be remembered that we held rule
over more Greeks than any other Greek state, that we
sustained the greatest wars against their united or separate
powers, and inhabited a city unrivalled by any other in
resources or magnitude." In the World's Classics edition of
the *History*, the editor, Sir R.W. Livingstone, drily adds the
comment (p. 128): "This sentence must have been written
after the disastrous end of the war."

There is nothing subtle about Pericles' conclusion. It is
virtually a command: decide now for honor and glory in days
to come, achieve both by hard work today, do not send
heralds to Sparta, don't show any signs of being down-
hearted. It's simply a case of getting the job done and the war
won, he concludes.

Pericles goes on begging the Assembly not to be led astray
by the aristocratic Peace Party pleas. His final sentences are
remarkable. They are full of passion and plausible reason.
They appeal to pride and tradition, the glories of the past,
and the hopes of the future. "These glories may incur the
censure of the slow and the unambitious; but in the breast of
energy they will awaken emulation, and in those who must
remain without them an obvious regret" (II 64.4).

The final paragraph of Pericles' third speech has echoes in the plays of Euripides, as Finley has so carefully shown (*Three Essays*, p. 28). Without repeating the citations from Euripides the references from the *History* concern the harangue about keeping up the fight (II 64.2), the fact that all great institutions pass away (II 64.3), and the value of perseverance when great ends are at stake (II 64.5). These concepts could not fail to strike home when stated by a man of Pericles' stature. Indeed, few others could have made them so credible.

The Greek word προθυμία may be roughly translated by zeal, earnestness, readiness, and willingness. Pericles closes (II 64.6) his third speech by implying that all these meanings of the word are demanded if the war is to be won.

Finally, in unmistakable language Pericles "makes his charge": no more thought about sending envoys with peace feelers; don't show signs of being depressed just now; the truly great men and nations do not buckle with misfortune; they are the most steadfast in meeting it.

This third speech of Pericles is distinctive in many ways. It reveals an uncanny knowledge of Athenian emotions. It shows the impact of one man's integrity as a form of appeal. It introduces the argument of the supremacy of naval power for the first time. It shows, as Finley points out, "the full implications of the doctrine of πολυπραγμοσύνη, the doctrine that the capacity and the will to do forever cause and justify change. ...To Thucydides, this will to do, which is thus identified with Athenian democracy, undoubtedly seemed fundamental to history."[3]

This is the speech more than any other that caused Aristophanes to say that Pericles "lightened, and thundered, and embroiled all Greece."[4] Cicero praised the grandeur and loftiness of Pericles (*Orator*, 119) and the explanation for his superior qualities probably is found in Plato's *Phaedrus* 269 e4, where Socrates argues that Pericles had profited from

3. John H. Finley, Jr. *Thucydides,* London, 1947, p. 154.
4. Archarnians 530-531.

his study with Anaxagoras. The view is confirmed by Cicero in the *Brutus* X. 44 — "but having been trained by Anaxagoras, the natural philosopher, he found it easy to transfer that mental discipline from obscure and abstruse problems to the business of the forum and the popular assembly."

In recent days when Americans were torn between the arguments of "doves" and "hawks" about the Viet Nam war it was speakers like Senator Fulbright and Senator McGovern who best represented the ability (not the arguments) of Pericles to explain and persuade by philosophic principles rather than by the tactics or the strategy of the moment. Unlike Pericles they were not widely popular speakers. But their arguments were compelling to those willing to listen. They both spoke as if they had *studied* Thucydides.

§

[60]. I was not unprepared for the indignation of which I have been the object, as I know its causes; and I have called an assembly for the purpose of reminding you upon certain points, and of protesting against your being unreasonably irritated with me, or cowed by your sufferings. I am of opinion that national greatness is more for the advantage of private citizens, than any individual well-being coupled with public humiliation. A man may be personally ever so well off, and yet if his country be ruined he must be ruined with it; whereas a flourishing commonwealth always affords chances of salvation to unfortunate individuals. Since then a state can support the misfortunes of private citizens, while they cannot support hers, it is surely the duty of every one to be forward in her defence, and not like you to be so confounded with your domestic afflictions as to give up all thoughts of the common safety, and to blame me for having counselled war and yourselves for having voted it. And yet if you are angry with me, it is with one who, as I believe, is second to no man either in knowledge of the proper policy, or in the ability to expound it, and who is moreover not only a patriot but an honest one. A man possessing that knowledge without that faculty of exposition might as well have no idea at all on the matter: if he had both these gifts, but no love for his country, he

would be but a cold advocate for her interests; while were his patriotism not proof against bribery, everything would go for a price. So that if you thought that I was even moderately distinguished for these qualities when you took my advice and went to war, there is certainly no reason now why I should be charged with having done wrong.

[61]. For those of course who have a free choice in the matter and whose fortunes are not at stake, war is the greatest of follies. But if the only choice was between submission with loss of independence, and danger with the hope of preserving that independence, — in such a case it is he who will not accept the risk that deserves blame, not he who will. I am the same man and do not alter, it is you who change, since in fact you took my advice while unhurt, and waited for misfortune to repent of it; and the apparent error of my policy lies in the infirmity of your resolution, since the suffering that it entails is being felt by every one among you, while its advantage is still remote and obscure to all, and a great and sudden reverse having befallen you, your mind is too much depressed to persevere in your resolves. For before what is sudden, unexpected, and least within calculation the spirit quails; and putting all else aside, the plague has certainly been an emergency of this kind. Born, however, as you are, citizens of a great state, and brought up, as you have been, with habits equal to your birth, you should be ready to face the greatest disasters and still to keep unimpaired the lustre of your name. For the judgment of mankind is as relentless to the weakness that falls short of a recognised renown, as it is jealous of the arrogance that aspires higher than its due. Cease then to grieve for your private afflictions, and address yourselves instead to the safety of the commonwealth.

[62]. If you shrink before the exertions which the war makes necessary, and fear that after all they may not have a happy result, you know the reasons by which I have often demonstrated to you the groundlessness of your apprehension. If those are not enough, I will now reveal an advantage arising from the greatness of your dominion, which I think has never yet suggested itself to you, which I never mentioned in my previous speeches, and which has so bold a sound that I should scarce adventure it now, were it not for the unnatural depression which I see around me. You perhaps think that your empire extends only over your allies; I will declare to you the truth. The visible field of action has two parts, land and sea. In the whole of one of these you are completely supreme, not merely as far as you use it at present,

but also to what further extent you may think fit: in fine, your naval resources are such that your vessels may go where they please, without the king or any other nation on earth being able to stop them. So that although you may think it a great privation to lose the use of your land and houses, still you must see that this power is something widely different; and instead of fretting on their account, you should really regard them in the light of the gardens and other accessories that embellish a great fortune, and as, in comparison, of little moment. You should know too that liberty preserved by your efforts will easily recover for us what we have lost, while, the knee once bowed, even what you have will pass from you. Your fathers receiving these possessions not from others, but from themselves, did not let slip what their labour had acquired, but delivered them safe to you; and in this respect at least you must prove yourselves their equals, remembering that to lose what one has got is more disgraceful than to be baulked in getting, and you must confront your enemies not merely with spirit but with disdain. Confidence indeed a blissful ignorance can impart, ay, even to a coward's breast, but disdain is the privilege of those who, like us, have been assured by reflexion of their superiority to their adversary. And where the chances are the same, knowledge fortifies courage by the contempt which is its consequence, its trust being placed, not in hope, which is the prop of the desperate, but in a judgment grounded upon existing resources, whose anticipations are more to be depended upon.

[63]. Again, your country has a right to your services in sustaining the glories of her position. These are a common source of pride to you all, and you cannot decline the burdens of empire and still expect to share its honours. You should remember also that what you are fighting against is not merely slavery as an exchange for independence, but also loss of empire and danger from the animosities incurred in its exercise. Besides, to recede is no longer possible, if indeed any of you in the alarm of the moment has become enamoured of the honesty of such an unambitious part. For what you hold is, to speak somewhat plainly, a tyranny; to take it perhaps was wrong, but to let it go is unsafe. And men of these retiring views, making converts of others, would quickly ruin a state; indeed the result would be the same if they could live independent by themselves; for the retiring and unambitious are never secure without vigorous protectors at their side; in fine, such qualities are useless to an imperial city, though they may help a dependency to an unmolested servitude.

[64]. But you must not be seduced by citizens like these nor be angry with me, — who, if I voted for war, only did as you did yourselves, — in spite of the enemy having invaded your country and done what you could be certain that he would do, if you refused to comply with his demands; and although besides what we counted for, the plague has come upon us — the only point indeed at which our calculation has been at fault. It is this, I know, that has had a large share in making me more unpopular than I should otherwise have been, — quite undeservedly, unless you are also prepared to give me the credit of any success with which chance may present you. Besides, the hand of Heaven must be borne with resignation, that of the enemy with fortitude; this was the old way at Athens, and do not you prevent it being so still. Remember, too, that if your country has the greatest name in all the world, it is because she never bent before disaster; because she has expended more life and effort in war than any other city, and has won for herself a power greater than any hitherto known, the memory of which will descend to the latest posterity; even if now, in obedience to the general law of decay, we should ever be forced to yield, still it will be remembered that we held rule over more Hellenes than any other Hellenic state, that we sustained the greatest wars against their united or separate powers, and inhabited a city unrivalled by any other in resources or magnitude. These glories may incur the censure of the slow and unambitious; but in the breast of energy they will awake emulation, and in those who must remain without them an envious regret. Hatred and unpopularity at the moment have fallen to the lot of all who have aspired to rule others; but where odium must be incurred, true wisdom incurs it for the highest objects. Hatred also is short-lived; but that which makes the splendour of the present and the glory of the future remains for ever unforgotten. Make your decision, therefore, for glory then and honour now, and attain both objects by instant and zealous effort: do not send heralds to Lacedaemon, and do not betray any sign of being oppressed by your present sufferings, since they whose minds are least sensitive to calamity, and whose hands are most quick to meet it, are the greatest men and the greatest communities.

§

Some Comments on the Three Speeches by Pericles

Demosthenes, alone among orators imitated Thucydides in many particulars, as he imitated all writers who appeared to him to have achieved greatness and distinction. He acquired from him, and added to his own political speeches, merits which neither Antiphon, nor Lysias, nor Isocrates, the foremost orators of the day possessed: I mean swiftness, concentration, intensity, acrid pungency, and the force that arouses emotion. On the other hand, he neglected the recondite side of Thucydides' style, its strangeness and its poetical tinge, considering these qualities ill adapted to practical issues. Nor did he approve of Thucydides' use of figures of speech, straying far from the natural sequence of ideas, nor his solecisms. He confined himself to the normal, while embellishing his diction with variety and diversity of expression, and absolutely never expressing an idea in a perfectly direct way. His intricate sentences, which express much in a few words, sustain a lengthy grammatical connection, and make their point by an unexpected turn, Demosthenes emulated and introduced into his political and forensic speeches, using them more lavishly in public, than in private, suits. (From Section 53 *De Thucydide* by Dionysius of Halicarnassus. Trans. by W. Rhys Roberts)

How much of this high opinion of the influence of Thucydides upon Demosthenes is true is a question that is most difficult to verify. We may naturally assume that Demosthenes found the three speeches by Pericles most to his liking. They may have been the ones he studied most. Were these speeches really as spoken by Pericles or were they composed from memory by Thucydides? There is good evidence that Thucydides was in Athens during the times when Pericles spoke and it is highly probable he heard the man he admired so much. This does not mean he made and used a stenographic report.

In any event, the qualities which Dionysius singled out in the quotation above do apply in a remarkable way to the style of Pericles. The three speeches (I 140-144; II 35-46; II 60-64) do possess "swiftness, concentration, intensity, acrid pungency, and the force that arouses emotion." They are probably the best models in the entire *History*.

What other generalizations can we make about the speaker and the three speeches? Two speeches were made to the Athenian Assembly where decisions were made and one, the Funeral Oration, was on a ceremonial occasion. Pericles was about 68 years old and not well. All three contain antitheses in about the same proportion. Each forcefully portrays the *ethos* of the speaker — but with different emphasis. All three were given within a two-year period (432-430 B.C.) before Gorgias visited Athens in 427 B.C. In fact, Pericles died in 429 B.C. The Three Periclean Speeches are each longer than those of others. Taken together they contain more abstractions, more substance, more profound axioms or maxims about man and government than those of any other speaker. Pericles is the only speaker accorded (at II 65) a long and laudatory appraisal — "who owed his influence to his recognized standing and ability, and had proved himself clearly incorruptible in the highest degree, restrained the multitude while respecting their liberties, and led them rather than was led by them, because he did not resort to flattery, seeking power by dishonest means, but was able on the strength of his high reputation to oppose them and even provoke their wrath" (Smith trans. in Loeb edition, II 65.8-9).

It is true that Thucydides does not tell us all about Pericles' private life and that unlike Plutarch, he portrays his character only in the most favorable light. If Thucydides was thus either partial or impartial let it be said that the facts must have warranted that treatment. Alcibiades, Nicias, Cleon, and the rest of the Athenian leaders did not receive entirely favorable treatment in the *History*. They had defects of character that were indeed laid bare.

For our purposes perhaps the most useful comments on the three speeches by Pericles can be made about their style. Much under this heading centers under the use of antithesis.

Fortunately for this purpose we have available the detailed doctoral study by Grover Cleveland Kenyan of the University of Chicago (1941). He reports that "the three speeches of Pericles are uniformly highly antithetic" (p. 49).[1] Curiously, he discovers that antitheses appear less frequently in the eight speeches Thucydides probably heard (including all three by Pericles). And there is less use of antithesis relatively in those speeches given before 427 B.C., the date of Gorgias' embassy, than in those after 427. But Finley has shown that the so-called Gorgianic figures were well known in Athens before 427 and they were a common feature of the teachings of the sophists. Further, we know that Thucydides may have composed some of the speeches long after the visit of Gorgias. Thus the influence of Gorgianic figures in the early speeches of the *History* may seem anachronistic to some persons.

Jebb complains that in the Funeral Oration alone the word-deed contrast is used eighteen times ("Speeches of Thucydides," p. 383 n. 1) and we are familiar with Plato's parody of that excess in the *Menexenus* (236b). But this is not the full story of the overstraining of antitheses by any means.

Kenyan identifies and cites some 282 uses of all kinds of antitheses in the three Periclean speeches — 108 in the Funeral Oration, 91 in the first speech, and 83 in the third. It is impossible to detail all the varieties here — but they include the Intraclausal, those expressed by means of οὐκ—ἀλλά and καὶ οὐ, those by means of coordinating conjunctions, those by means of comparison, those by means of prepositions, those by means of other normal relations, those between two coordinate clauses, conjunctions used with antithetic clauses, those with one clause subordinate, those with infinitive clauses, those with finite verbs, those with mixed constructions, those by partly implied antithesis, and those of extended antithetic writing.

---

1. *Antithesis in the Speeches of the Greek Historians,* University of Chicago Libraries, Chicago, 1941.

To go into detail, the most familiar contrasts fall under the headings of: Greeks and barbarians, Athenians and Spartans, the weaker and the stronger, people of the present and people of the past, the dead and the living, Pericles and the people, war and peace, win and lose, take and give, word and deed, plan and execute, good and bad, freedom and slavery, Athens and Peloponnesus, land and sea, one's own land and another's, power and weakness, living and dying, large and small, fortune and misfortune, and numerous others where the Greek words or expressions are not easily rendered into English.

Truly, this compilation is a formidable list. Is it any wonder that Dionysius of Halicarnassus complained of the excessive use of antitheses — which Jebb defines as "the opposition of words, or of ideas, or of both in the two corresponding clauses of a sentence" (Jebb, *Attic Orators* I 98 n.1). It is only when we study the sentence-structure of the Periclean orations in minute detail that we realize the extent of the antitheses used. But if they are repelling to us nowadays they were not to the Athenians of the Age of Pericles. They delighted in them.

Pericles is also well known for his famous metaphors. They are the parts of a speech that an audience remembers best. Aristotle cites three examples of Periclean metaphors "of the most taking kind" and I quote from the Rhys Roberts translation: "Thus Pericles, for instance, said that the vanishing from their country of the young men who had fallen in the war was 'as if the spring were taken out of the year' (1411a 3 and 1365a 32), and 'Pericles compared the Samians to children who take their pap, but go on crying; and the Boeotians to holm-oaks because they were ruining one another by civil wars just as one oak causes another oak's fall' " (1407a 1-5). Again, Plutarch in his sketch of Pericles (8) says that Pericles could see war sweeping forward from the Peloponnesus.

It was Cicero (*De Oratore* II 22) who pointed out that the peculiarities of the style of Pericles were also present in Alcibiades and Thucydides (in the narrative part of the *History*). Thus we see again the profound influence which the teachings of the Sophists and the rhetoricians had in fifth-century Athens.

Thucydides uses few figures other than the antithesis.[2] We find these examples cited in Longinus *On the Sublime:* use of hyperbaton (ch. i.3), of the historic present (ch. xxv), and of the hyperbole (ch. xxxviii.3): "The Syracusans," he says, "came down to the water's edge and began the slaughter of those chiefly who were in the river, and the water at once became polluted, but none the less it was swallowed although muddy and mixed with blood, and to most it was still worth fighting for" (VII 84).

Thucydides and Antiphon are sometimes compared because of the similarity of their styles. But, generally speaking, Thucydides is more complex in his word-arrangement; he usually brings more clauses into his sentences, and yet in spite of these attributes Thucydides is more succinctly brief.

Two critics of Thucydides, an ancient and a modern, can best conclude this essay on the style of Thucydides. What each says applies especially to the three speeches by Pericles.

Eupolis (c.446-c.411), an author of the Old Comedy, wrote of Pericles: "This man, whenever he came forward, proved himself the greatest orator among men: like a good runner, he could give the other speakers ten feet start and win. ...Rapid, you call him; but besides his swiftness, a certain persuasion sat upon his lips — such was his spell: and, alone of the speakers, he ever left his sting in the hearers" (Eupolis, Δῆμοι, Bothe, *Frag. Com.* 1 162).

The other critic, later famous as the author of the *Wealth of Nations,* devoted an entire lecture to Thucydides in the

---

2. See John C. Robertson, *The Georgianic Figures in Early Greek Prose,* Johns Hopkins University doctoral dissertation, Baltimore, 1893, pp. 35-40.

recently published volume on his notes called *Lectures on Rhetoric and Belles Lettres.* Adam Smith spoke these words on Friday, 21 January 1763: "Pericles, in the oration Thucydides gives us in the introduction to the Peloponnesian War (I 140-144) is more correct, less exuberant and extravagant than the former [Lysias]; strong and nervous, precise and pointed, and carries along not only a direct commendation of the Athenians, but an indirect discommendation of the Lacaedemonians, then their rivals. His beauties are so manifest that I shall not insist on them any longer" (*Lectures,* ed. by John M. Lothian, Nelson and Sons, London, 1963, p. 135).

Such are the comments of many on the words uttered by Pericles, a foremost orator of his day, whose strength rested not so much in his well developed arguments, but in his own probity and his love of country. He was at home in Athens as the first of good men speaking well. I consider him one of the best political leaders who ever lived.

§

Mytilenean Envoys to the Peloponnesians at Olympia
Book III 9-14
428 B.C.

In 428 B.C. Mytilene, capital city of Lesbos decided the time was ripe to revolt from Athens. When the Athenians heard the plans they sent a delegation to persuade against such action. It met with no success, however, and Athens responded by sending out a naval force. "The generals delivered their orders, and upon the Mytilenians refusing to obey, commenced hostilities." Meanwhile, the Mytilenians had sent envoys to the Spartans to plead for admission to the Spartan league and thus for help against Athens. We read their appeal in the speech below.

It is almost certain that Thucydides did not hear this speech. He writes therefore on the basis of what he thought the envoys should have said under the circumstances. He uses the speech to describe what an old ally thought of Athens now that the costs of war had soared and the plague had taken its toll. It may be considered also as a contrasting speech to that of the Athenian envoys to Sparta at I 73-78. The two entirely different speeches provide one more comparative study of human nature under the stress of war.

"When you wish to support the formation of an alliance, you must make it clear that the occasion for doing so exists, and show if possible, that the proposed allies are just men, and that they have previously conferred some benefit upon the state, and that they are possessed of considerable power, and that they are situated near at hand." This is the advice given by the writer of the *Rhetorica ad Alexandrum* (1424b 35-40). This formula seems to have been in the minds of the Mytilenean envoys when they spoke to the Spartans at Olympia.

This speech is short and without much embellishment. The speaker begins by saying that Justice and Honesty will be his opening topics. And although the Mytilenians complain of no injustice from Athens they are moved by their own great desire for independence.

The high plane of the argument centers on the requisites for a successful alliance: (1) each party should be equally afraid of the other, (2) sympathy is the best basis of confidence but it has been replaced by terror, (3) a strong navy is a help until the other side fears it may unite with an enemy force, (4) paying court to the leaders of a democracy is necessary but they change and may get worse.

So, largely because of fear of what might happen Lesbos wanted to get out from under Athenian domination. "But if you will frankly support us, you will add to your side a state that has a large navy, which is your want; you will smooth the way to the overthrow of the Athenians by depriving them of their allies, who will be greatly encouraged to come over; and you will free yourselves from the charge made against you of not supporting those who revolt" (III 13.4).

What effect did the speech have? Its dramatic qualities won over the Spartans. They voted to take in the Lesbians, decided to invade Attica, ordered their allies present "to march as quickly as possible to the Isthmus with two thirds of their forces" and themselves prepared to attack Athens by sea and land at once.

The speech is remarkable for its compactness, its arguments based on likelihood and fear of destruction, or put another way, the instinct for self-preservation. The Spartans understood these appeals.

§

[9]. Lacedaemonians and allies, the rule established among the Hellenes is not unknown to us. Those who revolt in war and forsake their former confederacy are favourably regarded by those who receive them, in so far as they are of use to them, but otherwise are thought less well of, through being considered traitors to their former friends. Nor is this an unfair way of judging, where the rebels and the power from whom they secede are at one in policy and sympathy, and a

match for each other in resources and power, and where no reasonable ground exists for the rebellion. But with us and the Athenians this was not the case; and no one need think the worse of us for revolting from them in danger, after having been honoured by them in time of peace.

[10]. Justice and honesty will be the first topics of our speech, especially as we are asking for alliance; because we know that there can never be any solid friendship between individuals, or union between communities that is worth the name, unless the parties be persuaded of each other's honesty, and be generally congenial the one to the other; since from difference in feeling springs also difference in conduct. Between ourselves and the Athenians alliance began, when you withdrew from the Median war and they remained to finish the business. But we did not become allies of the Athenians for the subjugation of the Hellenes, but allies of the Hellenes for their liberation from the Mede; and as long as the Athenians led us fairly we followed them loyally; but when we saw them relax their hostility to the Mede, to try to compass the subjection of the allies, then our apprehensions began. Unable, however, to unite and defend themselves, on account of the number of confederates that had votes, all the allies were enslaved, except ourselves and the Chians, who continued to send our contingents as independent and nominally free. Trust in Athens as a leader, however, we could no longer feel, judging by the examples already given; it being unlikely that she would reduce our fellow-confederates, and not do the same by us who were left, if ever she had the power.

[11]. Had we all been still independent, we could have had more faith in their not attempting any change; but the greater number being their subjects, while they were treating us as equals, they would naturally chafe under this solitary instance of independence as contrasted with the submission of the majority; particularly as they daily grew more powerful, and we more destitute. Now the only sure basis of an alliance is for each party to be equally afraid of the other: he who would like to encroach is then deterred by the reflexion that he will not have odds in his favour. Again, if we were left independent, it was only because they thought they saw their way to empire more clearly by specious language and by the paths of policy than by those of force. Not only were we useful as evidence that powers who had votes, like themselves, would not, surely, join them in their expeditions, against their will, without the party attacked being in the wrong; but the same system also enabled them to lead the stronger states against the weaker first,

and so to leave the former to the last, stripped of their natural allies, and less capable of resistance. But if they had begun with us, while all the states still had their resources under their own control, and there was a centre to rally round, the work of subjugation would have been found less easy. Besides this, our navy gave them some apprehension: it was always possible that it might unite with you or with some other power, and become dangerous to Athens. The court which we paid to their commons and its leaders for the time being, also helped us to maintain our independence. However, we did not expect to be able to do so much longer, if this war had not broken out, from the examples that we had had of their conduct to the rest.

[12]. How then could we put our trust in such friendship or freedom as we had here? We accepted each other against our inclination; fear made them court us in war, and us them in peace; sympathy, the ordinary basis of confidence, had its place supplied by terror, fear having more share than friendship in detaining us in the alliance; and the first party that should be encouraged by the hope of impunity was certain to break faith with the other. So that to condemn us for being the first to break off, because they delay the blow that we dread, instead of ourselves delaying to know for certain whether it will be dealt or not, is to take a false view of the case. For if we were equally able with them to meet their plots and imitate their delay, we should be their equals and should be under no necessity of being their subjects; but the liberty of offence being always theirs, that of defence ought clearly to be ours.

[13]. Such, Lacedaemonians and allies, are the grounds and reasons of our revolt; clear enough to convince our hearers of the fairness of our conduct, and sufficient to alarm ourselves, and to make us turn to some means of safety. This we wished to do long ago, when we sent to you on the subject while the peace yet lasted, but were baulked by your refusing to receive us; and now, upon the Boeotians inviting us, we at once responded to the call, and decided upon a twofold revolt, from the Hellenes and from the Athenians, not to aid the latter in harming the former, but to join in their liberation, and not to allow the Athenians in the end to destroy us, but to act in time against them. Our revolt, however, has taken place prematurely and without preparation — a fact which makes it all the more incumbent on you to receive us into alliance and to send us speedy relief, in order to show that you support your friends, and at the same time do harm to your enemies. You have an opportunity such as you never had before. Disease and

expenditure have wasted the Athenians: their ships are either cruising round your coasts, or engaged in blockading us; and it is not probable that they will have any to spare, if you invade them a second time this summer by sea and land; but they will either offer no resistance to your vessels, or withdraw from both our shores. Nor must it be thought that this is a case of putting yourselves into danger for a country which is not yours. Lesbos may appear far off, but when help is wanted she will be found near enough. It is not in Attica that the war will be decided, as some imagine, but in the countries by which Attica is supported; and the Athenian revenue is drawn from the allies, and will become still larger if they reduce us; as not only will no other state revolt, but our resources will be added to theirs, and we shall be treated worse than those that were enslaved before. But if you will frankly support us, you will add to your side a state that has a large navy, which is your great want; you will smooth the way to the overthrow of the Athenians by depriving them of their allies, who will be greatly encouraged to come over; and you will free yourselves from the imputation made against you, of not supporting insurrection. In short, only show yourselves as liberators, and you may count upon having the advantage in the war.

[14]. Respect, therefore, the hopes placed in you by the Hellenes, and that Olympian Zeus, in whose temple we stand as very suppliants; become the allies and defenders of the Mitylenians, and do not sacrifice us, who put our lives upon the hazard, in a cause in which general good will result to all from our success, and still more general harm if we fail through your refusing to help us; but be the men that the Hellenes think you, and our fears desire.

§

Cleon to the Athenian Ecclesia
Book III 37-40
427 B.C.

Cleon was the very opposite of Pericles in many ways. He was a tanner by trade, a self-made rough and violent man, a demagogue, and suspicious of those with education and learning — especially in the art of rhetoric. In his day the critic of a general's strategy could himself become a general — and this is what happened. Cleon's outbursts on the operations against Sphacteria led Nicias to offer to turn over his command to Cleon. Aristophanes satirized him as an illiterate buffoon in "The Babylonians" in 426. Cleon took reprisal and prosecuted Aristophanes on the charges of alien birth and high treason. He was, in short, an anti-intellectual.

The speeches of Cleon and Diodotus that appear below do not, as Zimmern suggests, represent a contrast between ideas and expediency, but between wisdom and folly. Thucydides may have heard these speeches — they show great care in the contrast of ideas, arrangement, and style. Jebb argues that "in the speeches of Cleon and Diodotus, Thucydides has given the real substance of the arguments which were found to be so 'nearly balanced' and which led to so close a division" (*Speeches of Thucydides,* p. 388).

Cleon attacks here the fair- and open-mindedness and consideration that education develops in a man. Since the chief means of higher learning is by discussion and debate they bear the brunt of Cleon's tirade. "Steadiness without education is more helpful than cleverness without character." "Ordinary men usually manage public affairs better than their more gifted fellows." "Bad laws which are never changed are better for a city than good ones that have no authority." These commonplaces are a sampling of Cleon's line of argument in the opening section. The difficult point to explain away is that Cleon was applauded by many Athenians.

The first part of Cleon's speech (III 37-38) is a classic indictment of what Pericles stood for — free and full discussion of public policy. The persons to blame for poor popular decisions are those "who go to see an oration as you would to see a sight, take your facts on hearsay, judge of the practicability of a project by the wit of its advocates, and trust for the truth as to past events not to the fact which you saw more than to the clever strictures which you heard; the easy victims of new-fangled arguments, unwilling to follow received conclusions; slaves to every new paradox, despisers of the commonplace; the first wish of every man being that he could speak himself, the next to rival those who can speak by seeming to be quite up with their ideas by applauding every hit almost before it is made, and by being as quick in catching an argument as you are slow in foreseeing its consequences; asking, if I may so say, for something different from the conditions under which we live, and yet comprehending inadequately those very conditions; very slaves to the pleasure of the ear, and more like the audience of a rhetorician than the council of a city" (III 38).

The second part of Cleon's eruption calls for punishing Mytilene by putting the whole population to death — a massacre. We must remember that only the day before the Assembly voted to do precisely this. A ship was dispatched to carry out the order. The speech we read is in effect an appeal to let the order stand. The speech by Diodotus that follows is in effect a motion to reconsider.

Cleon casts himself as a watchdog of the people. He implies he is better able to judge speakers than the ordinary voter who is easily duped by an orator's wit, "an easy victim of new-fangled arguments and is unwilling to follow approved conclusions" (III 38.2-3). Cleon pretends not to delight in words like others, he despises the softness which rhetoric engenders, he stands against all that Pericles believed and practiced. Yet even though he is untutored in rhetoric he is skillful in using its worst devices.

Cleon offers another classic definition that has come down through the ages as a mockery to Pericles. The sentence reads: "I therefore now as before persist against your reversing your first decision, or giving way to the three failings most fatal to empire — pity, pleasure in words, and decency" (III 40.2). Here then is the advocate of brutality using the very devices of rhetoric to stir the emotions of a morally deprived, war-weary people.

Aristotle gives Cleon harsh treatment in *The Athenian Constitution* (28.3) where he says he "seems, more than any one else, to have been the cause of the corruption of the democracy by his wild undertakings; and he was the first to use unseemly shouting and coarse abuse on the Bema [a raised step, a tribunal to speak from in the Pynx at Athens], and to harangue the people with his cloak girt up short about him, whereas all his predecessors had spoken decently and in order" (trans. by Sir Frederic G. Kenyon).

§

[37]. I have often before now been convinced that a democracy is incapable of empire, and never more so than by your present change of mind in the matter of Mitylene. Fears or plots being unknown to you in your daily relations with each other, you feel just the same with regard to your allies, and never reflect that the mistakes into which you may be led by listening to their appeals, or by giving way to your own compassion, are full of danger to yourselves, and bring you no thanks for your weakness from your allies; entirely forgetting that your empire is a despotism and your subjects disaffected conspirators, whose obedience is insured not by your suicidal concessions, but by the superiority given you by your own strength and not their loyalty. The most alarming feature in the case is the constant change of measures with which we appear to be threatened, and our seeming ignorance of the fact that bad laws which are never changed are better for a city than good ones that have no authority; that unlearned loyalty is more serviceable than quick-witted insubordination; and that ordinary men usually manage public affairs better than their more gifted fellows. The latter are always wanting to appear wiser than the laws, and to overrule every proposition brought forward, thinking that they cannot show their wit in more important matters, and by such behaviour too often ruin their country; while those who mistrust their own cleverness are content to be less learned than the laws, and less able to pick holes in the speech of a good speaker; and being fair judges rather than rival

athletes, generally conduct affairs successfully. These we ought to imitate, instead of being led on by cleverness and intellectual rivalry to advise your people against our real opinions.

[38]. For myself I adhere to my former opinion and wonder at those who have proposed to reopen the case of the Mitylenians, and who are thus causing a delay which is all in favour of the guilty, by making the sufferer proceed against the offender with the edge of his anger blunted; although where vengeance follows most closely upon the wrong, it best equals it and most amply requites it. I wonder also who will be the man who will maintain the contrary, and will pretend to show that the crimes of the Mitylenians are of service to us, and our misfortunes injurious to the allies. Such a man must plainly either have such confidence in his rhetoric as to adventure to prove that what has been once for all decided is still undetermined, or be bribed to try to delude us by elaborate sophisms. In such contests the state gives the rewards to others, and takes the dangers for herself. The persons to blame are you who are so foolish as to institute these contests; who go to see an oration as you would to see a sight, take your facts on hearsay, judge of the practicability of a project by the wit of its advocates, and trust for the truth as to past events not to the fact which you saw more than to the clever strictures which you heard; the easy victims of new-fangled arguments, unwilling to follow received conclusions; slaves to every new paradox, despisers of the commonplace; the first wish of every man being that he could speak himself, the next to rival those who can speak by seeming to be quite up with their ideas by applauding every hit almost before it is made, and by being as quick in catching an argument as you are slow in foreseeing its consequences; asking, if I may so say, for something different from the conditions under which we live, and yet comprehending inadequately those very conditions; very slaves to the pleasure of the ear, and more like the audience of a rhetorician than the council of a city.

[39]. In order to keep you from this, I proceed to show that no one state has ever injured you as much as Mitylene. I can make allowance for those who revolt because they cannot bear our empire, or who have been forced to do so by the enemy. But for those who possessed an island with fortifications; who could fear our enemies only by sea, and there had their own force of galleys to protect them; who were independent and held in the highest honour by you — to act as these have done, this is not revolt — revolt implies oppression; it is deliberate and wanton aggression; an attempt to ruin us by siding with our

bitterest enemies; a worse offence than a war undertaken on their own account in the acquisition of power. The fate of those of their neighbours who had already rebelled and had been subdued, was no lesson to them; their own prosperity could not dissuade them from affronting danger; but blindly confident in the future, and full of hopes beyond their power though not beyond their ambition, they declared war and made their decision to prefer might to right, their attack being determined not by provocation but by the moment which seemed propitious. The truth is that great good fortune coming suddenly and unexpectedly tends to make a people insolent: in most cases it is safer for mankind to have success in reason than out of reason; and it is easier for them, one may say, to stave off adversity than to preserve prosperity. Our mistake has been to distinguish the Mitylenians as we have done: had they been long ago treated like the rest, they never would have so far forgotten themselves, human nature being as surely made arrogant by consideration, as it is awed by firmness. Let them now therefore be punished as their crime requires, and do not, while you condemn the aristocracy, absolve the people. This is certain, that all attacked you without distinction, although they might have come over to us, and been now again in possession of their city. But no, they thought it safer to throw in their lot with the aristocracy and so joined their rebellion! Consider therefore! if you subject to the same punishment the ally who is forced to rebel by the enemy, and him who does so by his own free choice, which of them, think you, is there that will not rebel upon the slightest pretext; when the reward of success is freedom, and the penalty of failure nothing so very terrible? We meanwhile shall have to risk our money and our lives against one state after another; and if successful, shall receive a ruined town from which we can no longer draw the revenue upon which our strength depends; while if unsuccessful, we shall have an enemy the more upon our hands, and shall spend the time that might be employed in combating our existing foes in warring with our own allies.

[40]. No hope, therefore, that rhetoric may instil or money purchase, of the mercy due to human infirmity must be held out to the Mitylenians. Their offence was not involuntary, but of malice and deliberate; and mercy is only for unwilling offenders. I therefore now as before persist against your reversing your first decision, or giving way to the three failings most fatal to empire — pity, sentiment, and indulgence. Compassion is due to those who can reciprocate the feeling, not to those who will never pity us in return, but are our natural and

necessary foes: the orators who charm us with sentiment may find other less important arenas for their talents, in the place of one where the city pays a heavy penalty for a momentary pleasure, themselves receiving fine acknowledgments for their fine phrases; while indulgence should be shown towards those who will be our friends in future, instead of towards men who will remain just what they were, and as much our enemies as before. To sum up shortly, I say that if you follow my advice you will do what is just towards the Mitylenians, and at the same time expedient; while by a different decision you will not oblige them so much as pass sentence upon yourselves. For if they were right in rebelling, you must be wrong in ruling. However, if, right or wrong, you determine to rule, you must carry out your principle and punish the Mitylenians as your interest requires; or else you must give up your empire and cultivate honesty without danger. Make up your minds, therefore, to give them like for like; and do not let the victims who escaped the plot be more insensible than the conspirators who hatched it; but reflect what they would have done if victorious over you, especially as they were the aggressors. It is they who wrong their neighbour without a cause, that pursue their victim to the death, on account of the danger which they foresee in letting their enemy survive; since the object of a wanton wrong is more dangerous, if he escape, than an enemy who has not this to complain of. Do not, therefore, be traitors to yourselves, but recall as nearly as possible the moment of suffering and the supreme importance which you then attached to their reduction; and now pay them back in their turn, without yielding to present weakness or forgetting the peril that once hung over you. Punish them as they deserve, and teach your other allies by a striking example that the penalty of rebellion is death. Let them once understand this and you will not have so often to neglect your enemies while you are fighting with your own confederates.

§

Diodotus to the Athenian Ecclesia
Book III 42-48
427 B.C.

We know but little of Diodotus. He was the son of Eucrates, the Athenian statesman who first succeeded Pericles. His speech against Cleon, however, portrays a man of integrity and stands as a monument to decency, pity, and thoughtful discussion — the very things that Cleon railed against. He spoke under difficult conditions — following a highly popular speaker, to a highly wrought-up audience, and for *reason* as opposed to *passion*. That he was even heard is a compliment to his power to hold attention and interest. Every politician knows that votes once cast are hard to reverse.

Jebb argues that "the two things which the early Sicilian rhetoric most sought to teach were skill in marshalling facts and skill in arguing probabilities" (*Attic Orators,* vol. 1, p. cxviii ff.). These concepts are well exemplified in the speech of Diodotus. He comes up with a hard-headed reply based not on justice and mercy but on what is best for Athens. He defends discussion and debate. He speaks as an intellectual against Cleon's vulgarities. He echoes the noble sentiment of the Funeral Oration once more. But the Athens of Pericles is gone, mob spirit now prevails.

The Greeks have a word for slander or false accusation — διαβολή. This is what Cleon relies upon and it is up to Diodotus to disclose the method in III 42-43. He reaffirms his faith in serious debate (42.2) and scorns dishonesty and ignorance. He refutes Cleon in detail. He relies mostly on the arguments of expediency and the irresistibility of natural impulse (III 46-47).

The argument Diodotus uses against capital punishment is worth quoting: "Either then some means of terror more terrible than this must be discovered, or it must be owned that this restraint is useless; and that as long as poverty gives men the courage of necessity, or plenty fills them with the ambition which belongs to insolence and pride, and the other conditions of life remain each under the thraldom of some fatal and master passion, so long will the impulse never be wanting to drive men into danger" (III 45.4). In other words, as Finley suggests, human beings are "fundamentally irrational and cannot be deterred by any known means from following their inmost desire" (*Thucydides*, p. 176).

Diodotus is among the first men in Western History to state that severe punishment does not deter crime. Murdering the Mytileneans in mass will not stop other allies from revolting. What is really needed is to placate and keep the good will of the people. Leniency is the method, not barbaric cruelty.

It is notable that Diodotus does not use humane pleas of the civilized kind Pericles might have used. But he has adapted to the mood of his audience. Appeals to kindness would have fallen on deaf ears. Thucydides wants us to know that war simply reenforces the ugly, selfish, animal-like nature of men.

The fact remains, however, that Diodotus did persuade. The vote was close. The Assembly decided to kill only the leaders of the revolt. A second galley was manned and by Herculean effort overtook the first — just in time to countermand the order to wipe out the city.

"Finally, to say a word of the speech as a whole, it is noteworthy that Diodotus opposes Cleon's position of rigid justice with the same cool arguments from the laws of nature and from personal profit with which the Nurse in *Hippolytus* (433-81, 500-502) disputes Phaedra's more idealistic stand" (Finley, *Three Essays*, pp. 32-33).

In the speeches of Cleon and Diodotus Thucydides once more provides an antilogy, a contrast of men, morals, values, and means. What we lack is an understanding of how the individual member of the Ecclesia reacted to the two speakers — the points he applauded and the points he scorned. If we had such a tabulation it could not reveal the audience on this accasion as rational and reflective. The ethical and logical appeals that Aristotle stresses would probably have had slight effect in comparison with the greed and ambition which the desire for power inspires (III 83).

The two speeches of Cleon and Diodotus before the Ecclesia have been used to point up the tortures of making fair judgements about treating allies in time of war. In the cases of the speeches that follow by the Plataeans and the Thebans before the Spartan judges Thucydides drives home the fact that war and justice cannot exist together. In fact Book III of the *History* is an unparalleled source for arguments *against* war of any kind. Not a single good reason for war, other than self defense for survival can be found in these tightly packed pages. They describe human violence at its worst. Glory, honor, the excitement of brave deeds get almost no play.

§

[42]. I do not blame the persons who have reopened the case of the Mitylenians, nor do I approve the protests which we have heard against important questions being frequently debated. I think the two things most opposed to good counsel are haste and passion; haste usually goes hand in hand with folly, passion with coarseness and narrowness of mind. As for the argument that speech ought not to be the exponent of action, the man who uses it must be either senseless or interested: senseless if he believes it possible to treat of the uncertain future through any other medium; interested if wishing to carry a disgraceful measure and doubting his ability to speak well in a bad cause, he thinks to frighten opponents and hearers by well-aimed calumny. What is still more intolerable is to accuse a speaker of making a display in order to be paid for it. If ignorance only were imputed, an unsuccessful speaker might retire with a reputation for honesty, if not for wisdom; while the charge of dishonesty makes him suspected, if successful, and thought, if defeated, not only a fool but a rogue. The city is no gainer by such a system, since fear deprives it of its advisers; although in truth, if our speakers are to make such assertions, it would be better for the country

if they could not speak at all, as we should then make fewer blunders. The good citizen ought to triumph not by frightening his opponents but by beating them fairly in argument; and a wise city without over-distinguishing its best advisers, will nevertheless not deprive them of their due, and far from punishing an unlucky counsellor will not even regard him as disgraced. In this way successful orators would be least tempted to sacrifice their convictions to popularity, in the hope of still higher honours, and unsuccessful speakers to resort to the same popular arts in order to win over the multitude.

[43]. This is not our way; and, besides, the moment that a man is suspected of giving advice, however good, from corrupt motives, we feel such a grudge against him for the gain which after all we are not certain he will receive, that we deprive the city of its certain benefit. Plain good advice has thus come to be no less suspected than bad; and the advocate of the most monstrous measures is not more obliged to use deceit to gain the people, than the best counsellor is to lie in order to be believed. The city and the city only, owing to these refinements, can never be served openly and without disguise; he who does serve it openly being always suspected of serving himself in some secret way in return. Still, considering the magnitude of the interests involved, and the position of affairs, we orators must make it our business to look a little further than you who judge offhand; especially as we, your advisers, are responsible, while you, our audience, are not so. For if those who gave the advice, and those who took it, suffered equally, you would judge more calmly; as it is, you visit the disasters into which the whim of the moment may have led you, upon the single person of your adviser, not upon yourselves, his numerous companions in error.

[44]. However, I have not come forward either to oppose or to accuse in the matter of Mitylene; indeed, the question before us as sensible men is not their guilt, but our interests. Though I prove them ever so guilty, I shall not, therefore, advise their death, unless it be expedient; nor though they should have claims to indulgence, shall I recommend it, unless it be clearly for the good of the country. I consider that we are deliberating for the future more than for the present; and where Cleon is so positive as to the useful deterrent effects that will follow from making rebellion capital, I who consider the interests of the future quite as much as he, as positively maintain the contrary. And I require you not to reject my useful considerations for his specious ones: his speech may have the attraction of seeming the more just in your present temper against Mitylene; but we are not in a court of justice,

but in a political assembly; and the question is not justice, but how to make the Mitylenians useful to Athens.

[45]. Now of course communities have enacted the penalty of death for many offences far lighter than this: still hope leads men to venture, and no one ever yet put himself in peril without the inward conviction that he would succeed in his design. Again, was there ever city rebelling that did not believe that it possessed either in itself or in its alliances resources adequate to the enterprise? All, states and individuals, are alike prone to err, and there is no law that will prevent them; or why should men have exhausted the list of punishments in search of enactments to protect them from evil-doers? It is probable that in early times the penalties for the greatest offences were less severe, and that, as these were disregarded, the penalty of death has been by degrees in most cases arrived at, which is itself disregarded in like manner. Either then some means of terror more terrible than this must be discovered, or it must be owned that this restraint is useless; and that as long as poverty gives men the courage of necessity, or plenty fills them with the ambition which belongs to insolence and pride, and the other conditions of life remain each under the thraldom of some fatal and master passion, so long will the impulse never be wanting to drive men into danger. Hope also and cupidity, the one leading and the other following, the one conceiving the attempt, the other suggesting the facility of succeeding, cause the widest ruin, and, although invisible agents, are far stronger than the dangers that are seen. Fortune, too, powerfully helps the delusion, and by the unexpected aid that she sometimes lends, tempts men to venture with inferior means; and this is especially the case with communities, because the stakes played for are the highest, freedom or empire, and, when all are acting together, each man irrationally magnifies his own capacity. In fine, it is impossible to prevent, and only great simplicity can hope to prevent, human nature doing what it has once set its mind upon, by force of law or by any other deterrent force whatsoever.

[46]. We must not, therefore, commit ourselves to a false policy through a belief in the efficacy of the punishment of death, or exclude rebels from the hope of repentance and an early atonement of their error. Consider a moment! At present, if a city that has already revolted perceive that it cannot succeed, it will come to terms while it is still able to refund expenses, and pay tribute afterwards. In the other case, what city think you would not prepare better than is now done, and hold out to the last against its besiegers, if it is all one whether it

surrender late or soon? And how can it be otherwise than hurtful to us to be put to the expense of a siege, because surrender is out of the question; and if we take the city, to receive a ruined town from which we can no longer draw the revenue which forms our real strength against the enemy? We must not, therefore, sit as strict judges of the offenders to our own prejudice, but rather see how by moderate chastisements we may be enabled to benefit in future by the revenue-producing powers of our dependencies; and we must make up our minds to look for our protection not to legal terrors but to careful administration. At present we do exactly the opposite. When a free community, held in subjection by force, rises, as is only natural, and asserts its independence, it is no sooner reduced than we fancy ourselves obliged to punish it severely; although the right course with freemen is not to chastise them rigorously when they do rise, but rigorously to watch them before they rise, and to prevent their ever entertaining the idea, and, the insurrection suppressed, to make as few responsible for it as possible.

[47]. Only consider what a blunder you would commit in doing as Cleon recommends. As things are at present, in all the cities the people is your friend, and either does not revolt with the oligarchy, or, if forced to do so, becomes at once the enemy of the insurgents; so that in the war with the hostile city you have the masses on your side. But if you butcher the people of Mitylene, who had nothing to do with the revolt, and who, as soon as they got arms, of their own motion surrendered the town, first you will commit the crime of killing your benefactors; and next you will play directly into the hands of the higher classes, who when they induce their cities to rise, will immediately have the people on their side, through your having announced in advance the same punishment for those who are guilty and for those who are not. On the contrary, even if they were guilty, you ought to seem not to notice it, in order to avoid alienating the only class still friendly to us. In short, I consider it far more useful for the preservation of our empire voluntarily to put up with injustice, than to put to death, however justly, those whom it is our interest to keep alive. As for Cleon's idea that in punishment the claims of justice and expediency can both be satisfied, facts do not confirm the possibility of such a combination.

[48]. Confess, therefore, that this is the wisest course, and without conceding too much either to pity or to indulgence, by neither of which motives do I any more than Cleon wish you to be influenced,

upon the plain merits of the case before you, be persuaded by me to try calmly those of the Mitylenians whom Paches sent off as guilty, and to leave the rest undisturbed. This is at once best for the future, and most terrible to your enemies at the present moment; inasmuch as good policy against an adversary is superior to the blind attacks of brute force.

§

Plataeans to the Spartan Judges
Book III 53-59
427 B.C.

The speeches of the Plataeans and the Thebans to the Spartan judges are the only forensic-type speeches in the *History*. They probably represent the best effort at judicial speech composition. It seems certain that Thucydides did not hear them when spoken. Both speeches are elaborate in organization. They follow fairly well the division taught by the Sicilian rhetors: proem, prothesis, narrative, proof, and epilogue. Great care has been used in assembling the sub-topics for each speech. Here are some of the obvious generalizations that may be made.

The speeches are deliberately arranged to follow after those on what to do about Mytilene. We are thus forced to ponder the contrast in the attitudes and the outcomes of the two pairs. Athens had by a narrow margin voted against a rebellious ally to refrain from full genocide. The Spartans took far harsher action against a gallant enemy. The reader considering Cleon's and the Thebans' pleas may decide where the greater crime lies.

The Plataeans' speech is remarkable for its candor and clarity. There is no attempt to deceive or to sidestep the history and the conduct of the Spartans. The arguments of the two speakers are logical and factual. But one senses half-way through that they are pleading a hopeless cause. Like the dramatist he is Thucydides gives us a foreboding of the tragic end to come.

This speech is largely a summary of past favors (III 54.2-56). It starts out in a conciliatory way and goes into the fears the Plataeans suffer. It acknowledges the great reputation of the Spartans as soldiers and as honorable men. It concludes in the most pathetic tone: "we adjure you not to give us up...to the Thebans, our most hated enemies, — but to be our saviours, and not, while you free the rest of the Hellenes, to bring us to destruction" (III 59.4).

It is worthy of note that Dionysius of Halicarnassus gave this speech his high praise in these words: "I admire the speech of the Plataeans more than anything in the seven books of Thucydides; it has nothing artificial or far fetched; it is natural and true to life; the sentiments are full of pathos; the composition is pleasant" (*De Thucydide*, c.42).

Thucydides gives the unmistakable impression in this speech that he is portraying each statement and its proof in a way that is most appropriate for the presentation without regard to what preceded or what follows. He lets the facts speak for themselves and the embellishments of figures of thought or of speech are conspicuous by their absence.

On the other hand the use of antithesis is evident throughout the speech. A double antithesis may be defined as putting the wording and the sense in contrast. A verbal antithesis applies only to words in opposition. One of sense applies, for example, when actions are contrasted, e.g. "When we asked for your alliance against our Theban oppressors, you rejected our petition, and told us to go to the Athenians who were our neighbors, as you lived too far off" (III 55.1). The whole speech is replete with examples of this kind, tiresomely so. But they are effective to us as they accumulated. To the judge who heard the case they must have been time-consuming.

The Plataeans end by begging for a chance to prove themselves: "we say that we did not surrender our city to the Thebans (to that we would have preferred inglorious starvation), but trusted in and capitulated to you; and it would be just, if we fail to persuade you, to put us back to the same position and let us take the chance that falls to us" (III 59.6).

Never did such noble thoughts cogently expressed fall upon less judicial-like deciders of a fate.

§

[53]. Lacedaemonians, when we surrendered our city we trusted in you, and looked forward to a trial more agreeable to the forms of law than the present, to which we had no idea of being subjected; the judges also in whose hands we consented to place ourselves were you, and you only (from whom we thought we were most likely to obtain justice), and not other persons, as is now the case. As matters stand, we are afraid that we have been doubly deceived. We have good reason to suspect, not only that the issue to be tried is the most terrible of all, but that you will not prove impartial; if we may argue from the fact that no accusation was first brought forward for us to answer, but we had ourselves to ask leave to speak, and from the question being put so shortly, that a true answer to it tells against us, while a false one can be contradicted. In this dilemma, our safest, and indeed our only course, seems to be to say something at all risks: placed as we are, we could scarcely be silent without being tormented by the damning thought that speaking might have saved us. Another difficulty that we have to encounter is the difficulty of convincing you. Were we unknown to each other we might profit by bringing forward new matter with which you were unacquainted: as it is, we can tell you nothing that you do not know already, and we fear, not that you have condemned us in your own minds of having failed in our duty towards you, and make this our crime, but that to please a third party we have to submit to a trial the result of which is already decided. Nevertheless, we will place before you what we can justly urge, not only on the question of the quarrel which the Thebans have against us, but also as addressing you and the rest of the Hellenes; and we will remind you of our good services, and endeavour to prevail with you.

[54]. To your short question, whether we have done the Lacedaemonians and allies any service in this war, we say, if you ask us as enemies, that to refrain from serving you was not to do you injury; if as friends, that you are more in fault for having marched against us. During the peace, and against the Mede, we acted well: we have not now been the first to break the peace, and we were the only Boeotians who then joined in defending against the Mede the liberty of Hellas. Although an inland people, we were present at the action at Artemisium; in the battle that took place in our territory we fought by the side of yourselves and Pausanias; and in all the other Hellenic exploits of the time we took a part quite out of proportion to our strength. Besides, you, as Lacedaemonians, ought not to forget that at the time of the great panic at Sparta, after the earthquake, caused by

the secession of the Helots to Ithome, we sent the third part of our citizens to assist you.

[55]. On these great and historical occasions such was the part that we chose, although afterwards we became your enemies. For this you were to blame. When we asked for your alliance against our Theban oppressors, you rejected our petition, and told us to go to the Athenians who were our neighbours, as you lived too far off. In the war we never have done to you, and never should have done to you, anything unreasonable. If we refused to desert the Athenians when you asked us, we did no wrong; they had helped us against the Thebans when you drew back, and we could no longer give them up with honour; especially as we had obtained their alliance and had been admitted to their citizenship at our own request, and after receiving benefits at their hands; but it was plainly our duty loyally to obey their orders. Besides, the faults that either of you may commit in your supremacy must be laid, not upon the followers, but on the chiefs that lead them astray.

[56]. With regard to the Thebans, they have wronged us repeatedly, and their last aggression, which has been the means of bringing us into our present position, is within your own knowledge. In seizing our city in time of peace, and what is more at a holy time in the month, they justly encountered our vengeance, in accordance with the universal law which sanctions resistance to an invader; and it cannot now be right that we should suffer on their account. By taking your own immediate interest and their animosity as the test of justice, you will prove yourselves to be rather waiters on expediency than judges of right; although if they seem useful to you now, we and the rest of the Hellenes gave you much more valuable help at a time of greater need. Now you are the assailants, and others fear you; but at the crisis to which we allude, when the barbarian threatened all with slavery, the Thebans were on his side. It is just, therefore, to put our patriotism then against our error now, if error there has been; and you will find the merit outweighing the fault, and displayed at a juncture when there were few Hellenes who would set their valour against the strength of Xerxes, and when greater praise was theirs who preferred the dangerous path of honour to the safe course of consulting their own interest with respect to the invasion. To these few we belonged, and highly were we honoured for it; and yet we now fear to perish by having again acted on the same principles, and chosen to act well with Athens sooner than wisely with Sparta. Yet in justice the same cases should be decided in

the same way, and policy should not mean anything else than lasting gratitude for the service of a good ally combined with a proper attention to one's own immediate interest.

[57]. Consider also that at present the Hellenes generally regard you as a pattern of worth and honour; and if you pass an unjust sentence upon us in this which is no obscure cause, but one in which you, the judges, are as illustrious as we, the prisoners, are blameless, take care that displeasure be not felt at an unworthy decision in the matter of honourable men made by men yet more honourable than they, and at the consecration in the national temples of spoils taken from the Plataeans, the benefactors of Hellas. Shocking indeed will it seem for Lacedaemonians to destroy Plataea, and for the city whose name your fathers inscribed upon the tripod at Delphi for its good service, to be by you blotted out from the map of Hellas, to please the Thebans. To such a depth of misfortune have we fallen, that while the Medes' success had been our ruin, Thebans now supplant us in your once fond regards; and we have been subjected to two dangers, the greatest of any — that of dying of starvation then, if we had not surrendered our town, and now of being tried for our lives. So that we Plataeans, after exertions beyond our power in the cause of the Hellenes, are rejected by all, forsaken and unassisted; helped by none of our allies, and reduced to doubt the stability of our only hope, yourselves.

[58]. Still, in the name of the gods who once presided over our confederacy, and of our own good service in the Hellenic cause, we adjure you to relent; to recall the decision which we fear that the Thebans may have obtained from you; to ask back the gift that you have given them, that they disgrace not you by slaying us; to gain a pure instead of a guilty gratitude, and not to gratify others to be yourselves rewarded with shame. Our lives may be quickly taken, but it will be a heavy task to wipe away the infamy of the deed; as we are no enemies whom you might justly punish, but friends forced into taking arms against you. To grant us our lives would be, therefore, a righteous judgment; if you consider also that we are prisoners who surrendered of their own accord, stretching out our hands for quarter, whose slaughter Hellenic law forbids, and who besides were always your benefactors. Look at the sepulchres of your fathers, slain by the Medes and buried in our country, whom year by year we honoured with garments and all other dues, and the first fruits of all that our land produced in their season, as friends from a friendly country and allies to our old companions in arms! Should you not decide aright, your

conduct would be the very opposite to ours. Consider only: Pausanias buried them thinking that he was laying them in friendly ground and among men as friendly; but you, if you kill us and make the Plataean territory Theban, will leave your fathers and kinsmen in a hostile soil and among their murderers, deprived of the honours which they now enjoy. What is more, you will enslave the land in which the freedom of the Hellenes was won, make desolate the temples of the gods to whom they prayed before they overcame the Medes, and take away your ancestral sacrifices from those who founded and instituted them.

[59]. It were not to your glory, Lacedaemonians, either to offend in this way against the common law of the Hellenes and against your own ancestors, or to kill us your benefactors to gratify another's hatred without having been wronged yourselves: it were more so to spare us and to yield to the impressions of a reasonable compassion; reflecting not merely on the awful fate in store for us, but also on the character of the sufferers, and on the impossibility of predicting how soon misfortune may fall even upon those who deserve it not. We, as we have a right to do and as our need impels us, entreat you, calling aloud upon the gods at whose common altar all the Hellenes worship, to hear our request, to be not unmindful of the oahts which your fathers swore, and which we now plead — we supplicate you by the tombs of your fathers, and appeal to those that are gone to save us from falling into the hands of the Thebans and their dearest friends from being given up to their most detested foes. We also remind you of that day on which we did the most glorious deeds, by your fathers' sides, we who now on this are like to suffer the most dreadful fate. Finally, to do what is necessary and yet most difficult for men in our situation — that is, to make an end of speaking, since with that ending the peril of our lives draws near — in conclusion we say that we did not surrender our city to the Thebans (to that we would have preferred inglorious starvation), but trusted in and capitulated to you; and it would be just, if we fail to persuade you, to put us back in the same position and let us take the chance that falls to us. And at the same time we adjure you not to give us up, — your suppliants, Lacedaemonians, out of your hands and faith, Plataeans foremost of the Hellenic patriots, to Thebans, our most hated enemies, — but to be our saviours, and not, while you free the rest of the Hellenes, to bring us to destruction.

§

Thebans to the Spartan Judges
Book III 61-67
427 B.C.

No sooner had the Plataeans made their plea when the Thebans came forward to state their case. It is an acid-like rebuke to Astymachus and Lacon, the delegates from Plataea, for their country's bitter hostility to Thebes. The Thebans argue that it is when acts are in the wrong that highly emotional arguments are used to screen the wrongs (III 67.6). Even so, their own speaking is full of hatred and envy. The Thebans appeal to the emotions of their judges — not to pity and compassion but to fear and enmity.

In one of those insightful passages of the *Rhetoric*, Book II, Aristotle explains "(1) in what form of mind, (2) with what persons, and (3) on what grounds people grow angry" (1379a 9). In forensic cases, Aristotle warns, it is vital that the pleader should be able to influence the emotions of the jury of the judges. How do the Thebans undertake to do this? They say they will answer the charges of the Plataeans, "refute their self-praise, in order that neither our bad name nor their good may help them, but that you may hear the real truth on both points and so decide" (III 61.1-2).

This is essentially what takes place but, of course, the problem of discovering "the real truth" still remains when they conclude. One example of the subtlety of the Theban argument occurs at III 63.4: "Athens helped Plataea against an aggressor; it would have been dishonorable for Plataeans not to help Athens if she were attacked; it would not be dishonorable to refuse to help her to oppress others" (Oxford World's Classics translation ed. by Sir R.W. Livingstone, p. 178 note 2).

The peroration is a beautiful example of summing up and re-appeal to Spartan anger: "Do not be softened by tales of their [Plataea's] past virtues, if they had any; these may be fairly appealed to by the victims of injustice, but only aggravate the guilt of an offender, since they offend against their better nature. ...put one short question to all alike and decide accordingly" (III 67.4).

This last demand won out. The question put to the Plataeans was the same one used earlier: "Have you, citizens of Plataea, rendered any service to us in the war with Athens?" As the Plataeans had said in their speech — they were forced to submit to a trial "the result of which is already decided" (III 53.5). The Lacedaemonian judges ordered the question put and when the response was negative — i.e. no service had been made — they "took them out and killed them, all without exception." The women were sold as slaves.

The final sentences which Thucydides wrote of the episode are bitingly condemnatory: "The hostile attitude of the Lacedaemonians in the whole Plataean affair was mainly adopted to please the Thebans, who were thought to be useful in the war at that moment raging — such was the end of Plataea, ninety-three years after she became an ally of Athens" (III 68.5).

§

[61]. We should never have asked to make this speech if the Plataeans on their side had contented themselves with shortly answering the question, and had not turned round and made charges against us, coupled with a long defence of themselves upon matters outside the present inquiry and not even the subject of accusation, and with praise of what no one finds fault with. However, since they have done so, we must answer their charges and refute their self-praise, in order that neither our bad name nor their good may help them, but that you may hear the real truth on both points, and so decide.

The origin of our quarrel was this. We settled Plataea some time after the rest of Boeotia, together with other places out of which we had driven the mixed population. The Plataeans not choosing to recognise our supremacy, as had been first arranged, but separating themselves from the rest of the Boeotians, and proving traitors to their nationality, we used compulsion; upon which they went over to the Athenians, and with them did as much harm, for which we retaliated.

[62]. Next, when the barbarian invaded Hellas they say that they were the only Boeotians who did not Medise; and this is where they most glorify themselves and abuse us. We say that if they did not Medise, it was because the Athenians did not do so either; just as afterwards when the Athenians attacked the Hellenes they, the Plataeans, were again the only Boeotians who Atticised. And yet consider the forms of our respective governments when we so acted. Our city at that juncture had neither an oligarchical constitution in which all the nobles enjoyed equal rights nor a democracy, but that which is most opposed to law and good government and nearest a tyranny — the rule of a close cabal. These, hoping to strengthen their individual power by the success of the Mede, kept down by force the people, and brought him into the town. The city as a whole was not its own mistress when it so acted, and ought not to be reproached for the errors that it committed while deprived of its constitution. Examine only how we acted after the departure of the Mede and the recovery of the constitution; when the Athenians attacked the rest of Hellas and endeavoured to subjugate our country, of the greater part of which faction had already made them masters. Did not we fight and conquer at Coronea and liberate Boeotia, and do we not now actively contribute to the liberation of the rest, providing horses to the cause and a force unequalled by that of any other state in the confederacy?

[63]. Let this suffice to excuse us for our Medism. We will now endeavour to show that you have injured the Hellenes more than we, and are more deserving of condign punishment. It was in defence against us, say you, that you became allies and citizens of Athens. If so, you ought only to have called in the Athenians against us, instead of joining them in attacking others: it was open to you to do this if you ever felt that they were leading you where you did not wish to follow, as Lacedaemon was already your ally against the Mede, as you so much insist; and this was surely sufficient to keep us off, and above all to allow you to deliberate in security. Nevertheless, of your own choice and without compulsion you chose to throw your lot in with Athens. And you say that it had been base for you to betray your benefactors; but it was surely far baser and more iniquitous to sacrifice the whole body of the Hellenes, your fellow-confederates, who were liberating Hellas, than the Athenians only, who were enslaving it. The return that you made them was therefore neither equal nor honourable, since you called them in, as you say, because you were being oppressed yourselves, and then became their accomplices in oppressing others;

although baseness rather consists in not returning like for like than in not returning what is justly due but must be unjustly paid.

[64]. Meanwhile after thus plainly showing that it was not for the sake of the Hellenes that you alone then did not Medise, but because the Athenians did not do so either, and you wished to side with them and to be against the rest; you now claim the benefit of good deeds done to please your neighbours. This cannot be admitted: you chose the Athenians, and with them you must stand or fall. Nor can you plead the league then made and claim that it should now protect you. You abandoned that league, and offended against it by helping instead of hindering the subjugation of the Aeginetans and others of its members, and that not under compulsion, but while in enjoyment of the same institutions that you enjoy to the present hour, and no one forcing you as in our case. Lastly, an invitation was addressed to you before you were blockaded to be neutral and join neither party: this you did not accept. Who then merit the detestation of the Hellenes more justly than you, you who sought their ruin under the mask of honour? The former virtues that you allege you now show not to be proper to your character; the real bent of your nature has been at length damningly proved: when the Athenians took the path of injustice you followed them.

[65]. Of our unwilling Medism and your wilful Atticising this then is our explanation. The last wrong of which you complain consists in our having, as you say, lawlessly invaded your town in time of peace and festival. Here again we cannot think that we were more in fault than yourselves. If of our own proper motion we made an armed attack upon your city and ravaged your territory, we are guilty; but if the first men among you in estate and family, wishing to put an end to the foreign connexion and to restore you to the common Boeotian country, of their own free will invited us, wherein is our crime? Where wrong is done, those who lead, as you say, are more to blame than those who follow. Not that, in our judgment, wrong was done either by them or by us. Citizens like yourselves, and with more at stake than you, they opened their own walls and introduced us into their own city, not as foes but as friends, to prevent the bad among you from becoming worse; to give honest men their due; to reform principles without attacking persons, since you were not to be banished from your city, but brought home to your kindred, nor to be made enemies to any, but friends alike to all.

[66]. That our intention was not hostile is proved by our behaviour. We did no harm to any one, but publicly invited those who wished to

live under a national, Boeotian government to come over to us; which at first you gladly did, and made an agreement with us and remained tranquil, until you became aware of the smallness of our numbers. Now it is possible that there may have been something not quite fair in our entering without the consent of your commons. At any rate you did not repay us in kind. Instead of refraining, as we had done, from violence, and inducing us to retire by negotiation, you fell upon us in violation of your agreement, and slew some of us in fight, of which we do not so much complain, for in that there was a certain justice; but others who held out their hands and received quarter, and whose lives you subsequently promised us, you lawlessly butchered. If this was not abominable, what is? And after these three crimes committed one after the other — the violation of your agreement, the murder of the men afterwards, and the lying breach of your promise not to kill them, if we refrained from injuring your property in the country — you still affirm that we are the criminals and yourselves pretend to escape justice. Not so, if these your judges decide aright, but you will be punished for all together.

[67]. Such, Lacedaemonians, are the facts. We have gone into them at some length both on your account and on our own, that you may feel that you will justly condemn the prisoners, and we, that we have given an additional sanction to our vengeance. We would also prevent you from being melted by hearing of their past virtues, if any such they had: these may be fairly appealed to by the victims of injustice, but only aggravate the guilt of criminals, since they offend against their better nature. Nor let them gain anything by crying and wailing, by calling upon your fathers' tombs and their own desolate condition. Against this we point to the far more dreadful fate of our youth, butchered at their hands; the fathers of whom either fell at Coronea, bringing Boeotia over to you, or seated, forlorn old men by desolate hearths, with far more reason implore your justice upon the prisoners. The pity which they appeal to is rather due to men who suffer unworthily; those who suffer justly as they do, are on the contrary subjects for triumph. For their present desolate condition they have themselves to blame, since they wilfully rejected the better alliance. Their lawless act was not provoked by any action of ours; hate, not justice, inspired their decision; and even now the satisfaction which they afford us is not adequate; they will suffer by a legal sentence, not as they pretend as suppliants asking for quarter in battle, but as prisoners who have surrendered upon agreement to take their trial.

Vindicate, therefore, Lacedaemonians, the Hellenic law which they have broken; and to us, the victims of its violation, grant the reward merited by our zeal. Nor let us be supplanted in your favour by their harangues, but offer an example to the Hellenes, that the contests to which you invite them are of deeds, not words: good deeds can be shortly stated, but where wrong is done a wealth of language is needed to veil its deformity. However, if leading powers were to do what you are now doing, and putting one short question all alike were to decide accordingly, men would be less tempted to seek fine phrases to cover bad actions.

§

Lacedaemonian Envoys to the Athenian Ecclesia
Book IV 17-20
425 B.C.

The adjective *Laconic* means terse or sparing of words and comes from the Greek Λακωνικὸς which conveys the Spartan reputation for brevity. The speakers begin by reminding the Ecclesia that they can "speak at some length without any departure from the habit of our country. Men of few words where many are not wanted, we can be less brief when there is a matter of importance to be illustrated and an end to be served by its illustration" (IV 17.2).

Even so, the speech which Thucydides may well have heard, is succinct, reasonable in tone, and the very model of good sense under what may be called adverse Spartan circumstances — just having lost a major engagement of the war — the sea and land fight at Pylos. It is a brilliant composition, but again, as in previous good speeches, the ideas fell upon men with closed minds.

In spite of these facts — that the Athenians had been fighting nine seasons and were hard up for finances and their losses from both battle and disease were enormous — they rejected the Spartan offer of peace. Although Thucydides does not give his speech it was Cleon, "a popular speaker of the day and very powerful with the multitude," who spoke against peace.

Let us follow what the Spartan envoys said. They open in a conciliatory way. They offer what they term "the best course to be taken addressed to intelligent judges" (IV 17.4). Or as another translator renders the Greek "to men who know how to come to a good decision."

Thereupon, the speakers remind the Assembly that the Spartans were not "poor relations." At one time they were better entitled to confer the kind of favor they now begged for. Further, the fortunes of war change quickly. Now is the time to make peace while you are ahead in the game.

Specifically, the Spartans offered to end the war, to give their friendship, and an alliance — all for the return of their men on the island. The proof of their sincerity is a series of philosophical arguments that are startlingly true today after hundreds of years of warfare to look back upon.

Referring to allies on both sides the Spartans wisely say: "let us be reconciled, and for ourselves choose peace instead of war, and grant to the rest of the Hellenes a remission from their sufferings, for which be sure they have chiefly you to thank. The war that they labour under they know not which began, but the peace that concludes it, as it depends on your decision, will by their gratitude be laid to your door" (IV 20.2).

The Spartan envoys almost seem to be out of character in this speech. They are reasonable, open minded, willing to do more than their share to end the conflict. It is difficult to see why the Athenians, lovers of logic and good sense, failed to respond to an offer that would have saved thousands of lives and even more thousands of talents.

The Athenian Assembly under the spell of Cleon rejected the peace offer, broke the Pylos armistice agreement, and resumed the war with new vigor.

Cleon had painted a canvas of riches and ease — by taxing others and expanding the empire. The sentence "they held out for more" (IV 21.2) ominously foretells the doom to come.

Lovers of Athens to this day finish reading the speech with the sad wish: If only Pericles, the Olympian, were then alive and the leader — instead of Cleon, the tanner.

§

[17]. Athenians, the Lacedaemonians sent us to try to find some way of settling the affair of our men on the island, that shall be at once satisfactory to your interests, and as consistent with our dignity in our misfortune as circumstances permit. We can venture to speak at some length without any departure from the habit of our country. Men of few words where many are not wanted, we can be less brief when there is a matter of importance to be illustrated and an end to be served by its illustration. Meanwhile we beg you to take what we may say, not in

a hostile spirit, nor as if we thought you ignorant and wished to lecture you, but rather as a suggestion on the best course to be taken, addressed to intelligent judges. You can now, if you choose, employ your present success to advantage, so as to keep what you have got and gain honour and reputation besides, and you can avoid the mistake of those who meet with an extraordinary piece of good fortune, and are led on by hope to grasp continually at something further, through having already succeeded without expecting it. While those who have known most vicissitudes of good and bad, have also justly least faith in their prosperity; and to teach your city and ours this lesson experience has not been wanting.

[18]. To be convinced of this you have only to look at our present misfortune. What power in Hellas stood higher than we did? and yet we are come to you, although we formerly thought ourselves more able to grant what we are now here to ask. Nevertheless, we have not been brought to this by any decay in our power, or through having our heads turned by aggrandisement; no, our resources are what they have always been, and our error has been an error of judgment, to which all are equally liable. Accordingly the prosperity which your city now enjoys, and the accession that it has lately received, must not make you fancy that fortune will be always with you. Indeed sensible men are prudent enough to treat their gains as precarious, just as they would also keep a clear head in adversity, and think that war, so far from staying within the limit to which a combatant may wish to confine it, will run the course that its chances prescribe; and thus, not being puffed up by confidence in military success, they are less likely to come to grief, and most ready to make peace, if they can, while their fortune lasts. This, Athenians, you have a good opportunity to do now with us, and thus to escape the possible disasters which may follow upon your refusal, and the consequent imputation of having owed to accident even your present advantages, when you might have left behind you a reputation for power and wisdom which nothing could endanger.

[19]. The Lacedaemonians accordingly invite you to make a treaty and to end the war, and offer peace and alliance and the most friendly and intimate relations in every way and on every occasion between us; and in return ask for the men on the island, thinking it better for both parties not to stand out to the end, on the chance of some favourable accident enabling the men to force their way out, or of their being compelled to succumb under the pressure of blockade. Indeed if great enmities are ever to be really settled, we think it will be, not by the

system of revenge and military success, and by forcing an opponent to swear to a treaty to his disadvantage, but when the more fortunate combatant waives these his privileges, to be guided by gentler feelings, conquers his rival in generosity, and accords peace on more moderate conditions than he expected. From that moment, instead of the debt of revenge which violence must entail, his adversary owed a debt of generosity to be paid in kind, and is inclined by honour to stand to his agreement. And men oftener act in this manner towards their greatest enemies than where the quarrel is of less importance; they are also by nature as glad to give way to those who first yield to them, as they are apt to be provoked by arrogance to risks condemned by their own judgment.

[20]. To apply this to ourselves: if peace was ever desirable for both parties, it is surely so at the present moment, before anything irremediable befall us and force us to hate you eternally, personally as well as politically, and you to miss the advantages that we now offer you. While the issue is still in doubt, and you have reputation and our friendship in prospect, and we the compromise of our misfortune before anything fatal occur, let us be reconciled, and four ourselves choose peace instead of war, and grant to the rest of the Hellenes a remission from their sufferings, for which be sure they will think they have chiefly you to thank. The war that they labour under they know not which began, but the peace that concludes it, as it depends on your decision, will by their gratitude be laid to your door. By such a decision you can become firm friends with the Lacedaemonians at their own invitation, which you do not force from them, but oblige them by accepting. And from this friendship consider the advantages that are likely to follow: when Attica and Sparta are at one, the rest of Hellas, be sure, will remain in respectful inferiority before its heads.

§

Hermocrates in the Sicilian Congress at Gela
Book IV 50-64
424 B.C.

The preface to this speech describes Hermocrates, son of Hermon, the Syracusan, a most influential man, as speaking "to this effect" and we may presume that Thucydides did not hear the speech. It was made in 434 B.C. to the Congress at Gela, a city on the south coast of Sicily. We know little about Hermocrates and it seems odd to read the words attributed to a man from the birthplace of rhetoric — actually written by a Greek from the deme Halimus. We have indeed another instance of the historian making "the persons say what it seemed to me most opportune for them to say in view of each situation" (I 22).

Jebb uses this very speech to illustrate how Thucydides may have undertaken his task: "Suppose a report to have reached him in this shape: 'Hermocrates spoke to the Congress at Gela, urging the Sicilian cities to lay aside their feuds and unite against Athens.' In composing on this theme, the first thought of Thucydides would be, 'what arguments would Hermocrates have used?' The general rule would, of course, be liable to various degrees of modification in cases where the speaker was well known to the historian as having marked traits of character, opinion or style" (*Speeches of Thucydides,* p. 374). Thus, if Jebb is correct, we find Thucydides anticipating by several decades Aristotle's famous definition of rhetoric as "the faculty of observing in any given case the available means of persuasion" (*Rhetoric* Bk. I ch. 2 translated by W. Rhy Roberts).

What then are the available means Hermocrates uses to win over his audience? First, he says he argues on the basis of what is best for Sicily as a whole. The Athenians are really planning against Sicily and they are actually present "watching for our mistakes" and are trying to turn them to advantage. This is why Sicilian unity is imperative. Faction is the chief cause of ruin to most states. There must be therefore a common effort to defend Sicily in its entirety. The argument goes on. The Athenians are operating because our own dissidents asked them to interfere. If we all unite and forget our difference the Athenians will realize we are by no means easy to conquer and they will turn and go home. If we are wise we will conclude a truce for the longest practicable time and set aside our differences to some future date. Only in this way can we get rid of the Athenians and escape a civil war of our own.

This speech is in reality a character sketch of Hermocrates, a man not unlike Pericles in his military and civic virtues. He knew how to make good decisions quickly, he was gifted with political foresight, he was a first-class orator, and he was a talented leader of the people. Within his own sphere he was just as great a man as Pericles and a far better man than Nicias or Alcibiades.

It was an exceptionally diplomatic speech based largely on logical reasoning with enough emotional and ethical appeals to make it highly effective. The delegates did agree among themselves. The Athenian generals were notified and they agreed to withdraw their fleet. For this they paid a price on their return to Athens. Two were exiled and one was fined. The withdrawal was really a lucky break for Athens but as coming events will show the ignorant Athenians failed to recognize its value. They wanted more war.

§

[59]. If I now address you, Sicilians, it is not because my city is the least in Sicily or the greatest sufferer by the war, but in order to state publicly what appears to me to be the best policy for the whole island. That war is an evil is a proposition so familiar to every one that it would be tedious to develop it. No one is forced to engage in it by ignorance, or kept out of it by fear, if he fancies there is anything to be gained by it. To the former the gain appears greater than the danger, while the latter would rather stand the risk than put up with any

immediate sacrifice. But if both should happen to have chosen the wrong moment for acting in this way, advice to make peace would not be unserviceable; and this, if we did but see it, is just what we stand most in need of at the present juncture.

[60]. I suppose that no one will dispute that we went to war at first in order to serve our own several interests, that we are now, in view of the same interests, debating how we can make peace; and that if we separate without having as we think our rights, we shall go to war again. And yet, as men of sense, we ought to see that our separate interests are not alone at stake in the present congress: there is also the question whether we have still time to save Sicily, the whole of which in my opinion is menaced by Athenian ambition; and we ought to find in the name of that people more imperious arguments for peace than any which I can advance, when we see the first power in Hellas watching our mistakes with the few ships that she has at present in our waters, and under the fair name of alliance speciously seeking to turn to account the natural hostility that exists between us. If we go to war, and call in to help us a people that are ready enough to carry their arms even where they are not invited; and if we injure ourselves at our own expense, and at the same time serve as the pioneers of their dominion, we may expect when they see us worn out, that they will one day come with a larger armament, and seek to bring all of us into subjection.

[61]. And yet as sensible men, if we call in allies and court danger, it should be in order to enrich our different countries with new acquisitions, and not to ruin what they possess already; and we should understand that the intestine discords which are so fatal to communities generally, will be equally so to Sicily, if we, its inhabitants, absorbed in our local quarrels, neglect the common enemy. These considerations should reconcile individual with individual, and city with city, and unite us in a common effort to save the whole of Sicily. Nor should any one imagine that the Dorians only are enemies of Athens, while the Chalcidian race is secured by its Ionian blood; the attack in question is not inspired by hatred of one of two nationalities, but by a desire for the good things in Sicily, the common property of us all. This is proved by the Athenian reception of the Chalcidian invitation: an ally who has never given them any assistance whatever, at once receives from them almost more than the treaty entitles him to. That the Athenians should cherish this ambition and practise this policy is very excusable; and I do not blame those who wish to rule, but those who are over ready to serve. It is just as much in men's nature to rule those

who submit to them, as it is to resist those who molest them; one is not less invariable than the other. Meanwhile all who see these dangers and refuse to provide for them properly, or who have come here without having made up their minds that our first duty is to unite to get rid of the common peril, are mistaken. The quickest way to be rid of it is to make peace with each other; since the Athenians menace us not from their own country, but from that of those who invited them here. In this way instead of war issuing in war, peace quietly ends our quarrels; and the guests who come hither under fair pretences for bad ends, will have good reason for going away without having attained them.

[62]. So far as regards the Athenians such are the great advantages proved inherent in a wise policy. Independently of this, in the face of the universal consent that peace is the first of blessings, how can we refuse to make it amongst ourselves; or do you not think that the good which you have, and the ills that you complain of, would be better preserved and cured by quiet than by war; that peace has its honours and splendours of a less perilous kind, not to mention the numerous other blessings that one might dilate on, with the not less numerous miseries of war? These considerations should teach you not to disregard my words, but rather to look in them every one for his own safety. If there be any here who feels certain either by right or might to effect his object, let not this surprise be to him too severe a disappointment. Let him remember that many before now have tried to chastise a wrongdoer, and failing to punish their enemy have not even saved themselves; while many who have trusted in force to gain an advantage, instead of gaining anything more, have been doomed to lose what they had. Vengeance is not necessarily successful because wrong has been done, or strength sure because it is confident; but the incalculable element in the future exercises the widest influence, and is the most treacherous, and yet in fact the most useful of all things, as it frightens us all equally, and thus makes us consider before attacking each other.

[63]. Let us therefore now allow the undefined fear of this unknown future, and the immediate terror of the Athenians' presence to produce their natural impression, and let us consider any failure to carry out the programmes that we may each have sketched out for ourselves as sufficiently accounted for by these obstacles, and send away the intruder from the country; and if everlasting peace be impossible between us, let us at all events make a treaty for as long a term as possible, and put off our private differences to another day. In fine, let us recognise that the adoption of my advice will leave us each citizens

of a free state, and as such arbiters of our own destiny, able to return good or bad offices with equal effect; while its rejection will make us dependent on others, and thus not only impotent to repel an insult, but on the most favourable supposition, friends to our direst enemies, and at feud with our natural friends.

[64]. For myself, though, as I said at first, the representative of a great city, and able to think less of defending myself than of attacking others, I am prepared to concede something in prevision of these dangers. I am not inclined to ruin myself for the sake of hurting my enemies, or so blinded by animosity as to think myself equally master of my own plans and of fortune which I cannot command; but I am ready to give up anything in reason. I call upon the rest of you to imitate my conduct of your own free will, without being forced to do so by the enemy. There is no disgrace in connexions giving way to one another, a Dorian to a Dorian, or a Chalcidian to his brethren; above and beyond this we are neighbours, live in the same country, are girt by the same sea, and go by the same name of Sicilians. We shall go to war again, I suppose, when the time comes, and again make peace among ourselves by means of future congresses; but the foreign invader, if we are wise, will always find us united against him, since the hurt of one is the danger of all; and we shall never, in future, invite into the island either allies or mediators. By so acting we shall at the present moment do for Sicily a double service, ridding her at once of the Athenians, and of civil war, and in future shall live in freedom at home, and be less menaced from abroad.

§

Brasidas to the Acanthians
Book IV 85-87
424 B.C.

Brasidas has been called the only attractive and clever military figure the Spartans produced in the war. He was energetic, resourceful, and constantly aggressive. The absence of these qualities caused the exile of Thucydides, the Athenian general sent to relieve Amphipolis in 424 B.C. who arrived too late. As the speech begins we find Brasidas at Acanthus, a promontory in Macedonia between the Thermarc and the Storymonic gulfs with a force of Chalcidians. Brasidas asked the inhabitants to hear him and he was admitted. Thucydides says he was a very able speaker, for a Spartan.

The speech is short, in the direct form, and full of surprises. The argument is the old one — the Spartans are engaged in freeing Greece from the tyranny of Athens. For this reason it is hard to believe that the Acanthians have barred their gates to the Spartan troops. But if Acanthus should join with the Spartans they can expect full independence. Moreover, there will be no attempt to control local policies. If they reject the offer the people of Acanthus can only foresee their country ruined and their future wiped out. It was a blunt and painfully clear choice: Independence or Slavery. Join with us and survive or remain loyal to Athens and die.

The persuasive devices of Brasidas seduced the Acanthians. They fell for his line and soon paid the price. What Sparta promised not to do is precisely what she carried out. It was another bitter lesson that Spartan promises meant exactly nothing. Jebb reminds us that "this speech of Brasidas — composed by Thucydides after the close of the war — was inserted by him here, just at the moment when Sparta was making the first advances to the democratic cities of northern Greece for the purpose of bringing out the glaring contrast between Spartan promise and Spartan performance" (Jebb, "Speeches of Thucydides," p. 398).

Brasidas and Cleon were killed in the same engagement in the battle for the defense of Amphipolis in the year 422 B.C. This battle made possible the Peace of Nicias, concluded in 421, and since it was only partially observed it lasted but a short time.

Sir Frank E. Adcock, author of *The Greek and Macedonian Art of War* (Berkeley, 1967), calls Brasidas "the most resourceful officer Sparta ever produced" (p. 35). He could inspire confidence anywhere.

The Peace of Nicias brought sharp criticism in Sparta and Brasidas was unappreciated. Athens was expected to give up quickly and she did not. Brasidas here (IV 85.2) says the Spartans miscalculated in their hopes of quick victory. What Thucydides says of Brasidas at IV 81.1 is in sharp contrast with his estimate of Nicias. In this speech the historian gives high praise to the very man who caused his own downfall and ended his career as a general.

For another persuasive triumph by Brasidas we must look to IV 36 where he spurs on his troops about to panic just before a battle.

§

[85]. Acanthians, the Lacedaemonians have sent out me and my army to make good the reason that we gave for the war when we began it, viz. that we were going to war with the Athenians in order to free Hellas. Our delay in coming has been caused by mistaken expectations as to the war at home, which led us to hope, by our own unassisted efforts and without your risking anything, to effect the speedy downfall of the Athenians; and you must not blame us for this, as we are now come to the moment that we were able, prepared with your aid, to do our best to subdue them. Meanwhile I am astonished at finding your gates shut against me, and at not meeting with a better welcome. We Lacedaemonians thought of you as allies eager to have us, to whom we should come in spirit even before we were with you in body; and in this expectation undertook all the risks of a march of many days through a strange country, so far did our zeal carry us. It will be a terrible thing if after this you have other intentions, and mean

to stand in the way of your own and Hellenic freedom. It is not merely that you oppose me yourselves; but wherever I may go people will be less inclined to join me, on the score that you, to whom I first came — an important town like Acanthus, and prudent men like the Acanthians — refused to admit me. I shall have nothing to prove that the reason which I advance is the true one; it will be said either that there is something unfair in the freedom which I offer, or that I am here in insufficient force and unable to protect you against an attack from Athens. Yet when I went with the army which I now have to the relief of Nisaea, the Athenians did not venture to engage me although in greater force than I; and it is not likely they will ever send across sea against you an army as numerous as they had at Nisaea.

[86]. And for myself, I have come here not to hurt but to free the Hellenes, witness the solemn oaths by which I have bound my government that the allies that I may bring over shall be independent; and besides my object in coming is not by force or fraud to obtain your alliance, but to offer you mine to help you against your Athenian masters. I protest, therefore, against any suspicions of my intentions after the guarantees which I offer, and equally so against doubts of my ability to protect you, and I invite you to join me without hesitation. Some of you may hang back because they have private enemies, and fear that I may put the city into the hands of a party: none need be more tranquil than they. I am not come here to help this party or that; and I do not consider that I should be bringing you freedom in any real sense, if I should disregard your constitution, and enslave the many to the few or the few to the many. This would be heavier than a foreign yoke; and we Lacedaemonians instead of being thanked for our pains, should get neither honour nor glory, but contrariwise reproaches. The charges which strengthen our hands in the war against the Athenians would on our own showing be merited by ourselves, and more hateful in us than in those who make no pretensions to honesty; as it is more disgraceful for persons of character to take what they covet by fair-seeming fraud than by open force; the one aggression having for its justification the might which fortune gives, the other being simply a piece of clever roguery. A matter which concerns us thus nearly we naturally look to most jealously; and over and above the oaths that I have mentioned, what stronger assurance can you have, when you see that our words, compared with the actual facts, produce the necessary conviction that it is our interest to act as we say?

[87]. If to these considerations of mine you put in the plea of inability, and claim that your friendly feeling should save you from

being hurt by your refusal; if you say that freedom, in your opinion, is not without its dangers, and that it is right to offer it to those who can accept it, but not to force it on any against their will, then I shall take the gods and heroes of your country to witness that I came for your good and was rejected, and shall do my best to compel you by laying waste your land. I shall do so without scruple, being justified by the necessity which constrains me, first, to prevent the Lacedaemonians from being damaged by you, their friends, in the event of your non-adhesion, through the monies that you pay to the Athenians; and secondly, to prevent the Hellenes from being hindered by you in shaking off their servitude. Otherwise indeed we should have no right to act as we propose; except in the name of some public interest, what call should we Lacedaemonians have to free those who do not wish it? Empire we do not aspire to: it is what we are labouring to put down; and we should wrong the greater number if we allowed you to stand in the way of the independence that we offer to all. Endeavour, therefore, to decide wisely, and strive to begin the work of liberation for the Hellenes, and lay up for yourselves endless renown, while you escape private loss, and cover your commonwealth with glory.

§

Conference Between Athenian and Melian Negotiators
Book V 85-113
416 B.C.

Melos is an island about a hundred miles south of Athens. It is one of the Cyclades group and like Thera did not belong to the Delian Confederacy. It had remained independent even though attacked in 426 — but the Melians had strong ties with Sparta in the past.

Now in the sixteenth year of the war the Athenians, flexing muscles, sent a landing force to Melos under command of Cleomedes and Tisias. Soon after their arrival they sent envoys to the city demanding that Melos surrender and become a subject ally of Athens.

The Melian dialogue, as the passage below is known, is in effect an explanation of the ruthless compulsion of Athens to expand its empire. The setting is the island of Melos whose Dorian inhabitants were friendly to Sparta. They had refused to surrender to Athens or to pay tribute and the Athenians were now planning to make them see the light. The conversation that follows is fascinating for several reasons — its orderly form, its candor, its grim depravity on the part of Athens, and finally as an example of what fifteen years of warfare can do to a once idealistic and brilliant people.

The discussion that follows was not held in public. It was really a small affair with perhaps three or four Athenians and a dozen members of the Melian council. Thucydides was not present and whatever information he gives must have come from the Athenian side since all the Melians were slain soon after the talks. He probably did not get his report until some years later. What we have below therefore is a kind of dramatic reproduction of what may have taken place. It is highly condensed and in dialectical form — an unlikely form since diplomats are not known for their brevity or clarity. The Greeks had a word, *eristikos,* that meant fond of wrangling. Eristic was the art of making the worse argument appear the better. Aristotle says that "people were right in objecting to the training Protagoras undertook to give them (Cp. Plato, *Protagoras* 319 A). It was a fraud; the probability was not genuine but spurious, and has a place in no art except Rhetoric (in the perverted sense) and Eristic (i.e. non genuine Dialectic)" (*Rhetoric*, Book II 1402a 23-29, Roberts translation).

"Educated men," Aristotle says in the *Rhetoric*, "lay down broad general principles; uneducated men argue from common knowledge and draw obvious conclusions." Here the Melians try to present their case on abstract principles of justice but the Athenians just insist on discussing power and expediency. It is the Melians who talk like educated men. In simple terms the Athenians revert to the Sophist doctrine that might makes right — and for the Melians this meant that to survive they had better give in. Athens held the trump cards. But, as Edith Hamilton shrewdly says, "The Melians were unpractical and they decided to fight. They were conquered with little effort by Athens. She put the men to death and made slaves of the women and children" (*The Greek Way of Life*, p. 145).

Let us examine the import of the dialogue in more detail. First, it is the one extended example of dialectic, the art of question and answer, in the *History*. It is the longest discourse in the book. It consists of 27 short exchanges between Melians and Athenians. Their bluntness is startling at times. Aristotle says "Dialectic does not construct its syllogisms out of any haphazard materials such as the fancies of crazy people, but out of materials that call for discussion..." (*Rhetoric* 1356b 35). This is precisely the situation in the Melian dialogue and the Athenians lay down the ground rules at the start: (1) the purpose of the meeting is to look at existing facts, (2) to discuss the safety of the city, (3) with no surmises about the future, (4) there will be no long speeches, (5) each side will deal separately with each point, (6) only the speakers for both sides make up the audience, (7) the room must be kept secure. Under these conditions obviously a lopsided discussion proceeded. The youngest schoolboy reader can sense the outcome: When the Melians reject what the Athenian generals offered their doom is just a matter of time.

The Melian dialogue is an example of eristic and the Athenian spokesmen are the dishonest practitioners. They are adept at twisting facts and probabilities to their advantage. There are thirteen issues that arise and long before the end we sense that the Melians are not speaking to rational men — rather they are hopelessly appealing to men whose minds were already closed and made up. This is why the term dialogue does not accurately apply to the meeting.

The bluntest appraisal of the Spartans' untrustworthiness is found at V 105.4 where the Athenian speaker concludes "Such a way of thinking does not promise much for the safety (i.e. help from Sparta) which you now unreasonably count upon." The Athenians were right. Sparta did not lift a finger to help Melos.

The Melians attempt to put their trust in the Gods at another point but the Athenian emissary coldly replies: "of the gods we believe, and of men we know, that by a necessary law of their nature they rule wherever they can." They go on to say they did not make the law — but that you (the Melians) "having the same power as we have, would do the same as we have" (V 105.2).

Thucydides has chosen a dramatic way to portray the political reality that cities and states, and Athens especially, when minds are made up, are no more moved by ideas of justice than are individuals. Here we learn about Athenian motivation in its raw form. The drive to expand is far more powerful than any abstract political concept. Why was this so? Simply because colonies could be taxed and could provide jobs for Athenians and this was a way of keeping the Athenian economy at a high level. Even in the fifth century B.C. the deceptive notion was abroad that wars were good and that one conquest gave high promise for another.

Professor Finley makes the case that something like the Melian negotiations did take place since rhetoric and dialectic had trained men to think along these lines. Some scholars, on the other hand, argue that the whole incident is contrived and carefully put into words by Thucydides. Finley's argument is buttressed by the similarities of the points to be found in Euripides — *The Trojan Women, Heraclidae, Bellerophon, Orestes, Alcestis,* and *Medea.* He cites lines in all these plays that bear marked resemblance to the Athenian ideas of empire that the envoys utter at V 89-99, V 100, V 103, V 104, V 105.1-2, V 105.4, and V 105.3 The details are to be found in the celebrated essay, "Euripides and Thucydides," in *Three Essays,* pp. 40-42.

The Melian dialogue has been called "a sophistical little piece" and it is not included in some of the anthologies of Thucydides. It is indeed sophistical but not unreal or improbable. The very same arguments have cropped up for the past twenty-five centuries.

§

[85]. *Athenians.*—Since the negotiations are not to go on before the people, in order that we may not be able to speak straight on without interruption, and deceive the ears of the multitude by seductive arguments which would pass without refutation (for we know that this is the meaning of our being brought before the few), what if you who sit there were to pursue a method more cautious still! Make no set speech yourselves, but take us up at whatever you do not like, and settle that before going any farther. And first tell us if this proposition of ours suits you.

The Melian commissioners answered:—

[86]. *Melians.*—To the fairness of quietly instructing each other as you propose there is nothing to object; but your military preparations are too far advanced to agree with what you say, as we see you are come to be judges in your own cause, and that all we can reasonably expect from this negotiation is war, if we prove to have right on our side and refuse to submit, and in the contrary case, slavery.

[87]. *Athenians.*—If you have met to reason about presentiments of the future, or for anything else than to consult for the safety of your state upon the facts that you see before you, we will give over; otherwise we will go on.

[88]. *Melians.*—It is natural and excusable for men in our position to turn more ways than one both in thought and utterance. However, the question in this conference is, as you say, the safety of our country; and the discussion, if you please, can proceed in the way which you propose.

[89]. *Athenians.*—For ourselves we shall not trouble you with specious pretences — either of how we have a right to our empire because we overthrew the Mede, or are now attacking you because of wrong that you have done us — and make a long speech which would not be believed; and in return we hope that you, instead of thinking to influence us by saying that you did not join the Lacedaemonians, although their colonists, or that you have done us no wrong, will aim at what is feasible, holding in view the real sentiments of us both; since you know as well as we do that right, as the world goes, is only in question between equals in power, while the strong do what they can and the weak suffer what they must.

[90]. *Melians.*—As we think, at any rate, it is expedient — we speak as we are obliged, since you enjoin us to let right alone and talk only of interest — that you should not destroy what is our common protection, the privilege of being allowed in danger to invoke what is fair and right, and even to profit by arguments not strictly valid if they can be got to pass current. And you are as much interested in this as any, as your fall would be a signal for the heaviest vengeance and an example for the world to meditate upon.

[91]. *Athenians.*—The end of our empire, if end it should, does not frighten us: a rival empire like Lacedaemon, even if Lacedaemon was our real antagonist, is not so terrible to the vanquished as subjects who by themselves attack and overpower their rulers. This, however, is a risk that we are content to take. We will now proceed to show you that we are come here in the interest of our empire, and that we shall say what we are now going to say, for the preservation of your country; as we would fain exercise that empire over you without trouble, and see you preserved for the good of us both.

[92]. *Melians.*—And how, pray, could it turn out as good for us to serve as for you to rule?

[93]. *Athenians.*—Because you would have the advantage of submitting before suffering the worst, and we should gain by not destroying you.

[94]. *Melians.*—So that you would not consent to our being neutral, friends instead of enemies, but allies of neither side.

[95]. *Athenians.*—No; for your hostility cannot so much hurt us as your friendship will be an argument to our subjects of our weakness, and your enmity of our power.

[96]. *Melians.*—Is that your subjects' idea of equity, to put those who have nothing to do with you in the same category with peoples that are most of them your own colonists, and some conquered rebels?

[97]. *Athenians.*—As far as right goes they think one has as much of it as the other, and that if any maintain their independence it is because they are strong, and that if we do not molest them it is because we are afraid; so that besides extending our empire we should gain in security by your subjection; the fact that you are islanders and weaker than others rendering it all the more important that you should not succeed in baffling the masters of the sea.

[98]. *Melians.*—But do you consider that there is no security in the policy which we indicate? For here again if you debar us from talking about justice and invite us to obey your interest, we also must explain our, and try to persuade you, if the two happen to coincide. How can you avoid making enemies of all existing neutrals who shall look at our case and conclude from it that one day or another you will attack them? And what is this but to make greater the enemies that you have already, and to force others to become so who would otherwise have never thought of it?

[99]. *Athenians.*—Why, the fact is that continentals generally give us but little alarm; the liberty which they enjoy will prevent their taking precautions against us; it is rather islanders like yourselves, outside our empire, and subjects smarting under the yoke, who would be the most likely to take a rash step and lead themselves and us into obvious danger.

[100]. *Melians.*—Well then, if you risk so much to retain your empire, and your subjects to get rid of it, it were surely great baseness and cowardice in us who are still free not to try everything that can be tried, before submitting to your yoke.

[101]. *Athenians.*—Not if you are well advised, the contest not being an equal one, with honour as the prize and shame the penalty, but a question of self-preservation and of not resisting those who are far stronger than you are.

[102]. *Melians.*—But we know that the fortune of war is sometimes more impartial than the disproportion of numbers might lead one to

suppose; to submit is to give ourselves over to despair, while action still preserves for us a hope that we may stand erect.

[103]. *Athenians.*—Hope, danger's comforter, may be indulged in by those who have abundant resources, if not without loss at all events without ruin; but its nature is to be extravagant, and those who go so far as to put their all upon the venture see it in its true colours only when they are ruined; but so long as the discovery would enable them to guard against it, it is never found wanting. Let not this be the case with you, who are weak and hang on a single turn of the scale; nor be like the vulgar, who, abandoning such security as human means may still afford, when visible hopes fail them in extremity, turn to invisible, to prophecies and oracles, and other such inventions that delude men with hopes to their destruction.

[104]. *Melians.*—You may be sure that we are as well aware as you of the difficulty of contending against your power and fortune, unless the terms be equal. But we trust that the gods may grant us fortune as good as yours, since we are just men fighting against unjust, and that what we want in power will be made up by the alliance of the Lacedaemonians, who are bound, if only for very shame, to come to the aid of their kindred. Our confidence, therefore, after all is not so utterly irrational.

[105]. *Athenians.*—When you speak of the favour of the gods, we may as fairly hope for that as yourselves; neither our pretensions nor our conduct being in any way contrary to what men believe of the gods, or practise among themselves. Of the gods we believe, and of men we know, that by a necessary law of their nature they rule wherever they can. And it is not as if we were the first to make this law, or to act upon it when made: we found it existing before us, and shall leave it to exist for ever after us; all we do is to make use of it, knowing that you and everybody else, having the same power as we have, would do the same as we do. Thus, as far as the gods are concerned, we have no fear and no reason to fear that we shall be at a disadvantage. But when we come to your notion about the Lacedaemonians, which leads you to believe that shame will make them help you, here we bless your simplicity but do not envy your folly. The Lacedaemonians, when their own interests or their country's laws are in question, are the worthiest men alive; of their conduct towards others much might be said, but no clearer idea of it could be given than by shortly saying that of all the men we know they are most conspicuous in considering what is agreeable honourable, and what is expedient just. Such a way of thinking does not promise much for the safety which you now unreasonably count upon.

[106]. *Melians.*—But it is for this very reason that we now trust to their respect for expediency to prevent them from betraying the Melians, their colonists, and thereby losing the confidence of their friends in Hellas and helping their enemies.

[107]. *Athenians.*—Then you do not adopt the view that expediency goes with security, while justice and honour cannot be followed without danger; and danger the Lacedaemonians generally court as little as possible.

[108]. *Melians.*—But we believe that they would be more likely to face even danger for our sake, and with more confidence than for others, as our nearness to Peloponnese makes it easier for them to act, and our common blood insures our fidelity.

[109]. *Athenians.*—Yes, but what an intending ally trusts to, is not the goodwill of those who ask his aid, but a decided superiority of power for action; and the Lacedaemonians look to this even more than others. At least, such is their distrust of their home resources that it is only with numerous allies that they attack a neighbour; now is it likely that while we are masters of the sea they will cross over to an island?

[110]. *Melians.*—But they would have others to send. The Cretan sea is a wide one, and it is more difficult for those who command it to intercept others, than for those who wish to elude them to do so safely. And should the Lacedaemonians miscarry in this, they would fall upon your land, and upon those left of your allies whom Brasidas did not reach; and instead of places which are not yours, you will have to fight for your own country and your own confederacy.

[111]. *Athenians.*—Some diversion of the kind you speak of you may one day experience, only to learn, as others have done, that the Athenians never once yet withdrew from a siege for fear of any. But we are struck by the fact, that after saying you would consult for the safety of your country, in all this discussion you have mentioned nothing which men might trust in and think to be saved by. Your strongest arguments depend upon hope and the future, and your actual resources are too scanty, as compared with those arrayed against you, for you to come out victorious. You will therefore show great blindness of judgment, unless, after allowing us to retire, you can find some counsel more prudent than this. You will surely not be caught by that idea of disgrace, which in dangers that are disgraceful, and at the same time too plain to be mistaken, proves so fatal to mankind; since in too many cases the very men that have their eyes perfectly open to what they are rushing into, let the thing called disgrace, by the mere

influence of a seductive name, lead them on to a point at which they become so enslaved by the phrase as in fact to fall wilfully into hopeless disaster, and incur disgrace more disgraceful as the companion of error, than when it comes as the result of misfortune. This, if you are well advised, you will guard against; and you will not think it dishonourable to submit to the greatest city in Hellas, when it makes you the moderate offer of becoming its tributary ally, without ceasing to enjoy the country that belongs to you; nor when you have the choice given you between war and security, will you be so blinded as to choose the worse. And it is certain that those who do not yield to their equals, who keep terms with their superiors, and are moderate towards their inferiors, on the whole succeed best. Think over the matter, therefore, after our withdrawal, and reflect once and again that it is for your country that you are consulting, that you have not more than one, and that upon this one deliberation depends its prosperity or ruin.

The Athenians now withdrew from the conference; and the Melians, left to themselves, came to a decision corresponding with what they had maintained in the discussion, and answered.

[112]. Our resolution, Athenians, is the same as it was at first. We will not in a moment deprive of freedom a city that has been inhabited these seven hundred years; but we put our trust in the fortune by which the gods have preserved it until now, and in the help of men, that is, of the Lacedaemonians; and so we will try and save ourselves. Meanwhile we invite you to allow us to be friends to you and foes to neither party, and to retire from our country after making such a treaty as shall seem fit to us both.

Such was the answer of the Melians. The Athenians now departing from the conference said:

[113]. Well, you alone, as it seems to us, judging from these resolutions, regard what is future as more certain than what is before your eyes, and what is out of sight, in your eagerness, as already coming to pass; and as you have staked most on, and trusted most in, the Lacedaemonians, your fortune, and your hopes, so will you be most completely deceived.

§

Nicias to the Athenian Ecclesia
Book VI 9-14
415 B.C.

Book VI may be likened to a three-act play with a short epilogue added. Act I consists of the speeches of Nicias, Alcibiades, and Nicias again before the Athenian Ecclesia. Act II has speeches by Mermocrates, Athenagoras, and a Syracusan general to the Syracusan Assembly. Act III presents speeches by Hermocrates and Euphenus at Camarina. The epilogue and the final address of the *History* allows Alcibiades to give his advice at Sparta. To be sure there are some dozen military harangues scattered in Books II, IV, V, VI and VII but they are all very short exhortations to troops in the field and they deserve separate treatment.

This first address by Nicias opens the nine significant presentations of Book VI. They are essentially examples of the force of each speaker's *ethos.* Thucydides uses his words to reveal in each speech the kind of person the *speaker* is — his character and integrity or their lack, his honesty and sincerity or their lack, his strengths or weaknesses as the case may be. The result is a series of sketches producing credibility or non-credibility in each speaker. The reader reacts as that reasonable man in the audience in the year 415 must have reacted at the time. The task of deciding just how he responded to the speaker according to the appeals he used, assuming the speeches resemble those actually delivered, is a fascinating one. This is so because of the strange mixture of clarity and obscurity that pervades Book VI. More than any other part of the *History* it illustrates the truth of the heroic couplet: "The champ obscurant is old man Thucydides; every page in his book conceals the lucidites."

This speech demonstrates many familiar ways of thinking. Nicias says here that what was earlier fought for is now given without a struggle (VI 10.4). Fear is relative; the Athenians no longer were ten feet tall to the Spartans (VI 11.4). With the Spartans "military reputation is their oldest and chiefest study" (VI 11.7) and they do not easily fold up. The "generation-gap" looms up in VI 12.2-12 when Nicias discusses the differences between the old and the young. There is a real conflict of interests.

One of the most telling arguments Nicias makes in his speech is found at VI 11.7 when he says: "Our struggle, therefore, if we are wise, will not be for the barbarian Egestaeans in Sicily, but how to defend ourselves most effectively against the oligarchical machinations of Lacedaemon."

Nicias is a tragic figure. He was opposed to the Sicilian expedition from the start. He did not seek to command it (VI 8.4). He was a sick man and by nature a cautious general. He lost his two best deputies — Loinachus and Alcibiades, by death and desertion. He is the victim of chance and he calls forth our pity. But we cannot admire the man. His skill as a troop leader was hampered by his "stupidity, timidity, and incompetence" (David Grene, *Greek Political Theory*, Chicago, 1965, p. 71). These qualities are revealed in the speech below and more especially in the one after Alcibiades speaks (VI 20-23).

§

[9]. Although this assembly was convened to consider the preparations to be made for sailing to Sicily, I think, notwithstanding, that we have still this question to examine, whether it be better to send out the ships at all, and that we ought not to give so little consideration to a matter of such moment, or let ourselves be persuaded by foreigners into undertaking a war with which we have nothing to do. And yet, individually, I gain in honour by such a course, and fear as little as other men for my person — not that I think a man need be any the worse citizen for taking some thought for his person and estate; on the contrary, such a man would for his own sake desire the prosperity of his country more than others — nevertheless, as I have never spoken against my convictions to gain honour, I shall not begin to do so now,

but shall say what I think best. Against your character any words of mine would be weak enough; if I were to advise your keeping what you have got and not risking what is actually yours for advantages which are dubious in themselves, and which you may or may not attain. I will, therefore, content myself with showing that your ardour is out of season, and your ambition not easy of accomplishment.

[10]. I affirm, then, that you leave many enemies behind you here to go yonder and bring more back with you. You imagine, perhaps, that the treaty which you have made can be trusted; a treaty that will continue to exist nominally, as long as you keep quiet — for nominal it has become, owing to the practices of certain men here and at Sparta — but which in the event of a serious reverse in any quarter would not delay our enemies a moment in attacking us; first, because the convention was forced upon them by disaster and was less honourable to them than to us; and secondly, because in this very convention there are many points that are still disputed. Again, some of the most powerful states have never yet accepted the arrangement at all. Some of these are at open war with us; others (as the Lacedaemonians do not yet move) are restrained by truces renewed every ten days, and it is only too probable that if they found our power divided, as we are hurrying to divide it, they would attack us vigorously with the Siceliots, whose alliance they would have in the past valued as they would that of few others. A man ought, therefore, to consider these points, and not to think of running risks with a country placed so critically, or of grasping at another empire before we have secured the one we have already; for in fact the Thracian Chalcidians have been all these years in revolt from us without being yet subdued, and others on the continents yield us but a doubtful obedience. Meanwhile the Egestaeans, our allies, have been wronged, and we run to help them, while the rebels who have so long wronged us still wait for punishment.

[11]. And yet the latter, if brought under, might be kept under; while the Sicilians, even if conquered, are too far off and too numerous to be ruled without difficulty. Now it is folly to go against men who could not be kept under even if conquered, while failure would leave us in a very different position from that which we occupied before the enterprise. The Siceliots, again, to take them as they are at present, in the event of a Syracusan conquest (the favourite bugbear of the Egestaeans), would to my thinking be even less dangerous to us than before. At present they might possibly come here as separate states for love of Lacedaemon; in the other case one empire would scarcely attack

another; for after joining the Peloponnesians to overthrow ours, they could only expect to see the same hands overthrow their own in the same way. The Hellenes in Sicily would fear us most if we never went there at all, and next to this, if after displaying our power we went away again as soon as possible. We all know that that which is farthest off and the reputation of which can least be tested, is the object of admiration; at the least reverse they would at once begin to look down upon us, and would join our enemies here against us. You have yourselves experienced this with regard to the Lacedaemonians and their allies, whom your unexpected success, as compared with what you feared at first, has made you suddenly despise, tempting you further to aspire to the conquest of Sicily. Instead, however, of being puffed up by the misfortunes of your adversaries, you ought to think of breaking their spirit before giving yourselves up to confidence, and to understand that the one thought awakened in the Lacedaemonians by their disgrace is how they may even now, if possible, overthrow us and repair their dishonour; inasmuch as military reputation is their oldest and chiefest study. Our struggle, therefore, if we are wise, will not be for the barbarian Egestaeans in Sicily, but how to defend ourselves most effectually against the oligarchical machinations of Lacedaemon.

[12]. We should also remember that we are but now enjoying some respite from a great pestilence and from war, to the no small benefit of our estates and persons, and that it is right to employ these at home on our own behalf, instead of using them on behalf of these exiles whose interest it is to lie as fairly as they can, who do nothing but talk themselves and leave the danger to others, and who if they succeed will show no proper gratitude, and if they fail will drag down their friends with them. And if there be any man here, overjoyed at being chosen to command, who urges you to make the expedition, merely for ends of his own — especially if he be still too young to command — who seeks to be admired for his stud of horses, but on account of its heavy expenses hopes for some profit from his appointment, do not allow such an one to maintain his private splendour at his country's risk, but remember that such persons injure the public fortune while they squander their own, and that this is a matter of importance, and not for a young man to decide or hastily to take in hand.

[13]. When I see such persons now sitting here at the side of that same individual and summoned by him, alarm seizes me; and I, in my turn, summon any of the older men that may have such a person sitting next him, not to let himself be shamed down, for fear of being thought a

coward if he do not vote for war, but, remembering how rarely success is got by wishing and how often by forecast, to leave to them the mad dream of conquest, and as a true lover of his country, now threatened by the greatest danger in its history, to hold up his hand on the other side; to vote that the Siceliots be left in the limits now existing between us, limits of which no one can complain (the Ionian sea for the coasting voyage, and the Sicilian across the open main), to enjoy their own possessions and to settle their own quarrels; that the Egestaeans, for their part, be told to end by themselves with the Selinuntines the war which they began without consulting the Athenians; and that for the future we do not enter into alliance, as we have been used to do, with people whom we must help in their need, and who can never help us in ours.

[14]. And you, Prytanis, if you think it your duty to care for the commonwealth, and if you wish to show yourself a good citizen, put the question to the vote, and take a second time the opinions of the Athenians. If you are afraid to move the question again, consider that a violation of the law cannot carry any prejudice with so many abettors, that you will be the physician of your misguided city, and that the virtue of men in office is briefly this, to do their country as much good as they can, or in any case no harm that they can avoid.

§

Alcibiades to the Athenian Ecclesia
Book VI 16-18
415 B.C.

Finley believes that the speeches of Alcibiades "must be imagined farthest from their originals, because the trend to the new Atticism — the trend that the historian escaped through his exile — must then have been already under way" (*Three Essays*, p. x). But even if the style and diction are not true to the speaker we cannot doubt the validity of the ideas that Alcibiades utters. He is true in speech-content to the kind of character his public conduct revealed.

This is a short, blunt, and essentially candid speech. It comes from a popular hero, a man used to wealth — with a cultivated taste for wine, high living, and horses. He was not crude in manner or speech. Indeed he was brought up in the home of Pericles. Socrates was his friend. Socrates had saved his life at Potidaea (432) and he saved Socrates at Delium (424). The intellectuals of the day were his friends. If he seems arrogant in this speech remember that he was a superior speaker. He had a brilliant record as a commander and diplomat and was a general at the age of 30. Now at 35 he is at the peak of his power. Remember too, his audience. The Athenians were war-mad. They were ready to conquer their known world — first Sicily and then Carthage — everything up to the Pillars of Hercules. Alcibiades was young, bold, handsome — the ideal politician. He had the highest degree of credibility. He appealed to the gambling instinct of man.

So, true to the maxim, a bold attack is the best defense; this is how Alcibiades begins. He lists his qualifications — "the distinguished manner in which he represented the state at Olympia," his sponsorship of seven chariots — winning first, second, and fourth places (another account gives it first, second, and third); his fellow citizens are not his equals. Does his personal unpopularity interfere with his administrative capacity, and what about the choruses he provided? And so on to the final most arrogant reason of all — a boast that the Spartans at the battle of Mantinea (418 B.C.) "have never since fully regained confidence." Actually that battle was a disastrous Athenian defeat. Only an Alcibiades could have told the story in that upside-down way.

The speaker alludes again to the doctrine that those who deserve power should exercise it. Alcibiades considers himself pre-eminently qualified to lead (VI 18). This doctrine assumes that the power to lead induces change. And we may assume further that change is a prime feature of democracy.

But he does not argue that the Assembly should reject Nicias. No, he goes on: "And do not be afraid of my youth now, but while I am still in flower, and Nicias enjoys the reputation of success, avail yourselves to the utmost of the services of us both." Thus Alcibiades seems to conciliate. But in reality he pressed hard for quick action — on to Sicily. Inactivity is ruinous. So he concludes "the safest rule of life is to take one's character and institutions for better and for worse, and to live up to them as closely as one can" (VI 18.6).

Thus we have portraits of the two Athenian leaders. Their personalities were opposite. Their military skills were far apart, and their patriotism, as we shall soon discover, was even farther apart. In truth, as Professor Finley has so well analyzed them: "hence one returns again to Athens' calamity in having as rival leaders, two men whose virtues though complementary, were in each case marred by glaring faults" (*Thucydides*, p. 218).

§

[16]. Athenians, I have a better right to command than others — I must begin with this as Nicias has attacked me — and at the same time I believe myself to be worthy of it. The things for which I am abused, bring fame to my ancestors and to myself, and to the country profit besides. The Hellenes, after expecting to see our city ruined by the war,

concluded it to be even greater than it really is, by reason of the magnificence with which I represented it at the Olympic games, when I sent into the lists seven chariots, a number never before entered by any private person, and won the first prize, and was second and fourth, and took care to have everything else in a style worthy of my victory. Custom regards such displays as honourable, and they cannot be made without leaving behind them an impression of power. Again, any splendour that I may have exhibited at home in providing choruses or otherwise, is naturally envied by my fellow-citizens, but in the eyes of foreigners has an air of strength as in the other instance. And this is no useless folly, when a man at his own private cost benefits not himself only, but his city: nor is it unfair that he who prides himself on his position should refuse to be upon an equality with the rest. He who is badly off has his misfortunes all to himself, and as we do not see men courted in adversity, on the like principle a man ought to accept the insolence of prosperity; or else, let him first mete out equal measure to all, and then demand to have it meted out to him. What I know is that persons of this kind and all others that have attained to any distinction, although they may be unpopular in their lifetime in their relations with their fellow-men and especially with their equals, leave to posterity the desire of claiming connexion with them even without any ground, and are vaunted by the country to which they belonged, not as strangers or ill-doers, but as fellow-countrymen and heroes. Such are my aspirations, and however I am abused for them in private, the question is whether any one manages public affairs better than I do. Having united the most powerful states of Peloponnese, without great danger or expense to you, I compelled the Lacedaemonians to stake their all upon the issue of a single day at Mantinea; and although victorious in the battle, they have never since fully recovered confidence.

[17]. Thus did my youth and so-called monstrous folly find fitting arguments to deal with the power of the Peloponnesians, and by its ardour win their confidence and prevail. And do not be afraid of my youth now, but while I am still in its flower, and Nicias appears fortunate, avail yourselves to the utmost of the services of us both. Neither rescind your resolution to sail to Sicily, on the ground that you would be going to attack a great power. The cities in Sicily are peopled by motley rabbles, and easily change their institutions and adopt new ones in their stead; and consequently the inhabitants, being without any feeling of patriotism, are not provided with arms for their persons, and have not regularly established themselves on the land; every man

thinks that either by fair words or by party strife he can obtain something at the public expense, and then in the event of a catastrophe settle in some other country, and makes his preparations accordingly. From a mob like this you need not look for either unanimity in counsel or concert in action; but they will probably one by one come in as they get a fair offer, especially if they are torn by civil strife as we are told. Moreover, the Siceliots have not so many heavy infantry as they boast; just as the Hellenes generally did not prove so numerous as each state reckoned itself, but Hellas greatly over-estimated their numbers, and has hardly had an adequate force of heavy infantry throughout this war. The states in Sicily, therefore, from all that I can hear, will be found as I say, and I have not pointed out all our advantages, for we shall have the help of many barbarians, who from their hatred of the Syracusans will join us in attacking them; nor will the powers at home prove any hindrance, if you judge rightly. Our fathers with these very adversaries, which it is said we shall now leave behind us when we sail, and the Mede as their enemy as well, were able to win the empire, depending solely on their superiority at sea. The Peloponnesians had never so little hope against us at present; and let them be ever so sanguine, although strong enough to invade our country even if we stay at home, they can never hurt us with their navy, as we leave one of our own behind us that is a match for them.

[18]. In this state of things what reason can we give to ourselves for holding back, or what excuse can we offer to our allies in Sicily for not helping them? They are our confederates, and we are bound to assist them, without objecting that they have not assisted us. We did not take them into alliance to have them to help us in Hellas, but that they might so annoy our enemies in Sicily as to prevent them from coming over here and attacking us. It is thus that empire has been won, both by us and by all others that have held it, by a constant readiness to support all, whether barbarians or Hellenes, that invite assistance; since if all were to keep quiet or to pick and choose whom they ought to assist, we should make but few new conquests, and should imperil those we have already won. Men do not rest content with parrying the attacks of a superior, but often strike the first blow to prevent the attack being made. And we cannot fix the exact point at which our empire shall stop; we have reached a position in which we must not be content with retaining but must scheme to extend it, for, if we cease to rule others, we are in danger of being ruled ourselves. Nor can you look at inaction from the same point of view as others, unless you are prepared to change your habits and make them like theirs.

Be convinced then that we shall augment our power at home by this adventure abroad, and let us make the expedition, and so humble the pride of the Peloponnesians by sailing off to Sicily, and letting them see how little we care for the peace that we are now enjoying; and at the same time we shall either become masters, as we very easily may, of the whole of Hellas through the accession of the Sicilian Hellenes, or in any case ruin the Syracusans, to the no small advantage of ourselves and our allies. The faculty of staying if successful, or of returning, will be secured to us by our navy, as we shall be superior at sea to all the Siceliots put together. And do not let the do-nothing policy which Nicias advocates, or his setting of the young against the old, turn you from your purpose, but in the good old fashion by which our fathers, old and young together, by their united counsels brought our affairs to their present height, do you endeavour still to advance them; understanding that neither youth nor old age can do anything the one without the other, but that levity, sobriety, and deliberate judgment are strongest when united, and that, by sinking into inaction, the city, like everything else, will wear itself out, and its skill in everything decay; while each fresh struggle will give it fresh experience, and make it more used to defend itself not in word but in deed. In short, my conviction is that a city not inactive by nature could not choose a quicker way to ruin itself than by suddenly adopting such a policy, and that the safest rule of life is to take one's character and institutions for better and for worse, and to live up to them as closely as one can.

§

Nicias to the Athenian Ecclesia
Book VI 20-23
415 B.C.

Nicias sensed that his audience favored Alcibiades. Caution was out and the hawks were screaming. So, bold strategy was demanded. It comes now in a speech only half as long as that of Alcibiades.

Nicias may not appeal to readers nowadays as a forceful commander but in this speech he reveals a far better grasp of the difficulties of the Sicilian expedition than any other Athenian. Aside from the military problems he correctly foresaw he was aware of the psychological similarities of the Sicilians to the Athenians. They were tough, determined, willing to take risks and to innovate. They were not like the Spartans.

The argument of Nicias runs this way: Very well, you want to capture Sicily. This is what it will take: great numbers of heavy infantry (5,000), archers and slingers (in proportion), at least 100 galleys, corresponding transports for supplies, over 25,000 men in all. The ships and sailors must be first-class with high pay for all. The generals in command need to have full powers of decision at sea and in battle on land. These are the minimum requirements.

Such demands were intended to sound so preposterous as to give the Athenians a cause to hesitate — and pull out. But no, everything was agreed upon — by acclamation. As the saying goes, nobody batted an eyelash. Nicias completely misjudged his hearers — and found himself in command of the whole expedition — unwillingly, unwittingly, physically unfit, and militarily inept. The whole idea of the expedition was clearly doomed to fail even though the prospects for men, equipment, strategic concept appeared so bright. The offer of Nicias to turn over the command if he could not have all he asked boomeranged. As Thucydides says: "with this enthusiasm of the majority, the few that liked it not feared to appear unpatriotic by holding up their hands against it, and so kept quiet" (VI 24).

This is how Nicias is cast as the leading actor in what Thucydides later (VII 87.5) called the greatest tragedy ever to befall a state. Is it any wonder that Alcibiades appealed to younger Athenians as a more likely winner?

§

[20]. I see, Athenians, that you are thoroughly bent upon the expedition, and therefore hope that all will turn out as we wish, and proceed to give you my opinion at the present juncture. From all that I hear we are going against cities that are great and not subject to one another, or in need of change, so as to be glad to pass from enforced servitude to an easier condition, or in the least likely to accept our rule in exchange for freedom; and, to take only the Hellenic towns, they are very numerous for one island. Besides Naxos and Catana, which I expect to join us from their connexion with Leontini, there are seven others armed at all points just like our own power, particularly Selinus and Syracuse, the chief objects of our expedition. These are full of heavy infantry, archers, and darters, have galleys in abundance and crowds to man them; they have also money, partly in the hands of private persons, partly in the temples at Selinus, and at Syracuse first-fruits from some of the barbarians as well. But their chief advantage over us lies in the number of their horses, and in the fact that they grow their corn at home instead of importing it.

[21]. Against a power of this kind it will not do to have merely a weak naval armament, but we shall want also a large land army to sail with us, if we are to do anything worthy of our ambition, and are not to be shut out from the country by a numerous cavalry; especially if the cities should take alarm and combine, and we should be left without friends (except the Egestaeans) to furnish us with horse to defend ourselves with. It would be disgraceful to have to retire under compulsion, or to send back for reinforcements, owing to want of reflexion at first: we must therefore start from home with a competent force, seeing that we are going to sail far from our country, and upon an expedition not like any which you may have undertaken in the quality of allies, among your subject states here in Hellas, where any additional supplies needed were easily drawn from the friendly

territory; but we are cutting ourselves off, and going to a land entirely strange, from which during four months in winter it is not even easy for a messenger to get to Athens.

[22]. I think, therefore, that we ought to take great numbers of heavy infantry, both from Athens and from our allies, and not merely from our subjects, but also any we may be able to get for love or for money in Peloponnese, and great numbers also of archers and slingers, to make head against the Sicilian horse. Meanwhile we must have an overwhelming superiority at sea, to enable us the more easily to carry in what we want; and we must take our own corn in merchant vessels, that is to say, wheat and parched barley, and bakers from the mills compelled to serve for pay in the proper proportion; in order that in case of our being weather-bound the armament may not want provisions, as it is not every city that will be able to entertain numbers like ours. We must also provide ourselves with everything else as far as we can, so as not to be dependent upon others; and above all we must take with us from home as much money as possible, as the sums talked of as ready at Egesta are readier, you may be sure, in talk than in any other way.

[23]. Indeed, even if we leave Athens with a force not only equal to that of the enemy except in the number of heavy infantry in the field, but even at all points superior to him, we shall still find it difficult to conquer Sicily or save ourselves. We must not disguise from ourselves that we go to found a city among strangers and enemies, and that he who undertakes such an enterprise should be prepared to become master of the country the first day he lands, or failing in this to find everything hostile to him. Fearing this, and knowing that we shall have need of much good counsel and more good fortune — a hard matter for mortal men to aspire to — I wish as far as may be to make myself independent of fortune before sailing, and when I do sail, to be as safe as a strong force can make me. This I believe to be surest for the country at large, and safest for us who are to go on the expedition. If any one thinks differently I resign to him my command.

§

Hermocrates to the Syracusan Assembly
Book VI 33-34
415 B.C.

The next two speeches by Hermocrates and Athenagoras, Jebb tells us, "bear the impress of the Sicilian rhetoric in their conscious partition. Proem, prothesis, narrative, proof, epilogue succeed each other — with more or less completeness according to circumstances — as distinct parts" (*Attic Orators,* II, 422).

Hermocrates has judged the leadership of Nicias well. He knows his famous timidity, that he will weigh and delay, that he lacks boldness. So Hermocrates urges taking the Athenians by surprise. Catch them off guard. Scare their leaders by assuming the initiative. Show force and courage by attack — defending is far more costly. It is the kind of speech a military commander might give — and a good one.

Hermocrates, according to Thucydides, had that distinctive Periclean gift of foresight. He can take bold and decisive action. Here he urges his countrymen (VI 34) to head off the Athenian fleet and destroy it before it can reach the Sicilian beaches.

The listing of the democratic virtues of Syracuse in VI 34.6-8 is all the more effective when we recall that earlier Athens had been pictured as the sole possessor of these virtues.

It is a bitter pill for the Athenian troops to acknowledge that little Sicily was strong for the same reasons that had made Athens a great power.

Alcibiades had argued in support of the Sicilian expedition first, that the Sicilians were a "motley crew" as Jowett translates the Greek, made up of various bands of old Greeks not at all united, ready for easy conquest and second, that Athens reached greatness by constant expansion. This was no time to reverse that policy.

Hermocrates' speech provides intelligence of a different kind. He urged immediate plans for all-out war. He wanted to rouse the rest of Sicily to the danger. His arguments prevailed. Full military control was given to a board of three generals. The Sicilian Greeks tightened belts, made ready, and gathered their courage and strength. Defending the homeland was at least as good an argument as conquering a far-off land.

But we are ahead of the story. The word of the Athenian navy's coming was impossible to believe. Intelligence was slow and unreliable — in spite of the clear concluding words of Hermocrates: "That the Athenians are coming to attack us, and are already upon the voyage, and are but here — of this I am sure."

Jebb says ("Speeches of Thucydides," p. 420, n. 5) that the two features that Sicilian rhetoric most sought to teach were skill in marshalling the facts and skill in arguing probabilities (cf. *Attic Orators* I, p. cxviii ff.). Hermocrates clearly demonstrates these features in his brilliantly organized speech. But we shall see in the next speech by Athenagoras the opposition he met.

§

[33]. Although I shall perhaps be no better believed than others have been when I speak upon the reality of the expedition, and although I know that those who either make or repeat statements thought not worthy of belief not only gain no converts, but are thought fools for their pains, I shall certainly not be frightened into holding my tongue when the state is in danger, and when I am persuaded that I can speak with more authority on the matter than other persons. Much as you wonder at it, the Athenians nevertheless have set out against us with a large force, naval and military, professedly to help the Egestaeans and to restore Leontini, but really to conquer Sicily, and above all our city, which once gained, the rest, they think, will easily follow. Make up your minds, therefore, to see them speedily here, and see how you can best repel them with the means under your hands, and do not be taken off your guard through despising the news, or neglect the common weal through disbelieving it. Meanwhile those who believe me need not be dismayed at the force or daring of the enemy. They will not be able to do us more hurt than we shall do them; nor is the greatness of their

armament altogether without advantage to us. Indeed, the greater it is the better, with regard to the rest of the Siceliots, whom dismay will make more ready to join us; and if we defeat or drive them away, disappointed of the objects of their ambition (for I do not fear for a moment that they will get what they want), it will be a most glorious exploit for us, and in my judgment by no means an unlikely one. Few indeed have been the large armaments, either Hellenic or barbarian, that have gone far from home and been successful. They cannot be more numerous than the people of the country and their neighbours, all of whom fear leagues together; and if they miscarry for want of supplies in a foreign land, to those against whom their plans were laid none the less they leave renown, although they may themselves have been the main cause of their own discomfort. Thus these very Athenians rose by the defeat of the Mede, in a great measure due to accidental causes, from the mere fact that Athens had been the object of his attack; and this may very well be the case with us also.

[34]. Let us therefore confidently begin preparations here; let us send and confirm some of the Sicels, and obtain the friendship and alliance of others, and despatch envoys to the rest of Sicily to show that the danger is common to all, and to Italy to get them to become our allies, or at all events to refuse to receive the Athenians. I also think that it would be best to send to Carthage as well; they are by no means there without apprehension, but it is their constant fear that the Athenians may one day attack their city, and they may perhaps think that they might themselves suffer by letting Sicily be sacrificed, and be willing to help us secretly if not openly, in one way if not in another. They are the best able to do so, if they will, of any of the present day, as they possess most gold and silver, by which war, like everything else, flourishes. Let us also send to Lacedaemon and Corinth, and ask them to come here and help us as soon as possible, and to keep alive the war in Hellas. But the true thing of all others, in my opinion, to do at the present moment, is what you, with your constitutional love of quiet, will be slow to see, and what I must nevertheless mention. If we Siceliots, all together, or at least as many as possible besides ourselves, would only launch the whole of our actual navy with two months' provisions, and meet the Athenians at Tarentum and the Iapygian promontory, and show them that before fighting for Sicily they must first fight for their passage across the Ionian sea, we should strike dismay into their army, and set them on thinking that we have a base for our defensive — for Tarentum is ready to receive us — while they

have a wide sea to cross with all their armament, which could with difficulty keep its order through so long a voyage, and would be easy for us to attack as it came on slowly and in small detachments. On the other hand, if they were to lighten their vessels, and draw together their fast sailers and with these attack us, we could either fall upon them when they were wearied with rowing, or if we did not choose to do so, we could retire to Tarentum; while they, having crossed with few provisions just to give battle, would be hard put to it in desolate places, and would either have to remain and be blockaded, or to try to sail along the coast, abandoning the rest of their armament, and being further discouraged by not knowing for certain whether the cities would receive them. In my opinion this consideration alone would be sufficient to deter them from putting out from Corcyra; and what with deliberating and reconnoitring our numbers and whereabouts, they would let the season go on until winter was upon them, or, confounded by so unexpected a circumstance, would break up the expedition, especially as their most experienced general has, as I hear, taken the command against his will, and would grasp at the first excuse offered by any serious demonstration of ours. We should also be reported, I am certain, as more numerous than we really are, and men's minds are affected by what they hear, and besides the first to attack, or to show that they mean to defend themselves against an attack, inspire greater fear because men see that they are ready for the emergency. This would just be the case with the Athenians at present. They are now attacking us in the belief that we shall not resist, having a right to judge us severely because we did not help the Lacedaemonians in crushing them; but if they were to see us showing a courage for which they are not prepared, they would be more dismayed by the surprise than they could ever be by our actual power. I could wish to persuade you to show this courage; but if this cannot be, at all events lose not a moment in preparing generally for the war; and remember all of you that contempt for an assailant is best shown by bravery in action, but that for the present the best course is to accept the preparations which fear inspires as giving the surest promise of safety, and to act as if the danger was real. That the Athenians are coming to attack us, and are already upon the voyage, and all but here — this is what I am sure of.

§

Athenagoras to the Syracusan Assembly
Book VI 36-40
415 B.C.

This too is a speech of pregnant brevity. It reminds us of Cleon's speeches just as Hermocrates at his best has some of the characteristics of Pericles.

Again, the argument is most appealing especially since Thucydides describes the speaker as a "leader of the people who at that time had great influence with the masses." The general proposition is simple: the Athenians will not abandon the Peloponnesian War to take on another. They are really glad that the Sicilians do not attack them "being so many and so great cities as we are."

At VI 36.4 Athenagoras says that Athens could not under any stretch of imagination undertake another war when the one in Greece is still in progress. But a minute later he is emphasizing the strong resistance that the Syracusans are putting up (VI 34.6-8).

Thucydides makes us well aware that the "man of the people" is usually looking out for himself. Cleon and Athenagoras are alike in their self-serving attitudes. They are short-sighted, greedy, and unscrupulous. At VI 38.2 Athenagoras argues that "it is necessary to punish an enemy not only for what he does, but also beforehand for what he intends to do, if the first to relax precaution would not be also the first to suffer." At VI 39 we find the statement "that democracy is neither wise nor equitable, but...the holders of property are also the best fitted to rule. ...the word *demos*, or people, includes the whole, state, oligarchy only a part." A little later we read "under an oligarchy, while the masses take their share of dangers, the few claim not merely the largest share, but the whole of the profits." All these observations serve to point up the alarming fact that the people of Syracuse were a far different breed than the Spartans. The more the war went on the less they feared the Athenians.

And it follows the more the Athenians met their match the more they feared the Sicilian fighters.

But if the Athenian fleet and army do come they will find Syracuse more than a match. They will lack horses. They cannot bring supplies. They cannot get far for fear of our cavalry.

Athenagoras was clearly afraid of the dissidents within the state. He hints at attempts to overthrow the government. He promises quick arrest of those who get out of line — the young, in particular. He has generals who will repulse invaders. The speech is plainly a political reply to Hermocrates and his aristocrats.

When Athenagoras finished an unnamed Syracusan general arose and announced the preparations that would be taken — to collect horses, and arms, to reconnoiter the cities and "to do all else that may appear desirable." He was taking no chances.

Thucydides once again has created the suspense for which he is famous. We feel the tensions that rumor and surprise generate. We wonder about the leaders and the morale — on both sides. We have our doubts about the wisdom of operating on two fronts with long lines of communication. The "fog of war" has set in. Fears grow and hope slips away. Military virtues and political ambitions do not thrive together. There is a lull before the storm.

§

[36]. For the Athenians, he who does not wish that they may be as misguided as they are supposed to be, and that they may come here to become our subjects, is either a coward or a traitor to his country; while as for those who carry such tidings and fill you with so much alarm, I wonder less at their audacity than at their folly if they flatter themselves that we do not see through them. The fact is that they have their private reasons to be afraid, and wish to throw the city into consternation to have their own terrors cast into the shade by the public alarm. In short, this is what these reports are worth; they do not

arise of themselves, but are concocted by men who are always causing agitation here in Sicily. However, if you are well advised, you will not be guided in your calculation of probabilities by what these persons tell you, but by what shrewd men and of large experience, as I esteem the Athenians to be, would be likely to do. Now it is not likely that they would leave the Peloponnesians behind them, and before they have well ended the war in Hellas wantonly come in quest of a new war quite as arduous, in Sicily; indeed, in my judgment, they are only too glad that we do not go and attack them, being so many and so great cities as we are.

[37]. However, if they should come as is reported, I consider Sicily better able to go through with the war than Peloponnese, as being at all points better prepared, and our city by itself far more than a match for this pretended army of invasion, even were it twice as large again. I know that they will not have horses with them, or get any here, except a few perhaps from the Egestaeans; or be able to bring a force of heavy infantry equal in number to our own, in ships which will already have enough to do to come all this distance, however lightly laden, not to speak of the transport of the other stores required against a city of this magnitude, which will be no slight quantity. In fact, so strong is my opinion upon the subject, that I do not well see how they could avoid annihilation if they brought with them another city as large as Syracuse, and settled down and carried on war from our frontier; much less can they hope to succeed with all Sicily hostile to them, as all Sicily will be, and with only a camp pitched from the ships, and composed of tents and bare necessaries, from which they would not be able to stir far for fear of our cavalry.

[38]. But the Athenians see this as I tell you, and as I have reason to know are looking after their possessions at home, while persons here invent stories that neither are true nor ever will be. Nor is this the first time that I see these persons, when they cannot resort to deeds, trying by such stories and by others even more abominable to frighten your people and get into their hands the government: it is what I see always. And I cannot help fearing that trying so often they may one day succeed, and that we, as long as we do not feel the smart, may prove too weak for the task of prevention, or, when the offenders are known, of pursuit. The result is that our city is rarely at rest, but is subject to constant troubles and to contests as frequent against herself as against the enemy, not to speak of occasional tyrannies and infamous cabals. However, I will try, if you will support me, to let nothing of this

happen in our time, by gaining you, the many, and by chastising the authors of such machinations, not merely when they are caught in the act — a difficult feat to accomplish — but also for what they have the wish though not the power to do; as is necessary to punish an enemy not only for what he does, but also beforehand for what he intends to do, if the first to relax precaution would not be also the first to suffer. I shall also reprove, watch, and on occasion warn the few — the most effectual way, in my opinion, of turning them from their evil course. And after all, as I have often asked — What would you have, young men? Would you hold office at once? The law forbids it, a law enacted rather because you are not competent than to disgrace you when competent. Meanwhile you would not be on a legal equality with the many! But how can it be right that citizens of the same state should be held unworthy of the same privileges?

[39]. It will be said, perhaps, that democracy is neither wise nor equitable, but that the holders of property are also the best fitted to rule. I say, on the contrary, first, that the word *demos*, or people, includes the whole state, oligarchy only a part; next, that if the best guardians of property are the rich, and the best counsellors the wise, none can hear and decide so well as the many; and that all these talents, severally and collectively, have their just place in a democracy. But an oligarchy gives the many their share of the danger, and not content with the largest part takes and keeps the whole of the profit; and this is what the powerful and young among you aspire to, but in a great city cannot possibly obtain.

[40]. But even now, foolish men, most senseless of all the Hellenes that I know, if you have no sense of the wickedness of your designs, or most criminal if you have that sense and still dare to pursue them, — even now, if it is not a case for repentance, you may still learn wisdom, and thus advance the interest of the country, the common interest of us all. Reflect that in the country's prosperity the men of merit in your ranks will have a share and a larger share than the great mass of your fellow-countrymen, but that if you have other designs you run a risk of being deprived of all; and desist from reports like these, as the people know your object and will not put up with it. If the Athenians arrive, this city will repulse them in a manner worthy of itself; we have, moreover, generals who will see to this matter. And if nothing of this be true, as I incline to believe, the city will not be thrown into a panic by your intelligence, or impose upon itself a self-chosen servitude by choosing you for its rulers; the city itself will look into the matter, and

will judge your words as if they were acts, and instead of allowing itself to be deprived of its liberty by listening to you, will strive to preserve that liberty, by taking care to have always at hand the means of making itself respected.

§

A Syracusan General to the Syracusan Assembly
Book VI 41
415 B.C.

This speech is another very short one which presents a workmanlike appraisal by a military man. Perhaps the key sentence is best translated by Rex Warner as follows: "Instead, we should be giving our attention to the reports which have reached us and seeing how we can all of us — the State as a whole and each individual in it — best deal with the invaders." This sentiment was the keynote of the Syracusan war effort. It provided a unity that grew stronger every day and was far more significant that the corresponding effort by Athens.

§

[41]. It is not well for speakers to utter calumnies against one another or for their hearers to entertain them; we ought rather to look to the intelligence that we have received, and see how each man by himself and the city as a whole may best prepare to repel the invaders. Even if there be no need, there is no harm in the state being furnished with horses and arms and all other insignia of war; and we will undertake to see to and order this, and to send round to the cities to reconnoitre and do all else that may appear desirable. Part of this we have seen to already, and whatever we discover shall be laid before you.

§

Hermocrates as Envoy of Syracuse at Camarina
Book VI 76-80
415 B.C.

The character of Hermocrates is to be considered with that of Euphemus just as those of Cleon and Pericles had been contrasted earlier. However, Hermocrates the Sicilian is matched with Pericles the Athenian — both as men of great integrity. Only Hermocrates possesses all four of the qualities of the statesman which Pericles outlined in his last speech (II 60.5).

Sir George Cornewall Lewis observes that "many important transactions were conducted orally in an ancient state, which would now be contained in dispatches between the ministers of different courts and in collections of state papers." He cites the address of the Syracusan and Athenian envoys at Camarina as one of the examples and reminds us that the use of a common language, Greek, made it possible for ambassadors of one state to speak at the public assembly of another (*The Methods of Observation and Reasoning in Politics*, I, 242 note 126).

The setting is Camarina, a town on the southern coast of Sicily at the mouth of the Hipparis. The purpose of the meeting was to "raise prejudices against the Athenians." The Syracusans sensed that the Camarinians had not willingly agreed to support Athens. Hermocrates' speech is designed to test and confirm their suspicion. Once again we have appeals to conflicting loyalties.

Nicias had just technically "won" a battle but he threw away the victory by failing to pursue. He retired with his troops to Camarina and soon found himself engaged in wooing the natives to his side. The speaker from Syracuse is a knowledgeable and persuasive man. He is well aware of his audience and of Athenian ambitions.

Hermocrates had by now been appointed general. Thucydides says he had "given proofs of military capacity and brilliant courage in the war." He speaks a blunt warning. His picture of Athens is not altruistic.

In short Athens attacks Syracuse just as in the struggle against Persia "to exchange one master for another, wiser indeed than the first, but wiser for evil." And the strategy again is to divide and conquer. First one city, then another. Making alliances so we will war with each other and "injuring others in any possible way while flattering them with smooth words." In fact, Hermocrates argues the Athenians invade Sicily not especially to punish Syracuse but to *use* that city as a pretext to get the friendship of Camarina.

So, says the Syracusan envoy, instead of lukewarm support he wants the people of Camarina to offer the aid they would expect of Syracuse if they had been attacked first. He pleads as a fellow Dorian and recalls that Camarina has the choice of present security as against the "disgraceful submission to an Athenian master." Hermocrates thus puts his hearers in a tough spot. It is hard to imagine how they can decide against what is offered. The appeal is to reason, tradition, past fairness, and the known reputation of an honorable man. But compare these factors with those soon to be promoted by a *realpolitiker*, Euphemus, an empire-builder, who knows that might makes right.

§

[76]. Camarinaeans, we did not come on this embassy because we were afraid of your being frightened by the actual forces of the Athenians, but rather of your being gained by what they would say to you before you heard anything from us. They are come to Sicily with the pretext that you know, and the intention which we all suspect, in my opinion less to restore the Leontines to their homes than to oust us from ours; as it is out of all reason that they should restore in Sicily the cities that they lay waste in Hellas, or should cherish the Leontine Chalcidians because of their Ionian blood, and keep in servitude the Euboean Chalcidians, of whom the Leontines are a colony. No; but the same policy which has proved so successful in Hellas is now being tried in

Sicily. After being chosen as the leaders of the Ionians and of the other allies of Athenian origin, to punish the Mede, the Athenians accused some of failure in military service, some of fighting against each other, and others, as the case might be, upon any colourable pretext that could be found, until they thus subdued them all. In fine, in the struggle against the Medes, the Athenians did not fight for the liberty of the Hellenes, or the Hellenes for their own liberty, but the former to make their countrymen serve them instead of him, the latter to change one master for another, wiser indeed than the first, but wiser for evil.

[77]. But we are not now come to declare to an audience familiar with them the misdeeds of a state so open to accusation as is the Athenian, but much rather to blame ourselves, who, with the warnings we possess in the Hellenes in those parts that have been enslaved through not supporting each other, and seeing the same sophisms being now tried upon ourselves — such as restorations of Leontine kinsfolk and support of Egestaean allies — do not stand together and resolutely show them that here are no Ionians, or Hellespontines, or islanders, who change continually, but always serve a master. sometimes the Mede and sometimes some other, but free Dorians from independent Peloponnese, dwelling in Sicily. Or, are we waiting until we be taken in detail, one city after another; knowing as we do that in no other way can we be conquered, and seeing that they turn to this plan, so as to divide some of us by words, to draw some by the bait of an alliance into open war with each other, and to ruin others by such flattery as different circumstances may render acceptable? And do we fancy when destruction first overtakes a distant fellow-countryman that the danger will not come to each of us also, or that he who suffers before us will suffer in himself alone?

[78]. As for the Camarinaean, who says that it is the Syracusan, not he, that is the enemy of the Athenian, and who thinks it hard to have to encounter risk in behalf of my country, I would have him bear in mind that he will fight in my country, not more for mine than for his own, and by so much the more safely in that he will enter on the struggle not alone, after the way has been cleared by my ruin, but with me as his ally; and that the object of the Athenian is not so much to punish the enmity of the Syracusan as to use me as a blind to secure the friendship of the Camarinaean. As for him who envies or even fears us (and envied and feared great powers must always be), and who on this account wishes Syracuse to be humbled to teach us a lesson, but would still have her survive in the interest of his own security, the wish that he

indulges is not humanly possible. A man can control his own desires, but he cannot likewise control circumstances; and in the event of his calculations proving mistaken, he may live to bewail his own misfortune, and wish to be again envying my prosperity. An idle wish, if he now sacrifice us and refuse to take his share of perils which are the same, in reality though not in name, for him as for us; what is nominally the preservation of our power being really his own salvation. It was to be expected that you, of all people in the world, Camarinaeans, being our immediate neighbours and the next in danger, would have foreseen this, and instead of supporting us in the lukewarm way that you are now doing, would rather come to us of your own accord, and be now offering at Syracuse the aid which you would have asked for at Camarina, if to Camarina the Athenians had first come, to encourage us to resist the invader. Neither you, however, nor the rest have as yet bestirred yourselves in this direction.

79. Fear perhaps will make you study to do right both by us and by the invaders, and plead that you have an alliance with the Athenians. But you made that alliance, not against your friends, but against the enemies that might attack you, and to help the Athenians when they were wronged by others, not when as now they are wronging their neighbours. Even the Rhegians, Chalcidians though they be, refuse to help to restore the Chalcidian Leontines; and it would be strange if, while they suspect the gist of this fine pretence and are wise without reason, you, with every reason on your side, should yet choose to assist your natural enemies, and should join with their direst foes in undoing those whom nature has made your own kinsfolk. This is not to do right; but you should help us without fear of their armament, which has no terrors if we hold together, but only if we let them succeed in their endeavours to separate us; since even after attacking us by ourselves and being victorious in battle, they had to go off without effecting their purpose.

80. United, therefore, we have no cause to despair, but rather new encouragement to league together; especially as succours will come to us from the Peloponnesians, in military matters the undoubted superiors of the Athenians. And you need not think that your prudent policy of taking sides with neither, because allies of both, is either safe for you or fair to us. Practically it is not as fair as it pretends to be. If the vanquished be defeated, and the victor conquer, through your refusing to join, what is the effect of your abstention but to leave the former to perish unaided, and to allow the latter to offend unhindered?

And yet it were more honourable to join those who are not only the injured party, but your own kindred, and by so doing to defend the common interests of Sicily and save your friends the Athenians from doing wrong.

In conclusion, we Syracusans say that it is useless for us to demonstrate either to you or to the rest what you know already as well as we do; but we entreat, and if our entreaty fail, we protest that we are menaced by our eternal enemies the Ionians, and are betrayed by you our fellow Dorians. If the Athenians reduce us, they will owe their victory to your decision, but in their own name will reap the honour, and will receive as the prize of their triumph the very men who enabled them to gain it. On the other hand, if we are the conquerors, you will have to pay for having been the cause of our danger. Consider, therefore; and now make your choice between the security which present servitude offers and the prospect of conquering with us and so escaping disgraceful submission to an Athenian master and avoiding the lasting enmity of Syracuse.

Euphemus as Envoy of Athens at Camarina
Book VI 82-87
415 B.C.

Camarina was a Dorian colony on the south shore of Sicily at the mouth of the Hipparis.

Euphemus is the envoy sent by Athens to state her case. His task is to remind the Camarineans that they are not again likely to have such a powerful ally as Athens. He plays up the golden opportunity to join up with a victorious state.

This speech relates to the Melian dialogue which Thucydides placed just before the account of the Sicilian expedition. The same dramatic effect arises again. The Athenian envoy is brutally frank about motives and the whole purpose of the Sicilian adventure. But he begins by distorting history to make it fit his purpose. He knows the catastrophe that looms up and like a man condemned to die — truth no longer matters. Let us follow the argument.

Proem: to get attention and good will (82)

We come to renew our alliance. But the Syracusans force us to discuss our right to empire. We have it to survive. Besides, no one has the right to give us orders except the one who happens to be stronger at the time. The Ionian Greeks joined Persia against Athens and chose to be slaves and to make us slaves too. But as Sir Richard Livingstone points out: "The Ionian Greeks had been conquered in 494 and forced to supply contingents to the Persian army which invaded Greece in 480. The arguments of Euphemus are dishonest: the Ionian Greeks had voluntarily placed themselves under Athens and not been 'willingly subservient to Persia'; nor did 'Athens overthrow the foreigner single handed' " (Oxford World's Classics translation of *Thucydides* p. 318, n. 1).

Statement: the problem and the purpose (83)

"We, therefore, deserve to rule because we placed the largest fleet and an unflinching patriotism at the service of Greece, and because these, our subjects, injured us by their willing subservience to Persia; and desert apart, we seek to strengthen ourselves against the Peloponnesians." We are here in Sicily to protect our own safety and yours coincides with ours. This, in short, is what the war is all about.

Narration: giving necessary information (84)

Fear motivates us all. We want to hold our empire in Greece and that is why we come "to secure our position in Sicily." We don't want to enslave others. We simply want to save you from slavery. If you are preserved and can hold out against Syracuse they will not be aiding the Peloponnesians and so try to harm us. On the other hand, the Syracusans want to dominate you. They stir you up and if we withdraw "by force or through your isolation" they become your masters — and Sicily's too. As soon as we were gone they would be more than a match for you.

Proof: to refute allegations of opponent and
to demonstrate truth of Athenian position (85-87)

It emphasizes the superiority of the probable over the factual. Look at the intent of the Syracusans. The way despots and empires behave no one relative can be trusted. Friendship and enmity both depend on the moment. Expedience determines. With us now it is different. We simply want your strength to weaken Syracuse. We do not want to weaken you. We come here by invitation. We don't want the Sicilians to harm us or you either. We come as allies because we have so many enemies to guard against. The chances are far better if you join with us.

Epilogue: summarizes and restates (end of 87)

We have openly stated our position. Do not turn on us now. Judge us by our past conduct. We keep peace even where we do not have influence because our arrival can make any uprising dangerous. Do as others do and instead of being on the defensive against Syracuse, join us and threaten them.

The argument that the Spartans had always done their utmost to keep Athens weak crops up again (VI 82). Euphemus gives a characteristic Greek argument at VI 85.1 when he says: "Besides for despots and imperial cities nothing is unreasonable if expedient, no one a kinsman unless he can be trusted; friendship or enmity must depend on circumstances." With this generalization he proceeds to argue that in Sicily the Athenian objective is not to weaken friends but "to use their strength to cripple our enemies."

Can you imagine what happened after Hermocrates and Euphemus finished? Could you have made a quick and easy decision? Would you choose the devil or the deep blue sea? This was the fix in which the Camarineans found themselves. They faced the Supreme antithesis: Survival or slavery as against slavery and survival.

What did they do? In present-day idiom, they played it cool. They sent a few horsemen to Syracuse because they feared their neighbor. Since they were allies of both parties they thought it best to side with neither. At best it was a satisfactory solution — and only future events could determine its wisdom.

Jebb reminds us that in this speech Euphemus is relying on the same sophistical arguments used so cleverly by Callicles and Thrasymachus in Plato's dialogues. Hippias too in Xenophon's *Memorabilia* had argued that justice and law are in fact merely arbitrary and conventional. They are what men make them and may be changed at will (*Mem.* iv 4.14).

The Athenian envoy was indeed a student of human nature. He knew the fickleness of men and how easily they could be swayed when their selfish interest was at stake.

The final example on a far grander scale is found in the speech of Alcibiades at Sparta (415 B.C.) which follows that of Euphemus.

§

[82]. Although we came here only to renew the former alliance, the attack of the Syracusans compels us to speak of our empire and of the good right we have to it. The best proof of this the speaker himself furnished, when he called the Ionians eternal enemies of the Dorians. It is the fact; and the Peloponnesian Dorians being our superiors in numbers and next neighbours, we Ionians looked out for the best means of escaping their domination. After the Median war we had a fleet, and so got rid of the empire and supremacy of the Lacedae-monians, who had no right to give orders to us more than we to them, except that of being the strongest at that moment; and being appointed leaders of the king's former subjects, we continue to be so, thinking that we are least likely to fall under the dominion of the Pelopon-nesians, if we have a force to defend ourselves with, and in strict truth having done nothing unfair in reducing to subjection the Ionians and islanders, the kinsfolk whom the Syracusans say we have enslaved. They, our kinsfolk, came against their mother country, that is to say against us, together with the Mede, and instead of having the courage to revolt and sacrifice their property as we did when we abandoned our city, chose to be slaves themselves, and to try to make us so.

[83]. We, therefore, deserve to rule because we placed the largest fleet and an unflinching patriotism at the service of the Hellenes, and because these, our subjects, did us mischief by their ready subservience to the Medes; and, desert apart, we seek to strengthen ourselves against the Peloponnesians. We make no fine professions of having a right to rule because we overthrew the barbarian single-handed, or because we risked what we did risk for the freedom of the subjects in question any more than for that of all, and for our own: no one can be quarrelled with for providing for his proper safety. If we are now here in Sicily, it is equally in the interest of our security, with which we perceive that your interest also coincides. We prove this from the conduct which the Syracusans cast against us and which you somewhat too timorously suspect; knowing that those whom fear has made suspicious, may be carried away by the charm of eloquence for the moment, but when they come to act follow their interests.

[84]. Now, as we have said, fear makes us hold our empire in Hellas, and fear makes us now come, with the help of our friends, to order safely matters in Sicily, and not to enslave any but rather to prevent any from being enslaved. Meanwhile, let no one imagine that we are interesting ourselves in you without your having anything to do with us, seeing that if you are preserved and able to make head against the Syracusans, they will be less likely to harm us by sending troops to the Peloponnesians. In this way you have everything to do with us, and on this account it is perfectly reasonable for us to restore the Leontines, and to make them, not subjects like their kinsmen in Euboea, but as powerful as possible, to help us by annoying the Syracusans from their frontier. In Hellas we are alone a match for our enemies; and as for the assertion that it is out of all reason that we should free the Sicilian, while we enslave the Chalcidian, the fact is that the latter is useful to us by being without arms and contributing money only; while the former, the Leontines and our other friends, cannot be too independent.

[85]. Besides, for tyrants and imperial cities nothing is unreasonable if expedient, no one a kinsman unless sure; but friendship or enmity is everywhere an affair of time and circumstance. Here, in Sicily, our interest is not to weaken our friends, but by means of their strength to cripple our enemies. Why doubt this? In Hellas we treat our allies as we find them useful. The Chians and Methymnians govern themselves and furnish ships; most of the rest have harder terms and pay tribute in money; while others, although islanders and easy for us to take, are free altogether, because they occupy convenient positions round Peloponnese. In our settlement of the states here in Sicily, we should, therefore, naturally be guided by our interest, and by fear, as we say, of the Syracusans. Their ambition is to rule you, their object to use the suspicions that we excite to unite you, and then, when we have gone away without effecting anything, by force or through your isolation, to become the masters of Sicily. And masters they must become, if you unite with them; as a force of that magnitude would be no longer easy for us to deal with united, and they would be more than a match for you as soon as we were away.

[86]. Any other view of the case is condemned by the facts. When you first asked us over, the fear which you held out was that of danger to Athens if we let you come under the dominion of Syracuse; and it is not right now to mistrust the very same argument by which you claimed to convince us, or to give way to suspicion because we are come with a larger force against the power of that city. Those whom

you should really distrust are the Syracusans. We are not able to stay here without you, and if we proved perfidious enough to bring you into subjection, we should be unable to keep you in bondage, owing to the length of the voyage and the difficulty of guarding large, and in a military sense continental, towns: they, the Syracusans, live close to you, not in a camp, but in a city greater than the force we have with us, plot always against you, never let slip an opportunity once offered, as they have shown in the case of the Leontines and others, and now have the face, just as if you were fools, to invite you to aid them against the power that hinders this, and that has thus far maintained Sicily independent. We, as against them, invite you to a much more real safety, when we beg you not to betray that common safety which we each have in the other, and to reflect that they, even without allies, will, by their numbers, have always the way open to you, while you will not often have the opportunity of defending yourselves with such numerous auxiliaries; if, through your suspicions, you once let these go away unsuccessful or defeated, you will wish to see if only a handful of them back again, when the day is past in which their presence could do anything for you.

[87]. But we hope, Camarinaeans, that the calumnies of the Syracusans will not be allowed to succeed either with you or with the rest: we have told you the whole truth upon the things we are suspected of, and will now briefly recapitulate, in the hope of convincing you. We assert that we are rulers in Hellas in order not to be subjects; liberators in Sicily that we may not be harmed by the Sicilians; that we are compelled to interfere in many things, because we have many things to guard against; and that now, as before, we are come as allies to those of you who suffer wrong in this island, not without invitation but upon invitation. Accordingly, instead of making yourselves judges or censors of our conduct, and trying to turn us, which it were now difficult to do, so far as there is anything in our interfering policy or in our character, that chimes in with your interest, this take and make use of; and be sure that far from being injurious to all alike, to most of the Hellenes that policy is even beneficial. Thanks to it, all men in all places, even where we are not, who either apprehend or meditate aggression, from the near prospect before them, in the one case, of obtaining our intervention in their favour, in the other, of our arrival making the venture dangerous, find themselves constrained, respectively, to be moderate against their will, and to be preserved without trouble of their own. Do not you reject this security that is

open to all who desire it, and is now offered to you; but do like others, and instead of being always on the defensive against the Syracusans, unite with us, and in your turn at last threaten them.

§

Alcibiades at Sparta
Book VI 89-92
415 B.C.

So long, however, as Pericles was leader of the people, things went tolerably well with the state; but when he was dead there was a great change for the worse. Then for the first time did the people choose a leader who was of no reputation among men of good standing, whereas up to this time such men had always been found as leaders of the democracy. ...After the death of Pericles, Nicias, who subsequently fell in Sicily, appeared as leader of the aristocracy, and Cleon, son of Cleaenetus of the people (*Works of Aristotle*, Oxford edition, *The Athenian Constitution* [28.1-3] trans. by Sir Frederic G. Kenyon).

This famous speech relates back to the chapter on revolutions (III 82). It continues the analysis of the psychology of class war. Its echoes have been heard many times in the centuries since it was spoken. Alcibiades knew that his own high living could find support among the poor because he exemplified the taking of chances. This is what he urged.

Finley aptly says: "No other speech in the *History* faintly resembles it. ... As the great description of the departure of the fleet had brought to a climax all that the historian had said of Athens' enormous inherent strength, so this speech, even more than the Melian Dialogue, consummates his judgment of her inner decay" (*Thucydides*, p. 229).

Alcibiades first has the problem of cleaning up his own *ethos*. He is a traitor to Athens. He offers his military knowledge and skill for sale. Everybody knows he is a proven leader and winner. Indeed, if he had been commander-in-chief of the Sicilian expedition the war would have been over in the first year. He knows that the Spartans were aware of his bold concepts. That is why he heightens his audacity and stirs their imaginations. He talks like a sure-fire winner. Who can resist such a man?

Athens had been greatest and most free under democracy (VI 89.6) but "the men of sense among us knew what it was, and I perhaps as well as any, as I have the most cause to complain of it; it is an acknowledged folly and there is nothing new to be said of it — meanwhile, we did not think it safe to alter it under the pressure of your hostility."

Here is Alcibiades at his treacherous best. He "sells out". His price is his own safety. He offers his soul, his skill, and the fall of Athens at a relatively cheap consultant's fee: power to influence Spartan decisions. Here is what Alcibiades, the ward of Pericles and the friend of Socrates, wants:

1. Send by sea to Syracuse heavy infantry ready to fight as soon as they land.

2. Put a Spartan general in command and "to compel recusants to serve."

3. Carry on the war here more openly.

4. Fortify Decelea.

This in brief is the bold program. It is designed to help Syracuse, aid the Peloponnesians, confuse Athens, and make Sparta supreme. It appeals because it comes from a man who understood Athenian intentions and capabilities (under good leadership) far better than the Athenians themselves — and especially that clumsy, slow-witted Nicias.

We usually think of *ethos* as the appeal of the good man of high character who is believable because he exemplifies character and integrity. He is the man who abhors wrongdoing. His high principles are more persuasive than his words. His record speaks for itself.

But here is a man, as Plutarch has so well delineated his life, full of man's baser instincts, actually making himself believable to men who should know better and be able to resist his arguments. Even before Thucydides tells us what happened we know he will win over the Spartan Ephors. He was the greatest "fast talker" of the fifth century B.C.

Pericles had set forth the essential qualities of a great leader as one possessed (1) in knowledge of the proper policy, (2) the ability to expound it and, (3) being a patriot, (4) and an honest one (II 60.5). The German scholar G. F. Bender, has argued that Alcibiades was able to develop strategy and policy, that he was a gifted speaker — but that he was neither a good patriot nor above the influence of money (*Der Begriff des Staatsmannes bei Thukydides*, Wurzburg, 1938). Since Alcibiades had expensive tastes and loved the gay life it is easy to understand why he had to have money in large quantities. Somewhat like a dope addict he was willing to do almost anything for it.

Pericles died in 429 B.C. Now fourteen years later Alcibiades was selling his high talents to the most likely bidder. Both Socrates and Pericles would have wept if they had heard this speech.

The Spartans did exactly what Alcibiades told them to do "in the best and quickest way possible under the circumstances." Whoever said that evil men with evil intentions could not persuade men — regardless of their own principles? This is a monstrous speech by a monstrous man. The man won.

§

[89]. I am forced first to speak to you of the prejudice with which I am regarded, in order that suspicion may not make you disinclined to listen to me upon public matters. The connexion with you as your *Proxeni*, which the ancestors of our family by reason of some discontent renounced, I personally tried to renew by my good offices towards you, in particular upon the occasion of the disaster at Pylos. But although I maintained this friendly attitude, you yet chose to negotiate the peace with the Athenians through my enemies, and thus to strengthen them and to discredit me. You had therefore no right to complain if I turned to the Mantineans and Argives, and seized other occasions of thwarting and injuring you; and the time has now come when those among you, who in the bitterness of the moment may have

been then unfairly angry with me, should look at the matter in its true light, and take a different view. Those again who judged me unfavourably, because I *learned* rather to the side of the commons, must not think that their dislike is any better founded. We have always been hostile to tyrants, and all who oppose arbitrary power are called commons; hence we continued to act as leaders of the multitude; besides which, as democracy was the government of the city, it was necessary in most things to conform to established conditions. However, we endeavoured to be more moderate than the licentious temper of the times; and while there were others, formerly as now, who tried to lead the multitide astray, the same who banished me, our party was that of the whole people, our creed being to do our part in preserving the form of government under which the city enjoyed the utmost greatness and freedom, and which we had found existing. As for democracy, the men of sense among us knew what it was, and I perhaps as well as any, as I have the more cause to complain of it; but there is nothing new to be said of a patent absurdity — meanwhile we did not think it safe to alter it under the pressure of your hostility.

[90]. So much then for the prejudices with which I am regarded: I now can call your attention to the questions you must consider, and upon which superior knowledge perhaps permits me to speak. We sailed to Sicily first to conquer, if possible, the Siceliots, and after them the Italiots also, and finally to assail the empire and city of Carthage. In the event of all or most of these schemes succeeding, we were then to attack Peloponnese, bringing with us the entire force of the Hellenes lately acquired in those parts, and taking a number of barbarians into our pay, such as the Iberians and others in those countries, confessedly the most warlike known, and building numerous galleys in addition to those which we had already, timber being plentiful in Italy; and with this fleet blockading Peloponnese from the sea and assailing it with our armies by land, taking some of the cities by torm, drawing works of circumvallation round others, we hoped without difficulto to effect its reduction, and after this to rule the whole of the Hellenic name. Money and corn meanwhile for the better execution of these plans were to be supplied in sufficient quantities by the newly acquired places in those countries, independently of our revenues here at home.

[91]. You have thus heard the history of the present expedition from the man who most exactly knows what our objects were; and the remaining generals will, if they can, carry these out just the same. But that the states in Sicily must succumb if you do not help them, I will

now show. Although the Siceliots, with all their inexperience, might even now be saved if their forces were united, the Syracusans alone, beaten already in one battle with all their people and blockaded from the sea, will be unable to withstand the Athenian armament that is now there. But if Syracuse falls, all Sicily falls also, and Italy immediately afterwards; and the danger which I just now spoke of from that quarter will before long be upon you. None need therefore fancy that Sicily only is in question; Peloponnese will be so also, unless you speedily do as I tell you, and send on board ship to Syracuse troops that shall be able to row their ships themselves, and serve as heavy infantry the moment that they land; and what I consider even more important than the troops, a Spartan as commanding officer to discipline the forces already on foot and to compel recusants to serve. The friends that you have already will thus become more confident, and the waverers will be encouraged to join you. Meanwhile you must carry on the war here more openly, that the Syracusans seeing that you do not forget them, may put heart into their resistance, and that the Athenians may be less able to reinforce their armament. You must fortify Decelea in Attica, the blow of which the Athenians are always most afraid and the only one that they think they have not experienced in the present war; the surest method of harming an enemy being to find out what he most fears, and to choose this means of attacking him, since every one naturally knows best his own weak points and fears accordingly. The fortification in question, while it benefits you, will create difficulties for your adversaries, of which I shall pass over many, and shall only mention the chief. Whatever property there is in the country will most of it become yours, either by capture or surrender; and the Athenians will at once be deprived of their revenues from the silver mines at Laurium, of their present gains from their land and from the law courts, and above all of the revenue from their allies, which will be paid less regularly, as they lose their awe of Athens, and see you addressing yourselves with vigour to the war. The zeal and speech with which all this shall be done depends, Lacedaemonians, upon yourselves; as to its possibility, I am quite confident, and I have little fear of being mistaken.

[92]. Meanwhile I hope that none of you will think any the worse of me if after having hitherto passed as a lover of my country, I now actively join its worst enemies in attacking it, or will suspect what I say as the fruit of an outlaw's enthusiasm. I am an outlaw from the iniquity of those who drove me forth, not, if you will be guided by me, from

your service: my worst enemies are not you who only harmed your foes, but they who forced their friends to become enemies; and love of country is what I do not feel when I am wronged, but what I felt when secure in my rights as a citizen. Indeed I do not consider that I am now attacking a country that is still mine; I am rather trying to recover one that is mine no longer; and the true lover of his country is not he who consents to lose it unjustly rather than attack it, but he who longs for it so much that he will go all lengths to recover it. For myself, therefore, Lacedaemonians, I beg you to use me without scruple for danger and trouble of every kind, and to remember the argument in every one's mouth, that if I did you great harm as an enemy, I could likewise do you good service as a friend, inasmuch as I know the plans of the Athenians, while I only guessed yours. For yourselves I entreat you to believe that your most capital interests are now under deliberation; and I urge you to send without hesitation the expeditions to Sicily and Attica; by the presence of a small part of your forces you will save important cities in that island, and you will destroy the power of Athens both present and prospective; after this you will dwell in security and enjoy the supremacy over all Hellas, resting not on force but upon consent and affection.

§

Letter of Nicias to the Athenian Ecclesia
Book VII 11-15
414 B.C.

The letter Nicias sent to Athens when the Sicilians were strongly resisting is not usually treated as a speech. It was read by a clerk to the Athenian Ecclesia and strictly judged is not in the same class with the five speeches Nicias gives in the *History*. Yet it is a personal report from the commander-in-chief. It is in every sense a rhetorical document and deserves consideration here.

If ancient Athens preserved its records there is a good chance that Thucydides actually copied the letter. If he did it is the one item in the *History* that we may be sure was not composed by the historian some years after an event. On the other hand Gomme thinks the style is Thucydidean. He argues against the possibility of a copy being filed in the Athenian archives and states that Thucydides "is relying...on men's memories (including, of course, those among Nicias' companions in Sicily whom he interviewed and who might have known the gist of what he wrote). It is on all fours with the Speeches" (*Essays in Greek History and Literature*, Oxford, 1931, p. 167 n. 2).

Nicias was a man of many fears and the Athenian Assembly was one of them. As the war gets worse we sense that he feared going back to Athens. Although he had several chances to save his army from complete destruction he let them slip. Was it because he did not want his own officers and men revealing his failures as a commander? Was he putting the blame in the letter for lack of discipline of the soldiers to counter the argument he could not maintain discipline? Why does he stress the unexpected resistance of the Sicilians? Why does he refer to the information he sends as necessary but unpleasant?

Ferdinand Schevill has well observed that the speeches of Nicias in the History are "invariably honest and invariably uninspiring." Thus Thucydides "permits Nicias to draw his own portrait, which is strikingly realized in its hopeless mediocrity as is the criminal portrait Alcibiades obligingly gives of himself" (*Six Historians,* Chicago, 1956, p. 26). It may be added that the Letter of Nicias really does little to enhance his qualifications. The Athenian Ecclesia, by its action, does even less to enhance its qualifications for reappraising the military leader of its choice.

Once more the Ecclesia did not react as Nicias hoped. They did not accept his resignation. Instead they sent him two more deputies, voted more replacements — both in men and ships, and made ready for fighting to the last man. And this is what ultimately was forced upon them.

§

[11]. Our past operations, Athenians, have been made known to you by many other letters; it is now time for you to become familiar with our present condition, and to take your measures accordingly. We had defeated in most of our engagements with them the Syracusans, against whom we were sent, and we had built the works which we now occupy, when Gylippus arrived from Lacedaemon with an army obtained from Peloponnese and from some of the cities in Sicily. In our first battle with him we were victorious; in the battle on the following day we were overpowered by a multitude of cavalry and darters, and compelled to retire within our lines. We have now, therefore, been forced by the numbers of those opposed to us to discontinue the work of circumvallation, and to remain inactive; being unable to make use even of all the force we have, since a large portion of our heavy infantry is absorbed in the defence of our lines. Meanwhile the enemy have carried a single wall past our lines, thus making it impossible for us to invent them in future, until this cross wall be attacked by a strong force and captured. So that the besieger in name has become, at least from the land side, the besieged in reality; as we are prevented by their cavalry from even going for any distance into the country.

[12]. Besides this, an embassy has been despatched to Peloponnese to procure reinforcements, and Gylippus has gone to the cities in Sicily, partly in the hope of inducing those that are at present neutral to join

him in the war, partly of bringing from his allies additional contingents for the land forces and material for the navy. For I understand that they contemplate a combined attack upon our lines with their land forces and with their fleet by sea. You must none of you be surprised that I say by sea also. They have discovered that the length of the time we have now been in commission has rotted our ships and wasted our crews, and that with the entireness of our crews and the soundness of our ships the pristine efficiency of our navy has departed. For it is impossible for us to haul our ships ashore and careen them, because, the enemy's vessels being as many or more than our own, we are constantly anticipating an attack. Indeed, they may be seen exercising, and it lies with them to take the initiative; and not having to maintain a blockade, they have greater facilities for drying their ships.

[13]. This we should scarcely be able to do, even if we had plenty of ships to spare, and were freed from our present necessity of exhausting all our strength upon the blockade. For it is already difficult to carry in supplies past Syracuse; and were we to relax our vigilance in the slightest degree it would become impossible. The losses which our crews have suffered and still continue to suffer arise from the following causes. Expeditions for fuel and for forage, and the distance from which water has to be fetched, cause our sailors to be cut off by the Syracusan cavalry; the loss of our previous superiority emboldens our slaves to desert; our foreign seamen are impressed by the unexpected appearance of a navy against us, and the strength of the enemy's resistance; such of them as were pressed into the service take the first opportunity of departing to their respective cities; such as were originally seduced by the temptation of high pay, and expected little fighting and large gains, leave us either by desertion to the enemy or by availing themselves of one or other of the various facilities of escape which the magnitude of Sicily affords them. Some even engage in trade themselves and prevail upon the captains to take Hyccaric slaves on board in their place; thus they have ruined the efficiency of our navy.

[14]. Now I need not remind you that the time during which a crew is in its prime is short, and that the number of sailors who can start a ship on her way and keep the rowing in time is small. But by far my greatest trouble is, that holding the post which I do, I am prevented by the natural indocility of the Athenian seaman from putting a stop to these evils; and that meanwhile we have no source from which to recruit our crews, which the enemy can do from many quarters, but are compelled to depend both for supplying the crews in service and for

making good our losses upon the men whom we brought with us. For our present confederates, Naxos and Catana, are incapable of supplying us. There is only one thing more wanting to our opponents, I mean the defection of our Italian markets. If they were to see you neglect to relieve us from our present condition, and were to go over to the enemy, famine would compel us to evacuate, and Syracuse would finish the war without a blow.

I might, it is true, have written to you something different and more agreeable than this, but nothing certainly more useful, if it is desirable for you to know the real state of things here before taking your measures. Besides I know that it is your nature to love to be told the best side of things, and then to blame the teller if the expectations which he has raised in your minds are not answered by the result; and I therefore thought it safest to declare to you the truth.

[15]. Now you are not to think that either your generals or your soldiers have ceased to be a match for the forces originally opposed to them. But you are to reflect that a general Sicilian coalition is being formed against us; that a fresh army is expected from Peloponnese, while the force we have here is unable to cope even with our present antagonists; and you must promptly decide either to recall us or to send out to us another fleet and army as numerous again, with a large sum of money, and some one to succeed me, as a disease in the kidneys unfits me for retaining my post. I have, I think, some claim on your indulgence, as while I was in my prime I did you much good service in my commands. But whatever you mean to do, do it at the commencement of spring and without delay, as the enemy will obtain his Sicilian reinforcements shortly, those from Peloponnese after a longer interval; and unless you attend to the matter the former will be here before you, while the latter will elude you as they have done before.

§

Part Two

Military Harangues

An Introduction to the Military Harangues

Polybius wrote in his *History* that "war is a fearful thing, but not so fearful that we should submit to anything in order to avoid it" (IV 31). Later he explains that the real purpose of history is to distinguish the values of events and speeches. The historian is obligated to discover in the case of speeches the words actually spoken and then to decide why what was done or spoken resulted in success or failure (XII 25 b1). Speech in Greek and Roman times was the basis of all political life. In war it was not only a means of communication but vital as a means of inspiration.

This belief makes clear why Thucydides saw fit to include some thirteen military harangues in his *History*. They not only help explain the battles but they suggest to the reader why the Greeks or their enemies won or lost. There are some clear cases where the generals' words did affect the outcomes.

These thirteen military speeches are distinctly unlike the others in the *History*. They are much shorter, less dependent on structure or devices of style (especially antithesis) for effect, and far less studied in the use of word-sounds and rhythms. Quintilian has an explanation for some of these features in his statement: "Again, history, which should move with speed and impetuosity, would have been ill-suited by the halts imposed by the rounding off of the period, by the pauses for breath inevitable in oratory, and the elaborate methods of opening sentences and bringing them to a close" (Butler translation, IX 4.18).

Nowhere better than in the military speeches is "the reluctance to speak at superfluous length" (as expressed in I 68, II 36, IV 39) better illustrated. The figures of speech which Quintilian and Cicero catalogue are seldom used in the addresses of the troop commanders. Bluntness, candid explanation of difficulties, clear directions, inspiring predictions generally characterize the way the generals talk. Thus they are often believable. They cannot waste time. The good speakers sound like winners. The losers like Nicias sound like worry-weary men defeated before they begin. Did Thucydides plan the speeches this way or is this the way it was? The answer is affirmative to both parts.

In the final analysis before the general says a word his *ethos* counts most. If he had not established his military reputation before the battle even his choicest phrases beautifully spoken could not work magic. Generals like Pericles, Brasidas, and even Nicias until the Sicilian expedition had images, as we would say today, that made them highly persuasive. Much as we may disapprove of the speeches of Cleon and Alcibiades they too by their known reputations as strong-willed leaders were highly effective.

Adcock generalizes that Thucydides "in his generals' speeches before battle...is not so much concerned with their emotional appeal as with the factors which govern not the battle alone, but the essential character of war, and at times the military quality of the general concerned" (*The Greek and Macedonian Art of War*, pp. 99-100).

Since Thucydides almost certainly never heard a single one of the thirteen military harangues he reported we can conclude that his principal purpose in the speeches was to make the history dramatically move along. Inspiring the troops was incidental to reporting the progress of the battle. The speeches are worth our study for their invention and their understanding of the way men react under fear and danger. Most of all they tell us something about those imponderables of the battlefield — courage and bravery, skill and daring, chance and confusion. When we try to grasp why battles are lost we find hints under poor intelligence, misinformation, lack of planning, failure to organize and control troops and movements, and of course, lack of zeal and hot pursuit. When we recall that commands were given almost entirely by voice it is a miracle that the Athenians won as often as they did. Once a battle starts the common soldier has no time to remember what the general said.

Self-preservation depends on prior training and combat experience. The words of petty officers and lieutenants probably did more good than those of the generals and admirals. Nevertheless, we cannot ignore the fact that Thucydides had good reasons for telling us what Phormio and Pogandas and Gylippus were like in something like their own words. This means again what Thucydides thought was appropriate under all the circumstances. We must not forget that the writer had himself been a general and that he had many years to reflect on the art of generalship. In a sense these thirteen speeches represent a chapter of Thucydides' own memoirs — on "What I would have said if I had been in command at the time."

§

Archidamus to the Peloponnesian Officers
before invading Attica
Book II 11
431 B.C.

This is a speech by the fifth king of Sparta called Archidamus. He had an army of 100,000 men. He began a war that raged for 27 years during the greater part of which his country never really appeared as a winner. But we all have heard of the Spartan "virtues." They finally won out and this brief speech throws some light on why men fight.

The king gives weight to δέος, the Spartan concept of fear or terror "oftentimes a smaller force, made cautious by fear, overmatches a larger number that is caught unprepared because it despises the foe" (II 4-5, Smith trans. in Loeb ed).

Again, the idea of φόβας, the concept of fear inducing preparedness, is expressed in the passage "always be bold in spirit, but in action cautious and therefore prepared" (II 5).

This kind of thinking makes us believe that Archidamus had grave doubts about a Spartan victory over Athens. A real troop leader never suggests his troops may lose.

Of course, the speech must have been symbolic and given only to the generals and the headquarters troops. Whether it was relayed to the whole command by written word or by reading aloud we do not know. In any event it is full of good sense and not at all like a do-or-die oration. In fact, it comes from an opponent of the war. And it is hard to understand how a common soldier could have been inspired by it.

The chief appeal is to the reputation of ancestors, "both within and without Peloponnese." We must not show ourselves inferior to our fathers. It is easy to be over-confident. Events cannot be foreseen. Confidence must be tempered by a wise apprehension. Discipline and vigilance are of first importance. Obey orders promptly. Credit and safety are direct products of a single discipline.

This is the gist of the speech. It is so full of wisdom as to sound platitudinous. It contains no memorable phrases, however, and the troops will not rush into battle after hearing it. In fact Archidamus, an old man, warns of the troubles ahead for his own army. But the advice is countered by a young man, Melesippus, the herald sent to Athens to warn that the Spartans were on the march. Pericles refused to admit him and instead had him escorted to the Athenian frontier that same day. It is his words when the escort turned back that linger in the minds of Thucydides' readers to this day: "This day will be the beginning of great misfortunes to the Greeks." Truer words were never spoken.

§

[11]. Peloponnesians and allies, our fathers made many campaigns both within and without Peloponnese, and the elder men among us here are not without experience in war. Yet we have never set out with a larger force than the present; and if our numbers and efficiency are remarkable, so also is the power of the state against which we march. We ought not then to show ourselves inferior to our ancestors, or unequal to our own reputation. For the hopes and attention of all Hellas are bent upon the present effort, and its sympathy is with the enemy of the hated Athens. Therefore, numerous as the invading army may appear to be, and certain as some may think it that our adversary will not meet us in the field, this is no sort of justification for the least negligence upon the march; but the officers and men of each particular city should always be prepared for the advent of danger in their own quarters. The course of war cannot be foreseen, and its attacks are generally dictated by the impulse of the moment; and where overweening self-confidence has despised preparation, a wise apprehension has often been able to make head against superior numbers. Not that confidence is out of place in an army of invasion, but in an enemy's country it should also be accompanied by the precautions of apprehension: troops will by this combination be best inspired for dealing a blow, and best secured against receiving one. In the present instance, the city against which we are going, far from being so impotent for defence, is on the contrary most excellently equipped at all points; so that we have every reason to expect that they will take the field against us, and that if they have not set out already before we are

there, they will certainly do so when they see us in their territory wasting and destroying their property. For men are always exasperated at suffering injuries to which they are not accustomed, and on seeing them inflicted before their very eyes; and where least inclined for reflexion, rush with the greatest heat to action. The Athenians are the very people of all others to do this, as they aspire to rule the rest of the world, and are more in the habit of invading and ravaging their neighbours' territory, than of seeing their own treated in the like fashion. Considering, therefore, the power of the state against which we are marching, and the greatness of the reputation which, according to the event, we shall win or lose for our ancestors and ourselves, remember as you follow where you may be led to regard discipline and vigilance as of the first importance, and to obey with alacrity the orders transmitted to you; as nothing contributes so much to the credit and safety of an army as the union of large bodies by a single discipline.

§

Peloponnesian Commanders to their crews
before an action in the Corinthian Gulf
Book II 87
429 B.C.

This is the first speech in a series of two. Phormio who speaks next (II 89) must have heard what Brasidas and Cnemus said in this speech because he refutes it practically point by point. Of course we know that Phormio did *not* hear what was said. It is merely Thucydides giving us the antithesis again.

The speech as usual has several memorable generalizations, e.g. "Inexperience is more than offset by superiority in daring" (II 87.4); "Without valor no amount of proficiency avails against dangers" (*Ibid.*); "Fear drives presence of mind away" (*Ibid.*); and "Victory is generally on the side of those who are the more numerous and better prepared" (II 87.7).

Whether these same arguments could be used by Phormio to his men is a nice question. The fact remains that he uses opposite arguments to make his exhortation.

The speakers are "Cnemus and Brasidas and the rest of the Peloponnesian commanders." Their theme is simple — although naval skill is important it cannot overcome courage. This is in the tradition of exhortation and the ordinary sailor understands it even though the ship captains and boatswains may not believe it. And yet many a battle has been won just because men refuse to give up. Leadership and military know-how may not be everything, after all.

The fact is cowardice didn't produce the first defeat. True, there was not enough time for preparation. We do lack experience. But this is never an excuse for poor performance.

Fear must be avoided. It ruins presence of mind. Without valor skill is useless. Superior daring counts and so do superior numbers. We will recognize and reward the heroes, misconduct will be punished.

This is the gist of the speech. It is in the deliberately underdog manner. The common sailor will get the message and, chances are, respond far better than he would to the cautious words of Archidamus.

But listen to the next speaker, Phormio. He has another side to tell.

§

[87]. Peloponnesians, the late engagement which may have made some of you afraid of the one now in prospect, really gives no just ground for apprehension. Preparation for it, as you know, there was little enough; and the object of our voyage was not so much to fight at sea as an expedition by land. Besides this, the chances of war were largely against us; and perhaps also inexperience had something to do with our failure in our first naval action. It was not, therefore, cowardice that produced our defeat, nor ought the determination which force has not quelled, but which still has a word to say with its adversary, to lose its edge from the result of an accident; but admitting the possibility of a chance miscarriage, we should know that brave hearts must be always brave, and while they remain so can never put forward inexperience as an excuse for misconduct. Nor are you so behind the enemy in experience as you are ahead of him in courage; and although the science of your opponents would, if valour accompanied it, have also the presence of mind to carry out at an emergency the lesson it has learnt, yet a faint heart will make all art powerless in the face of danger. For fear takes away presence of mind, and without valour art is useless. Against their superior experience set your superior daring, and against the fear induced by defeat the fact of your having been then unprepared; remember, too, that you have always the advantage of superior numbers, and of engaging off your own coast, supported by your heavy infantry; and as a rule, numbers and equipment give victory. At no point, therefore, is defeat likely; and as for our previous mistakes, the very fact of their occurrence will teach us better for the future. Steersmen and sailors may, therefore, confidently attend to their several duties, none quitting the station assigned to them: as for ourselves, we promise to prepare for the engagement at least as well as your previous commanders, and to give no excuse for

any one misconducting himself. Should any insist on doing so, he shall meet with the punishment he deserves, while the brave shall be honoured with the appropriate rewards of valour.

§

Phormio to the men of the Athenian Fleet
before an action in the Corinthian Gulf
Book II 89
429 B.C.

Phormio won two naval victories in one year, 429 B.C. In any age this is a good record. Here he demonstrates once more that Athenian knowledge of sea warfare gained from hard experience, the best teacher, was a formidable resource.

The explanation Thucydides gives before the battle provides an insight into the way in which the Spartans and the Athenians thought about their men and their battle-worthiness: "this was their [the Spartans'] first attempt at a sea fight, and they could not believe that their fleet was so greatly inferior, but thought that there had been cowardice somewhere, failing to take into account the long experience of the Athenians as compared with their own brief practice" (II 85.2, Smith trans. in Loeb ed.).

Phormio knew what was going on in the minds of his men. He sensed their fears when they began forming into small groups. Even though Athenian sailors had been trained to believe they were better than any, even numerical superiority gave them cause to think. Troop leaders know that too much reflective thinking before a battle is fatal. So this is what Phormio, the admiral, reminds his men: The enemy knows land-warfare best. They do not know how to fight at sea. We have just drubbed them and here they are in larger numbers asking for more. Their men are conscripts and ours are volunteers. We have them badly frightened and we mean to do it again. We know how to maneuver and I will not get caught at close quarters without a way to retire. I know the importance of ramming from a long way off. This will not turn into a land battle. Remember that "beaten men do not face a danger twice with the same determination."

It is a good speech, spoken by a winner. Again, it is in the language sailors understand. It is designed to inspire confidence in the ship's officers. They know their business. At this stage it is, as so often is the case in the *History* when opposing sides are presented, a toss-up. There is good reason for believing either side will win — or lose.

The reader must follow the exciting events in II 90-92 to understand the brilliance of the Athenian victory. No one can excel the description which Thucydides paints.

§

[89]. I see, my men, that you are frightened by the number of the enemy, and I have accordingly called you together, not liking you to be afraid of what is not really terrible. In the first place, the Peloponnesians, already defeated, and not even themselves thinking that they are a match for us, have not ventured to meet us on equal terms, but have equipped this multitude of ships against us. Next, as to that upon which they most rely, the courage which they suppose constitutional to them, their confidence here only arises from the success which their experience in land service usually gives them, and which they fancy will do the same for them at sea. But this advantage will in all justice belong to us on this element, if to them on that; as they are not superior to us in courage, but we are each of us more confident, according to our experience in our particular department. Besides, as the Lacedaemonians use their supremacy over the allies to promote their own glory, they are most of them being brought into danger against their will, or they would never, after such a decided defeat, have ventured upon a fresh engagement. You need not, therefore, be afraid of their dash. You, on the contrary, inspire a much greater and better founded alarm, both because of your late victory and also of their belief that we should not face them unless about to do something worthy of a success so signal. An adversary numerically superior, like the one before us, comes into action trusting more to strength than to resolution; while he who voluntarily confronts tremendous odds must have very great internal resources to draw upon. For these reasons the Peloponnesians fear our irrational audacity more than they would ever have done a more commensurate preparation. Besides, many armaments have before now succumbed to an inferior through want of skill or sometimes of courage; neither of which defects certainly are ours. As to the battle, it shall not be, if I can help it, in the strait, nor will I sail in there at all; seeing that in a contest between a number of clumsily managed vessels

and a small, fast, well-handled squadron, want of sea room is an undoubted disadvantage. One cannot run down an enemy properly without having a sight of him a good way off, nor can one retire at need when pressed; one can neither break the line nor return upon his rear, the proper tactics for a fast sailer; but the naval action necessarily becomes a land one, in which numbers must decide the matter. For all this I will provide as far as can be. Do you stay at your posts by your ships, and be sharp at catching the word of command, the more so as we are observing one another from so short a distance; and in action think order and silence all important — qualities useful in war generally, and in naval engagements in particular—; and behave before the enemy in a manner worthy of your past exploits. The issues you will fight for are great — to destroy the naval hopes of the Peloponnesians or to bring nearer to the Athenians their fears for the sea. And I may once more remind you that you have defeated most of them already; and beaten men do not face a danger twice with the same determination.

§

Teutiaplus the Elean to Alcidas and the
Peloponnesian Leaders at Embatum
Book III 30
427 B.C.

Jebb does not include this speech in his list of the twelve
military harangues but says it is "virtually of this class." I
have included it because of its high merit. Finley calls it a
"unique little speech" and cites it as another example of
Thucydides' admiration of capacity for incisive action.

Embatum is on the coast of Asia Minor, opposite Chios.
We know no more about Teutiaplus and Alcidas than
Thucydides tells us. Alcidas was the commander of an
expedition of forty ships "which should have gone at once to
Mytilene" but they dawdled about the Peloponnese and
finally arrived at Delos "before they were heard of at
Athens." They touched at Icarus, an island in the Aegean
Sea, and Myconus, another island, where they "found too
late that Mytilene was taken." So they sailed for Embatum,
near Erythrae, one of the Ionian cities. They arrived just a
week after Mytilene had fallen. So a conference was called to
decide the next course of action. The speech below is not a
talk to troops; it is an "appreciation" as the British staff
officers would say, or as Americans would call it "an estimate
of the situation" — with a recommendation. It all took place
at Command Headquarters.

The English translators of III 30 take four sentences,
except for Rex Warner, who needs five. The speech exemplifies the principles officers are taught at the command and
staff colleges: pursue, make use of surprise, catch the enemy
off guard, victorious troops always celebrate and this is the
best time to attack, never be afraid of danger. The speaker
concludes with a piece of great wisdom, as Rex Warner
translates it: "let us remember that this is an example of the
unknown factor in warfare, and that the good general is the
one who guards against such unknown factors in his own

case, but exploits them for attack in the case of the enemy."

For troop commanders who had been "goofing off" for several weeks this was a remarkable prescription and a chance to redeem themselves. But Alcidas was like Nicias. He rejected the idea Teutiaplus offered. He turned down other suggestions to take one of the Ionian cities or Cymae in Aeolia. Instead, he headed for the town of Myonneses "where he put to death most of the prisoners he had taken on the voyage."

This little account should explain why the name of Alcidas is not included in any of the "Great Captains" series of military exploits.

§

[30]. Alcidas and Peloponnesians who share with me the command of this armament, my advice is to sail just as we are to Mitylene, before we have been heard of. We may expect to find the Athenians as much off their guard as men generally are who have just taken a city: this will certainly be so by sea, where they have no idea of any enemy attacking them, and where our strength, as it happens, mainly lies; while even their land forces are probably scattered about the houses in the carelessness of victory. If therefore we were to fall upon them suddenly and in the night, I have hopes, with the help of the well-wishers that we may have left inside the town, that we shall become masters of the place. Let us not shrink from the risk, but let us remember that this is just the occasion for one of the baseless panics common in war; and that to be able to guard against these in one's own case, and to detect the moment when an attack will find an enemy at this disadvantage, is what makes a successful general.

§

Demosthenes to his troops at Pylos
Book IV 10
425 B.C.

Pylos is the name of a town on the west coast of Peloponnesus in Messenia. There is a bay of Pylos and an island of Sphacteria which almost closes the mouth of the bay. The island is about 1¾ miles long and there are narrow entrances at each end. The Athenians had built a fort on the cliffs of Coryphasium, south of the old city of Pylos and just within the mouth entrance to the harbor. It was here that the action took place.

Demosthenes, the Athenian general in command, had few resources. He had five ships left from the fleet that sailed for Corcyra. But two had already been dispatched to Zacynthus. With the three galleys left he made a stockade around them. The sailors used shields made of osier, the small branches of willow trees. The Spartans had 43 ships and greatly outnumbered the Athenians. The problem therefore was to make the most of the slightly high ground at the rocky shore while the unskilled sailors forced their ships up the narrow channel. This was the situation when Demosthenes spoke to the 60 heavy infantry assigned to stop the landing.

Here is the way the speech developed: Don't start worrying about the odds against us. You will do better to knock down each landing party before it gains a foothold. "The sooner the danger is faced the better." Our great advantage is in their awkwardness. They must slow down and stop. If we run away they succeed. It is far easier to drive the enemy off while he is still crowded on his ships. And even though he has lots of ships we can pick them off one or two at a time. We all know that a land defender determined to stand fast has the odds greatly in his favor. We can save ourselves and the place too if nobody panics.

It was a splendid little speech — just what was needed. The Spartan ships advanced one by one, meeting stones and javelins and finding confusion in their ranks. When Brasidas made a brave effort to smash his own ship to effect a landing he was hit and lost his shield. It quickly became an Athenian trophy and as Brasidas fell back in faint his own men lost their nerve.

The Greek word *epiteichismos* refers to the fortification of a place so as to put pressure on the enemy. This is exactly what Demosthenes did with his few ships. His strategy worked, the Spartans were captured, and ultimately Pylos became a place where Spartan helots could escape to from their serfdom.

Twice later in commenting on the strategy Thucydides emphasizes that "it was a strange reversal of things for Athenians to be fighting from the land...against Lacedaemonians coming from the sea" (IV 12.3) and "the Lacedaemonians in their excitement and dismay were actually engaged in a sea fight on land, while the Athenians, in their eagerness to push their success as far as possible, were carrying on a land fight from their ships" (IV 14.3).

Professor Finley has argued (*Three Essays*, pp. 145-146) that these chapters of Book IV were composed very late in the war after the Athenian sea power had faded and probably when Thucydides had found the identical situation in the final battle of the Sicilian war (see VII 75.7).

As Thucydides tells us the fight was full of paradoxes. Here were Athenians, sailors by tradition, fighting on enemy land against Spartans trying to take back their own harbor. The arrival of the Athenian fleet soon put the Spartans to complete rout. The truce involved the surrender of sixty ships to Athens. It is a miracle that sixty courageous men in the beginning could determine a great Athenian victory.

§

[10]. Soldiers and comrades in this adventure, I hope that none of you in our present strait will think to show his wit by exactly calculating all the perils that encompass us, but that you will rather

hasten to close with the enemy, without staying to count the odds, seeing in this your best chance of safety. In emergencies like ours calculation is out of place; the sooner the danger is faced the better. To my mind also most of the chances are for us, if we will only stand fast and not throw away our advantages, overawed by the numbers of the enemy. One of the points in our favour is the awkwardness of the landing. This, however, only helps us if we stand our ground. If we give way it will be practicable enough, in spite of its natural difficulty, without a defender; and the enemy will instantly become more formidable from the difficulty he will have in retreating, supposing that we succeed in repulsing him, which we shall find it easier to do, while he is on board his ships, than after he has landed and meets us on equal terms. As to his numbers, these need not too much alarm you. Large as they may be he can only engage in small detachments, from the impossibility of bringing to. Besides, the numerical superiority that we have to meet is not that of an army on land with everything else equal, but of troops on board ship, upon an element where many favourable accidents are required to act with effect. I therefore consider that his difficulties may be fairly set against our numerical deficiencies, and at the same time I charge you, as Athenians who know by experience what landing from ships on a hostile territory means, and how impossible it is to drive back an enemy determined enough to stand his ground and not to be frightened away by the surf and the terrors of the ships sailing in, to stand fast in the present emergency, beat back the enemy at the water's edge, and save yourselves and the place.

§

Pagondas to the Boeotian troops
before the battle of Delium
Book IV 92
424 B.C.

The next two speeches illustrate how two commanders entreat their troops to do their utmost at the battle of Delium. Pagondas, a Theban, was in command of the Boeotians and Hippocrates, the nephew of Pericles, was general in charge of the Athenians. The battle took place on the coast of Boeotia in the territory of Tanagra near the Attic border. The place was named after the Temple of Apollo similar to that at Delos. Possibly the speech took place on the steps of the temple.

Pagondas begins by surmising that the Greeks intended to annoy Boeotia by crossing the frontier to build the fort.

The Greeks had clearly violated amity by invading Boeotia. All Boeotians oppose invaders. It is doubly imperative to repel the Greeks — since they mean to make slaves of "near and far alike." The Euboeans and most of the rest of Hellas are examples.

If we stand meekly by they will run over us but if we meet them outside and strike the first blow the advantage is all ours. What we did at Coronea proves the value of attacking first.

So let us remember what our fathers did in 417 against the army of Tolmides. Delos will help us. We must teach these Greeks that we are always ready to give battle for our liberty and they cannot get off without a struggle.

The advice that Pericles gave about not expanding the war is echoed and re-echoed in a half dozen or more places in the *History*. It was, Thucydides subtly keeps telling us, the rejection of this advice that brought Athens to her downfall. Professor Finley (*Three Essays*, p. 157) has observed the use of almost the same words by Cleon after Pylos, again describing the attack on Melos, and now before the battle of

Delium. We are thus reminded of what can happen when greed exceeds a country's capabilities. Here are the words in this speech: "For where men are attacked prudence does not admit of such nice calculation regarding their own land as is permitted to those who, secure in their own possessions, in their greed for more want only to attack others" (IV 92.2 Smith trans. in Loeb ed.).

Here again is a good speech for a good cause. The appeals are classic and time tested.

The speech is unique in the *History* in that Thucydides makes no use of antithesis.

As the troops prepared to clash the Thebans formed a column "twenty-five shields deep" and the remainder as they pleased. "Such was the strength and the disposition of the Boeotian army."

§

[92]. Boeotians, the idea that we ought not to give battle to the Athenians unless we came up with them in Boeotia, is one which should never have entered into the head of any of us, your generals. It was to annoy Boeotia that they crossed the frontier and built a fort in our country; and they are therefore, I imagine, our enemies wherever we may come up with them, and from wheresoever they may have come to act as enemies do. And if any one has taken up with the idea in question for reasons of safety, it is high time for him to change his mind. The party attacked, whose own country is in danger, can scarcely discuss what is prudent with the calmness of men who are in full enjoyment of what they have got, and are thinking of attacking a neighbour in order to get more. It is your national habit, in your country or out of it, to oppose the same resistance to a foreign invader; and when that invader is Athenian, and lives upon your frontier besides, it is doubly imperative to do so. As between neighbours generally, freedom means simply a determination to hold one's own; and with neighbours like these, who are trying to enslave near and far alike, there is nothing for it but to fight it out to the last. Look at the condition of the Euboeans and of most of the rest of Hellas, and be convinced that others have to fight with their neighbours for this frontier or that, but

that for us conquest means one frontier for the whole country, about which no dispute can be made, for they will simply come and take by force what we have. So much more have we to fear from this neighbour than from another. Besides, people who, like the Athenians in the present instance, are tempted by pride of strength to attack their neighbours, usually march most confidently against those who keep still, and only defend themselves in their own country, but think twice before they grapple with those who meet them outside their frontier and strike the first blow if opportunity offers. The Athenians have shown us this themselves; the defeat which we inflicted upon them at Coronea, at the time when our quarrels had allowed them to occupy the country, has given great security to Boeotia until the present day. Remembering this, the old must equal their ancient exploits, and the young, the sons of the heroes of that time, must endeavour not to disgrace their native valour; and trusting in the help of the god whose temple has been sacrilegiously fortified, and in the victims which in our sacrifices have proved propitious, we must march against the enemy, and teach him that he must go and get what he wants by attacking some one who will not resist him, but that men whose glory it is to be always ready to give battle for the liberty of their own country, and never unjustly to enslave that of others, will not let him go without a struggle.

§

Hippocrates to the Athenian troops
before the battle of Delium
Book IV 95
424 B.C.

This contrasting speech was given a little differently. Pagondas had called the troops to him a company at a time so as to prevent a surprise attack. But Hippocrates, the nephew of Pericles, passed along the Athenian lines and gave this little speech until half his men heard it. Then the Boeotian attack began. The imminence of the attack probably explains why the speech is only four sentences long.

There is no point in trying to condense the speech because it is so short — one of the shortest in the *History.* The fact that Hippocrates makes the same kind of appeal as Pagondas is of interest. He urges his men to fight as their fathers did "at Oenophyta [456 B.C.] with Myronides and thus gained possession of Boeotia."

The traditions of regimental feats of the past live on today in every army. Commanders always exhort on the basis of victories and never on the basis of defeats. Soldiers never want to be reminded about the prospect of their side losing.

Delium was a town on the coast of Boeotia in Tanagra and near the Attic border. It was named after a temple of Apollo similar to the one at Delos. The battle terrain was rugged and this fact hampered the movement of cavalry — a key factor in the outcome.

It is difficult to find good accounts of the troop movements in the battles of the Peloponnesian War. Thucydides is our best contemporary historian of what took place. Among present-day scholars, Sir Frank E. Adcock has written the best account of what transpired at Delium and I am going to reproduce below his analysis:

> The Theban Pagondas, who won the one considerable land battle in the first decade of the Peloponnesian War, namely the battle of Delium, may not wholly deserve the praise he has

received. I do not wish to be unjust to Pagondas, who had at least that strong desire to fight which goes a good way to make a good general. And so I may be allowed to discuss this battle. (see Thuc. IV, 90ff.; Diod. XII, 69f., adds little of value.) A substantial part of the Athenian field army was on its way home after establishing a strongpoint at Delium just inside the Boeotian border. Pagondas with rather more than an equal force of Boeotian troops was able to intercept them, and insisted on doing so. This was good strategy, for it was important to show that Athenian hoplites could not march in and out of Boeotia unchallenged. Hippocrates, the Athenian general, had left behind at Delium part of his small force of cavalry and had no light-armed troops of military value. Pagondas had one thousand Boeotian cavalry, which was always pretty good. He could presumably have retired until he found a battleground to suit his cavalry. As it was, he barred the way of the Athenians at a point where, in the normal formation of eight deep, they could fight with their flanks protected by watercourses on either side, if he attacked at once. And as he did attack before the Athenian general had finished going along his line addressing his troops, the moment of attack was of Pagondas' choosing. The Athenian line of hoplites in the normal depth had to meet the charge, in which the right wing of the Thebans was ranged twenty-five men deep, so that the remainder of the Boeotian infantry army was inferior in numbers to the Athenians opposed to them. The result was that the Thebans had the best of it and their Boeotian comrades the worst of it, and it was a nice question whether the Athenian advantage in one part of the battle would not compensate for their disadvantage in the other. The battle seems to have reached an equilibrium, if an unstable one. Pagondas then sent a force of cavalry to make a *détour* round a hill and come to the help of his left wing. This was a wise move, and, had the ground permitted it, this cavalry might have intervened with good effect. But it was not a good terrain for cavalry, (G.C. Grundy, *Thucydides and the History of His Age*, II, pp. 134ff.) and it is at least doubtful if this would have happened. What did happen was that the victorious Athenian right wing saw the cavalry appear on the skyline, believed it was the advance guard of a new Boeotian army, and broke in panic, and the battle was over. The intelligent Athenian hoplites had put two and two together and made it five. Had they been unimaginative Boeotians they would perhaps have arrived at the answer four (or even possibly three), and continued the battle so as to get a draw if not a win. It is hard to believe that Pagondas reckoned on producing this psychological effect on the Athenians, and it is possible to think that his generalship was better rewarded than it deserved to be. But it is only fair to repeat that the decision to fight, if not at that particular place, would have been right even if it had not resulted in a clear-cut victory, as in fact it did (from *The Greek and Macedonian Art of War*, Berkeley, 1967, pp. 84-85).

If ever there was a lucky general it was Pagondas of Thebes. It was the soldiers of Athens who made him look far better than he was.

§

[95]. Athenians, I shall only say a few words to you, but brave men require no more, and they are addressed more to your understanding than to your courage. None of you must fancy that we are going out of our way to run this risk in the country of another. Fought in their territory the battle will be for ours: if we conquer, the Peloponnesians will never invade your country without the Boeotian horse, and in one battle you will win Boeotia and in a manner free Attica. Advance to meet them then like citizens of a country in which you all glory as the first in Hellas, and like sons of the fathers who beat them at Oenophyta with Myronides and thus gained possession of Boeotia.

§

Brasidas to his troops on the
campaign against Arrhibaeus
Book IV 126
423 B.C.

Brasidas had recovered from his defeat at Pylos two years before. We find him now in command of the Peloponnesians "whom he still had with him and the Chalcidians, Ascansians, and others." With the troops of Peridaccas he had 3000 Hellenic heavy infantry (hoplites), the Macedonian cavalry, 1000 Chalcidians, and "an immense crowd of barbarians."

The events preceding the battle are described by Thucydides at IV 125. He tells us that just before the enemy came up Brasidas "sought to sustain the courage of his soldiers with the following hasty exhortation" which I give in essence.

> I speak because I know you are surprised at being left alone to fight this battle. But bravery does not depend on having allies near you. It depends on your own courage. Don't be fooled by those barbarians. They may yell and brandish weapons — but before an enemy standing fast they are different. They may look tough but they really are not. So, stand your ground, retire in good order if you must. They only show courage if they can pursue those who run away.

A short speech — not a very inspiring one to read. But it worked. The young soldiers of Brasidas repulsed the attacks one after another and finally won the day. It was an example of what good leadership can do in the face of a superior but less disciplined enemy.

In his Sather lectures at the University of California, Berkeley, Sir Frank E. Adcock praises Brasidas in this fashion: "The career of Brasidas the Spartan presents a long succession of resolute, at times vehement, feats of leadership, coupled with an adroit management of men and events. He seemed able to do more with fewer men than any other general in Greek history" (*The Greek and Macedonian Art of War*, Berkeley, 1967, p. 86).

The whole account before and after the battle serves to show the contrast between the organized attack of the Hellenes and the hit-or-miss plans of the barbarians. The speech of Brasidas that follows goes into the tactics in more detail.

§

[126]. Peloponnesians, if I did not suspect you of being dismayed at being left alone to sustain the attack of a numerous and barbarian enemy, I should just have said a few words to you as usual without further explanation. As it is, in the face of the desertion of our friends and the numbers of the enemy, I have some advice and information to offer, which, brief as they must be, will, I hope, suffice for the more important points. The bravery that you habitually display in war does not depend on your having allies at your side in this or that encounter, but on your native courage; nor have numbers any terrors for citizens of states like yours, in which the many do not rule the few, but rather the few the many, owing their position to nothing else than to superiority in the field. Inexperience now makes you afraid of barbarians; and yet the trial of strength which you had with the Macedonians among them, and my own judgment, confirmed by what I hear from others, should be enough to satisfy you that they will not prove formidable. Where an enemy seems strong but is really weak, a true knowledge of the facts makes his adversary the bolder, just as a serious antagonist is encountered most confidently by those who do not know him. Thus the present enemy might terrify an inexperienced imagination, they are formidable in outward bulk, their loud yelling is unbearable, and the brandishing of their weapons in the air has a threatening appearance. But when it comes to real fighting with an opponent who stands his ground, they are not what they seemed; they have no regular order that they should be ashamed of deserting their positions when hard pressed; flight and attack are with them equally honourable, and afford no test of courage; their independent mode of fighting never leaving any one who wants to run away without a fair excuse for so doing. In short, they think frightening you at a secure distance a surer game than meeting you hand to hand; otherwise they would have done the one and not the other. You can thus plainly see that the terrors with which they were at first invested are in fact

trifling enough, though to the eye and ear very prominent. Stand your ground therefore when they advance, and again wait your opportunity to retire in good order, and you will reach a place of safety all the sooner, and will know for ever afterwards that rabble such as these, to those who sustain their first attack, do but show off their courage by threats of the terrible things that they are going to do, at a distance, but with those who give way to them are quick enough to display their heroism in pursuit when they can do so without danger.

§

Brasidas to his troops
before the Battle at Amphipolis
Book V 9
422 B.C.

Amphipolis has a special significance. It was here that Thucydides lost his command because his relieving force did not arrive in time. So began his twenty years of banishment and so he was able to write the *History*.

The town is on the eastern bank of the Strymon in Macedonia, about three miles from the Aegean Sea. The speech below explains the stratagem by which Brasidas outwitted Cleon and gained a great victory.

The Spartan order of battle included 500 Thracian mercenaries, the Edonians, horse and targeteers, 1000 Myrcinean and Chalcidian targeteers, those already in Amphipolis, 2000 heavy infantry, 300 Hellenic cavalry.

Brasidas had 1500 with him at Cerdylium. When he had reports the Athenians were advancing he proceeded towards Amphipolis. But he wanted to keep secret his real strength. So he decided to attack suddenly and catch Cleon by surprise. This is how Brasidas told his plan to his men:

> You are Dorians. You have always beaten the Ionians whom you are about to meet. We are going to trick them — so don't be alarmed at our small force. We are seizing an opportunity of the moment — we will take them by surprise and run into their center. Then the Amphipolitans under Clearidas will rush in so as to create a panic.
>
> You have everything to gain — life and freedom if we win and slavery to Athens if we lose. So — I want no show of cowardice. Act like Spartans should. I will show you that what I preach I practice.

There is little classical antithesis in the speech. It is without the usual flourishes and yet its very brevity is inspiring. It is a soldier's speech to soldiers.

Ferdinand Schevill pays Thucydides a high compliment for his honest military appraisal of the man who caused his own loss of command. "It is plain that what caught Thucydides' fancy about Brasidas was that he had cast off the Spartan provincial dullness and that he boasted a swift intelligence and employed a novel military tactic of a daring that represented a complete reversal of the habitual Spartan mentality" (*Six Historians*, Chicago, 1956, p. 29).

This speech provides another instance for Thucydides to praise Spartan discipline. He makes Brasidas say "Show yourself a brave man, as a Spartan should; and do you, allies, follow him like men, and remember that zeal, honour, and obedience mark the good soldier, and that this day will make you either free men and allies of Lacedaemon, or slaves of Athens; even if you escape without personal loss of liberty or life, your bondage will be on harsher terms than before, and you will also hinder the liberation of the rest of Greece" (V 9.6, Crawley trans.).

Brasidas was wounded and was carried off the field. "He lived to hear the victory of his troops, and not long after expired." The battle went exactly as he predicted. The troops of Cleon, except for the Athenian right, simply were beaten before they had a chance to start.

§

[9]. Peloponnesians, the character of the country from which we have come, one which has always owed its freedom to valour, and the fact that you are Dorians and the enemy you are about to fight Ionians, whom you are accustomed to beat, are things that do not need further comment. But the plan of attack that I propose to pursue, this it is as well to explain, in order that the fact of our adventuring with a part instead of with the whole of our forces may not damp your courage by the apparent disadvantage at which it places you. I imagine it is the poor opinion that he has of us, and the fact that he has no idea of any one coming out to engage him, that has made the enemy march up to the place and carelessly look about him as he is doing, without noticing

us. But the most successful soldier will always be the man who most happily detects a blunder like this, and who carefully consulting his own means makes his attack not so much by open and regular approaches, as by seizing the opportunity of the moment; and these stratagems, which do the greatest service to our friends by most completely deceiving our enemies, have the most brilliant name in war. Therefore, while their careless confidence continues, and they are still thinking, as in my judgment they are now doing, more of retreat than of maintaining their position, while their spirit is slack and not high-strung with expectation, I with the men under my command will, if possible, take them by surprise and fall with a run upon their centre; and do you, Clearidas, afterwards, when you see me already upon them, and, as is likely, dealing terror among them, take with you the Amphipolitans, and the rest of the allies, and suddenly open the gates and dash at them, and hasten to engage as quickly as you can. That is our best chance of establishing a panic among them, as a fresh assailant has always more terrors for an enemy than the one he is immediately engaged with. Show yourself a brave man, as a Spartan should; and do you, allies, follow him like men, and remember that zeal, honour, and obedience mark the good soldier, and that this day will make you either free men and allies of Lacedaemon, or slaves of Athens; even if you escape without personal loss of liberty or life, your bondage will be on harsher terms than before, and you will also hinder the liberation of the rest of the Hellenes. No cowardice then on your part, seeing the greatness of the issues at stake, and I will show that what I preach to others I can practise myself.

§

Nicias to the Athenian troops
before the last sea-fight
Book VI 61-64
413 B.C.

There is a grim seriousness in this speech and in the one at VII 77 where Nicias speaks to the troops before their retreat from Syracuse. The cost of the war to Athens in men, money, ships, pride and prestige had been enormous and there is no attempt to hide the facts at this stage.

The greatest virtue of Nicias, his uprightness, was not enough to save him in the final weeks of the war. In the speech below all his past weaknesses and military ineptitudes must have been in the minds of his hearers. Yet he spoke more courageously than the circumstances gave him a right to do. If he had only developed a reputation early as a strong winner he might have pulled through. But time and tide were against him.

The scene is now quite different. Nicias describes it as "a land fight that we are forced to make from ship board." It is full of perils that Nicias plainly warns about. His men are trapped in a narrow wedge — we cannot "back water ourselves, nor...let the enemy do so, especially as the shore, except so much of it as may be held by our troops, is hostile ground." And so the commander tells his men that their fleet is all that is left of Athens and her glorious name. He seems to be forecasting the doom that all hands must have sensed.

Nonetheless this is one of the speeches that Dionysius of Halicarnassus approves of. He later transcribes the analytical passage (VII 69-72) and gives it the highest praise. In general, Dionysius admires the narrative parts of the *History* but is unwilling to recommend the *speeches* for models to imitate (*De Thucydide* c. 55). The speeches of Nicias in VI 9-14 and 20-23, this speech, and his letter (VII 11-15) are exceptions.

Professor Finley points out that portions of this speech referring to the "privileges of Attic life" call to mind similar ideas from the Funeral Oration of Pericles. The contrast with Spartan life is apparent by suggestion in the speech that follows — but it is by the Syracusan general Gylippus, as this biting passage reveals: "When men are once checked in what they consider their special excellence, their whole opinion of themselves suffers more than if they had not at first believed in their superiority, the unexpected shock to their pride causing them to give way more than their real strength warrants, and this is probably now the case with the Athenians" (VII 66.3).

The pathos mounts again after the speech of Gylippus. Nicias knew full well the terrible fate that hung in balance. So we learn (VII 69.1) that he, "appalled by the position of affairs, realizing the greatness and the nearness of the danger now that they were on the point of putting out from shore, and thinking as men are apt to think in great crises, that when all has been done they have still something left to do, and when all has been said that they have not yet said enough, again called on the captains one by one, addressing each by his father's name and by his own, and by that of his tribe, and adjured them not to belie their own personal renown, or to obscure the hereditary virtues for which their ancestors were illustrious; he reminded them of their country, first of the free, and of the unfettered discretion allowed in it to all to live as they pleased; and added other arguments such as men would use at such a crisis, and which, with little alteration are made to serve on all occasions alike — appeals to wives, children, and national gods — without caring whether they are thought commonplace, but loudly invoking them in the belief that they will be of use in the consternation of the moment."

We must now contrast this attitude with the adversary using his own peculiar appeals.

§

[61]. Soldiers of the Athenians and of the allies, we have all an equal interest in the coming struggle, in which life and country are at stake for us quite as much as they can be for the enemy; since if our fleet wins the day, each can see his native city again, wherever that city may be. You must not lose heart, or be like men without any experience, who fail in a first essay, and ever afterwards fearfully forebode a future as disastrous. But let the Athenians among you who have already had experience of many wars, and the allies who have joined us in so many expeditions, remember the surprises of war, and with the hope that fortune will not be always against us, prepare to fight again in a manner worthy of the number which you see yourselves to be.

[62]. Now, whatever we thought would be of service against the crush of vessels in such a narrow harbour, and against the force upon the decks of the enemy, from which we suffered before, has all been considered with the helmsmen, and, as far as our means allowed, provided. A number of archers and darters will go on board, and a multitude that we should not have employed in an action in the open sea, where our science would be crippled by the weight of the vessels; but in the present land-fight that we are forced to make from shipboard all this will be useful. We have also discovered the changes in construction that we must make to meet theirs; and against the thickness of their cheeks, which did us the greatest mischief, we have provided grappling-irons, which will prevent an assailant backing water after charging, if the soldiers on deck here do their duty; since we are absolutely compelled to fight a land battle from the fleet, and it seems to be our interest neither to back water ourselves, nor to let the enemy do so, especially as the shore, except so much of it as may be held by our troops, is hostile ground.

[63]. You must remember this and fight on as long as you can and must not let yourselves be driven ashore, but once alongside must make up your minds not to part company until you have swept the heavy infantry from the enemy's deck. I say this more for the heavy infantry than for the seamen, as it is more the business of the men on deck; and our land forces are even now on the whole the strongest. The sailors I advise, and at the same time implore, not to be too much daunted by their misfortunes, now that we have our decks better armed and a greater number of vessels. Bear in mind how well worth preserving is the pleasure felt by those of you who through your knowledge of our language and imitation of our manners were always considered Athenians, even though not so in reality, and as such were honoured

throughout Hellas, and had your full share of the advantages of our empire, and more than your share in the respect of our subjects and in protection from ill treatment. You, therefore, with whom alone we freely share our empire, we now justly require not to betray that empire in its extremity, and in scorn of Corinthians, whom you have often conquered, and of Siceliots, none of whom so much as presumed to stand against us when our navy was in its prime, we ask you to repel them, and to show that even in sickness and disaster your skill is more than a match for the fortune and vigour of any other.

[64]. For the Athenians among you I add once more this reflexion: — you left behind you no more such ships in your docks as these, no more heavy infantry in their flower; if you do aught but conquer, our enemies here will immediately sail thither, and those that are left of us at Athens will become unable to repel their home assailants, reinforced by these new allies. Here you will fall at once into the hands of the Syracusans — I need not remind you of the intentions with which you attacked them — and your countrymen at home will fall into those of the Lacedaemonians. Since the fate of both thus hangs upon this single battle — now, if ever, stand firm, and remember, each and all, that you who are now going on board are the army and navy of the Athenians, and all that is left of the state and the great name of Athens, in whose defence if any man has any advantage in skill or courage, now is the time for him to show it, and thus serve himself and save all.

§

Nicias to his troops
before the first battle at Syracuse
Book VI 68
415 B.C.

The battle following this speech was notable for its cavalry action. Tactics were not well developed in the fifth century B.C. Commanders used their horsemen mainly to pursue a phalanx in flight. They could also harass the infantry and overtake them on forced marches. Here the Sicilian cavalry was put to good use in the first battle before the city. Let Thucydides describe the action: "At last the Argives drove in the Syracusan left, and after them the Athenians routed the troops opposed to them, and the Syracusan army was thus cut in two and fled. The Athenians did not pursue far, being held in check by the numerous and undefeated Syracusan horse, who attacked and drove back any advance detachments of the heavy infantry; in spite of this the victors pursued in a body so far as was safe, and then went back and set up a trophy" (VI 70.3).

Soon, however, the Athenians threw away their victory; they retired to Camarina, where they prepared for their ultimate defeat.

This is the third of five speeches by Nicias in the *History*. He is represented for the first time as a military commander and a rather sorry figure he is. The speech is so brief, four sentences, that it need not be abstracted. But it cannot be ignored. Its chief argument seems to be — fight like hell or they'll bury us here. If they're fighting for their homeland the Syracusans may make our return home impossible. So, go forth boldly, my men.

Despite his brevity Nicias does use antithesis forcefully and pointedly compares the prospects for the enemy and for his own troops, depending on how each may do in the battle. Perhaps the contrast did get through to his officers and men after all. They acted as if their lives depended precisely on how well they fought. Fortune too was on their side.

§

[68] . Soldiers, a long exhortation is little needed by men like ourselves, who are here to fight in the same battle, the force itself being, to my thinking, more fit to inspire confidence than a fine speech with a weak army. Where we have Argives, Mantineans, Athenians, and the first of the islanders in the ranks together, it were strange indeed, with so many and so brave companions in arms, if we did not feel confident of victory; especially when we have mass-levies opposed to our picked troops, and what is more, Siceliots, who may disdain us but will not stand against us, their skill not being at all commensurate to their rashness. You may also remember that we are far from home and have no friendly land near, except what your own swords shall win you; and here I put before you a motive just the reverse of that which the enemy are appealing to; their cry being that they shall fight for their country, mine that we shall fight for a country that is not ours, where we must conquer or hardly get away, as we shall have their horse upon us in great numbers. Remember, therefore, your renown, and go boldly against the enemy, thinking the present strait and necessity more terrible than they.

§

Gylippus to the Syracusan troops
before the last sea-fight
Book VII 66-68
413 B.C.

Gylippus, the Spartan commander sent to Syracuse to oppose the Athenians in 414 B.C., shines like Brasidas as the other military tactician his side produced. He had exactly the qualities which Nicias lacked — imagination, prompt decision, and energy. Those qualities are revealed in the speech below. Fortunately for the Spartans, his tragic flaw developed after the war was over.

The speech begins by recalling to the Syracusans why the Athenians came — to conquer Sicily, and "after that, if successful, of Peloponnese and the rest of Hellas."

Then follows the allusion to the Athenian weakness (VII 66.3) quoted in the introduction to the speech of Nicias just preceding.

There is an example in this speech of an antithesis of one clause subordinate to the other at VII 68.3 as follows: "None should therefore relent or think it gain if they go away without further danger to us. This they will do just the same, even if they get the victory; while if we succeed, as we may expect in chastising them, and in handing down to all Sicily her ancient freedom strengthened and confirmed, we shall have achieved no mean triumph."

Gylippus accurately predicts the confusion that the close quarters of shipboard fighting are bound to produce. They are "landsmen put into a ship, who in a cramped position will not find means of discharging their darts." The rest of the speech sounds as if it was written by a keen observer after the battle. It describes in the most vivid language the desperate fight that the men of Nicias actually fall into. These details as given in VII 69.4-72.1 bear out the picture Gylippus foresaw.

This is the passage which Dionysius of Halicarnassus cites as an example of Thucydides at his best. The speech and the narrative combine to instill fear and pity in the greatest measure to the first-time reader as well as to devoted admirers of Thucydides, the readers who go back to relive this great sea-battle.

The contrasts provided in the antithesis in VII 63.3-68 between the Athenians and the Spartans provide one of the great passages in rhetorical writing. Gylippus knew he had morale-advantages on his side and he managed to exploit them to the utmost. Nothing succeeds like success and he extracted every ounce of price that the proverb inspires.

Several weeks before the battle in the great Harbor of Syracuse Demosthenes and Eurymedon, the other Athenian generals, had urged Nicias to withdraw the fleet. Once again Nicias delayed a decision and he was trapped. His enemy's leader was a tough-minded Spartan who knew what to do when luck was with him. In this speech he outlines his plan and forecasts the result.

§

[66]. Syracusans and allies, the glorious character of our past achievements and the no less glorious results at issue in the coming battle are, we think, understood by most of you, or you would never have thrown yourselves with such ardour into the struggle; and if there be any one not as fully aware of the facts as he ought to be, we will declare them to him. The Athenians came to this country first to effect the conquest of Sicily, and after that, if successful, of Peloponnese and the rest of Hellas, possessing already the greatest empire yet known, of present or former times, among the Hellenes. Here for the first time they found in you men who faced their navy which made them masters everywhere; you have already defeated them in the previous sea-fight, and will in all likelihood defeat them again now. When men are once checked in what they consider their special excellence, their whole opinion of themselves suffers more than if they had not at first believed in their superiority, the unexpected shock to their pride causing them

to give way more than their real strength warrants; and this is probably now the case with the Athenians.

[67]. With us it is different. The original estimate of ourselves which gave us courage in the days of our unskilfulness has been strengthened, while the convictions super-added to it that we must be the best seamen of the time, if we have conquered the best, has given us a double measure of hope to every man among us; and, for the most part, where there is the greatest hope, there is also the greatest ardour for action. The means to combat us which they have tried to find in copying our armament are familiar to our warfare, and will be met by proper provisions; while they will never be able to have a number of heavy infantry on their decks, contrary to their custom, and a number of darters (born landsmen, one may say, Acarnanians and others, embarked afloat, who will not know how to discharge their weapons when they have to keep still), without hampering their vessels and falling all into confusion among themselves through fighting not according to their own tactics. For they will gain nothing by the number of their ships — I say this to those of you who may be alarmed by having to fight against odds — as a quantity of ships in a confined space will only be slower in executing the movements required, and most exposed to injury from our means of offence. Indeed, if you would know the plain truth, as we are credibly informed, the excess of their sufferings and the necessities of their present distress have made them desperate; they have no confidence in their force, but wish to try their fortune in the only way they can, and either to force their passage and sail out, or after this to retreat by land, it being impossible for them to be worse off than they are.

[68]. The fortune of our greatest enemies having thus betrayed itself, and their disorder being what I have described, let us engage in anger, convinced that, as between adversaries, nothing is more legitimate than to claim to sate the whole wrath of one's soul in punishing the aggressor, and nothing more sweet, as the proverb has it, than the vengeance upon an enemy which it will now be ours to take. That enemies they are and mortal enemies you all know, since they came here to enslave our country, and if successful had in reserve for our men all that is most dreadful, and for our children and wives all that is most dishonourable, and for the whole city the name which conveys the greatest reproach. None should therefore relent or think it gain if they go away without further danger to us. This they will do just the same, even if they get the victory; while if we succeed, as we may

expect, in chastising them, and in handing down to all Sicily her ancient freedom strengthened and confirmed, we shall have achieved no mean triumph. And the rarest dangers are those in which failure brings little loss and success the greatest advantage.

§

Nicias to his troops
before the retreat from Syracuse
Book VII 77
413 B.C.

The retreat took eight days, each one a little worse than the last. Food and water were almost gone. There was no chance to forage — the enemy javelin men and cavalry continually harassed the columns. Medical supplies were non-existent. Morale was at the lowest ebb.

This sad short speech spells the end. Nicias, the unwilling commander, the hesitant and unsure man, the cautious and upright man, whom Thucydides suggests deserved a better fate, has a few words to say before the curtain drops down.

"The tenor of my life has been loyal to the Gods, just and without offense among men" (Jebb, "Speeches of Thucydides," p. 403). For this reason Nicias argues his faith in the future "and our misfortunes do not terrify me as much as they might."

Expiation is the ancient doctrine of atonement or reconciliation of making amends for past excesses. This is the basis Nicias uses for his final plea. He tells his soldiers they have suffered enough and good fortune will now come to them (VII 77.1-4).

The hope sounds false, however, and common sense dictates that sick, tired, hungry, beaten men cannot put forth the super-human effort he called for. But the religious side of Nicias rises once more in a final plea: "Our enemies have had good fortune enough; and if any of the gods was offended at our expedition, we have been already amply punished. Others before us have attacked their neighbors and have done what men will do without suffering more than they could bear; for we may now justly expect to find the gods more kind, for we have become fitter objects for their pity than their jealousy" (VII 77.3-4). These were the words of a man out of step with the realities of war.

Within a matter of hours and days what was once an elite corps, the soldiers and sailors of the Athenian army and navy, were slaughtered and forced to quench their thirst in the water of the Assinarus river mixed with the blood of their own dead. Demosthenes met a horrible death according to Thucydides but according to Plutarch both Nicias and Demosthenes were enabled to put an end to themselves.

The four qualities Athenians prized most in themselves are cited at various places in the *History*. They are high enthusiasm or spirit, courage, ability to innovate and solve problems, and a willingness to work long and hard. Again and again in the *History* a combination of these attributes had pulled citizens and soldiers through both in policy making and waging war. Now when Nicias needed superhuman efforts just to survive he found his officers and men unable to sustain themselves. Who was to blame? The leaders in Athens, the citizens who voted for the Sicilian expedition, poor generals like Nicias, Pericles for his own machinations. Or, was it Alcibiades, the traitor who finally sold out? Was it the fact that the democratic Sicilians had the four proved Athenian qualities in larger supply?

All told, Nicias makes five speeches and writes one letter in the *History*. Thucydides treats of him with compassion — failure though he is. Jebb says that "The ἀρετή of Nicias was that which consists in fidelity to the established observances of religion and to received notions of duty — as distinguished from the ἀρετή, less in conformity with popular conceptions, which Thucydides can still recognize in such a man as Antiphon" (VIII 68). ("Speeches," p. 403, note 3).

I prefer the cool judgment of Plutarch to the harsh condemnation of Nicias for all his faults of character and moral indecision. Here is what Plutarch says: "In actual service, Nicias deserves high praise. He frequently defeated the enemy in battle, and he was on the very point of capturing Syracuse; nor should he bear the whole blame of the disaster, which may fairly be ascribed in part to his want

of health and to the jealousy entertained of him at home.
...Yet the fault of over-caution, supported by old and general
opinion, better deserves forgiveness than that of self-willed
and lawless transgression" (Plutarch, *Lives*, Crassus and Nicias
Compared, penultimate paragraph).

When Longinus discusses Hyperboles in Section 38 of *A
Treatise Concerning Sublimity* he argues that "the best
hyperboles are those which are not noticed as hyperboles at
all." Then he gives as a striking example the sentence from
Thucydides (VII 68), describing the terrible grandeur of these
words: "For the Syracusans also came down and butchered
them, but especially those in the water, which was thus
immediately spoiled, but which they went on drinking just
the same, mud and all, bloody as it was, even fighting to have
it." "That blood and mud were drunk together, and yet were
things fought over, passes for credible in the intensity of the
feeling and in the crisis" (Trans. by A.O. Prickard).

In a sense the whole final description of the Sicilian
expedition is a consummate hyperbole. How could a man
who was not present paint such a picture without artistic
exaggeration and yet even if we are not to take the scenes
literally such is the imagery that we do believe what passes
before our eyes. We give ourselves utterly to the emotional
catharsis that Thucydides creates.

Sir Edward S. Creasy, writing in 1850, considered Syracuse
one of *The Fifteen Decisive Battles of the World*, as his
famous book is called. Chapter II goes into some detail that
cannot be found elsewhere. The arrival of the general
Demosthenes, for example, gave the troops under Nicias great
hope of a possible victory. Demosthenes did attempt to
recapture Epipolae and his new men had practically taken
over when a brigade of Boeotian allies "coolly and steadily...
formed their line, and, undismayed by the current of flight
around them, advanced against the advancing Athenians"
(Creasy, p. 54). The Athenians could not resist in time to
avoid a complete rout. This was the crisis of the battle; Nicias
was of no help. Soon he and Demosthenes were put to death.

It was the end of the Athenian empire — all brought on by the steadfast determination of a thousand or more well disciplined soldiers. This sentence from Creasy is worth repeating: "When once the tide was thus turned, the Syracusans passed rapidly from the extreme of panic to the extreme of vengeful daring, and with all their forces they now fiercely assailed the embarrassed and receding Athenians. ...All danger from Athens to the independent nations of the west was now for ever at an end" (Creasy, p. 55).

But for the pathos of defeat one should not fail to read the words of Thucydides himself in VIII 70-86: "They were beaten at all points and altogether; their sufferings in every way were great. They were totally destroyed — their fleet, their army, everything — and few out of many returned home. So ended the Sicilian expedition" (VIII 87).

§

[77]. Athenians and allies, even in our present position we must still hope on, since men have ere now been saved from worse straits than this; and you must not condemn yourselves too severely either because of your disasters or because of your present unmerited sufferings. I myself who am not superior to any of you in strength — indeed you see how I am in my sickness — and who in the gifts of fortune am, I think, whether in private life or otherwise, the equal of any, am now exposed to the same danger as the meanest among you; and yet my life has been one of much devotion towards the gods, and of much justice and without offence towards men. I have, therefore, still a strong hope for the future, and our misfortunes do not terrify me as much as they might. Indeed we may hope that they will be lightened: our enemies have had good fortune enough; and if any of the gods was offended at our expedition, we have been already amply punished. Others before us have attacked their neighbours and have done what men will do without suffering more than they could bear; and we may now justly expect to find the gods more kind, for we have become fitter objects for their pity than their jealousy. And then look at yourselves, mark the numbers and efficiency of the heavy infantry marching in your ranks, and do not give way too much to despondency, but reflect that you are

yourselves at once a city wherever you sit down, and that there is no other in Sicily that could easily resist your attack, or expel you when once established. The safety and order of the march is for yourselves to look to; the one thought of each man being that the spot on which he may be forced to fight must be conquered and held as his country and stronghold. Meanwhile we shall hasten on our way night and day alike, as our provisions are scanty; and if we can reach some friendly place of the Sicels, whom fear of the Syracusans still keeps true to us, you may forthwith consider yourselves safe. A message has been sent on to them with directions to meet us with supplies of food. To sum up, be convinced, soldiers, that you must be brave, as there is no place near for your cowardice to take refuge in, and that if you now escape from the enemy, you may all see again what your hearts desire, while those of you who are Athenians will raise up again the great power of the state, fallen though it be. Men make the city and not walls or ships without men in them.

§

Appendices

A
The Speeches of Thucydides
(Sir Richard C. Jebb)

B
Intellectual Background
(John H. Finley, Jr.)

C
A Chronology of Principal Events

D
A List of References

E
Maps

Appendix A
The Speeches of Thucydides[1]*
Sir Richard C. Jebb

§ 1. THE famous phrase in which Thucydides claims a lasting value for his work has had the fate of many striking expressions : it is often quoted apart from the words which explain it. " A possession for ever," not " the rhetorical triumph of an hour ": taken by itself this has a ring of exultation, noble perhaps, yet personal, as if the grave self-mastery of the historian had permitted this one utterance in the tone of the Roman poet's confident retrospect or the English poet's loftier hope, speaking of a monument more enduring than brass, of things so written that men should not willingly let them die. It is the context that reduces the meaning to a passionless precision. " The absence of fable in the History," he says, " will perhaps make it less attractive to hearers ; but it will be enough if it is found profitable by those who desire an exact knowledge of the past as a key to the future, which in all human probability will repeat or resemble the past. The work is meant to be a possession for ever, not

---

[1] A table of the Speeches will be found at the end of the Essay.

* Reprinted from *Hellenica, A collection of Essays on Greek Poetry, Philosophy, History, and Religion ; Edited by Evelyn Abbott* (Rivingtons 1880).

the rhetorical triumph of an hour[1]." That the
intention of Thucydides has been fulfilled in his own
sense is due largely to the speeches which form
between a fourth and fifth of the whole work. It is
chiefly by these that the facts of the Peloponnesian
war are transformed into typical examples of
universal laws and illuminated with a practical
significance for the students of politics in every age
and country. The scope of the speeches is seen
best if we consider what the History would be without them. The narrative would remain, with a few
brief comments on great characters or events, and
those two passages in which Thucydides describes
the moral effects of pestilence and of party-strife.
But there would be little or no light on the inner
workings of the Greek political mind, on the courses
of reasoning which determined the action, on the
whole play of feeling and opinion which lay behind
the facts.

§ 2. The introduction of speeches became a
regular part of ancient historiography, and came in
again at the revival of literature, not quite going
out, in Italy and France at least, till the end of the
last century. But the followers of Thucydides were
obeying an established tradition ; he was the writer
who had done most to establish it ; indeed, he might
properly be called its founder. The place of the

---

[1] i. 22. The τε after κτῆμα in the original marks the connection of the thought: "and *so.*" Cp. i. 4, Μίνως . . . ἐκράτησε
. . . τό τε λῃστικόν, ὡς εἰκός, καθῄρει: so 5, τό τε σιδηροφορεῖσθαι:
6, ἐγυμνώθησάν τε : 9, Ἀγαμέμνων τε.

speeches in his design was due to special influences of the age as well as to the peculiar bent of his mind ; we have to consider what had been done before him, and the plan on which he went to work. At the beginning of the Peloponnesian war a Greek prose literature scarcely yet existed. The Ionian prose-writers before Herodotus, or contemporary with him, are known to us only from scanty fragments. But the Augustan age possessed all, or nearly all, their writings ; and Dionysius of Halicarnassus has described their general characteristics, comparing them collectively with Herodotus and Thucydides¹. These Ionian writers, he says, treat the annals of cities and people separately²,— not combining them into a large picture, as Herodotus does. Their common object was to diffuse a knowledge of the legends which lived in oral tradition (ὅσαι διεσώζοντο μνῆμαι), and of the written records (γραφαί) preserved in temples or state-

---

¹ Dionys. *de Thuc.* c. 5. Dionysius concedes the more dignified name of συγγραφεῖς to the Ionian logographers. He names, (1) as anterior to the age of Thucydides,—Eugaeon of Samos, Deiochos of Proconnesos, Eudemos of Paros, Democles of Phigaleia, Hecataeus of Miletus, Acusilaus of Argos, Charon of Lampsacus, Amelesagoras of Chalcedon; (2) as elder contemporaries of Thucydides,—Hellanicus of Lesbos, Damastes of Sigeion, Xenomedes of Chios, Xanthos of Lydia. His words imply that these, "and many more" (ἄλλοι συχνοί), were then extant.

² *Ib.* οὐ συνάπτοντες ἀλλήλαις (τὰς ἱστορίας), ἀλλὰ κατ' ἔθνη καὶ κατὰ πόλεις διαιροῦντες: whereas Herodotus is said πολλὰς καὶ διαφόρους πράξεις ἐς μίαν περιγραφὴν πραγματείας ἀγαγεῖν.

archives ; and to publish these "such as they received them," without adding anything, and on the other hand without omitting "myths" and "theatrical episodes" which appear childish to a more critical age[1]. As to style, it is much the same for all of them,—plain, concise, "strictly to the point[2]," without artificial display ; but with a certain freshness, he adds, and some degree of charm, which has been the secret of their survival. The meagre fragments which remain, such as those of Xanthus and Charon, Hecataeus and Hellanicus, consist chiefly of short, jerky sentences, strung together in the baldest possible fashion[3]. If these Ionian writers introduced dialogues or speeches—as the example of

---

[1] Dionys. *de Thuc.* c. 5, ἐν αἷς καὶ μῦθοί τινες ἐνῆσαν ὑπὸ τοῦ πολλοῦ πεπιστευμένοι χρόνου (cp. Thuc. i. 21, of the stories told by the logographers, ὑπὸ χρόνου ... ἐπὶ τὸ μυθῶδες ἐκνενικηκότα) καὶ θεατρικαί τινες περιπέτειαι, πολὺ τὸ ἠλίθιον ἔχειν τοῖς νῦν δοκοῦσαι.

[2] *Ib.* τοῖς πράγμασι προσφυῆ. In Herodotus (i. 27, etc.) προσφυέως λέγειν is simply "to speak pertinently." But the phrase of Dionysius seems to mean, not merely "adapted to the subject," but *closely adhering to the facts of the story* (whether mythical or not), without attempt at *verbal* embellishment. It is illustrated by the dry and absolutely matter-of-fact style of the extant fragments.

[3] Müller, *Fragm. Histor. Graec.* i. 1—68. The longest fragment of Hecataeus may serve as a specimen :—"Orestheus, son of Deucalion, arrived in Aetolia in search of a kingdom ; and a dog produced him a green plant ; and he ordered the dog to be buried in the earth ; and from it sprang a vine fertile in grapes. Wherefore he called his son Phytius. Now the son of Phytius was Oeneus, so named after the vine-plant; for the ancient Greeks called the vine Oena: and the son of Oeneus was Aetolus." (*Frag.* 341, p. 26.)

the epic poets might have led them to do—it may
be conjectured that these were of the simplest kind.
There is one, indeed, who has left proof that he
could write dialogue with the ease and grace of
Herodotus himself[1]. But Ion of Chios was a poet
as well as a chronicler; he knew the Athens of
Pericles; and his memoirs, with their sprightly
gossip, must have been very unlike the normal type
of Ionian chronicle.

Herodotus is distinguished from his predecessors,
first of all, by an epic unity of plan. It is hard to
say exactly how far he was superior to them in his
method of verifying facts; his diligence and his
honesty are both unquestionable, and we know that
he attempted—not very scientifically, perhaps—to
decide between conflicting versions of the same
story. But in the dramatic element of his narrative
he shows the true freedom of an epic poet. In his
History, as in the *Iliad* and the *Odyssey*, the author
seldom speaks when there is a fair pretext for
making the characters speak. The habitual use of
"direct speech," or easy dialogue, is evidently a
different thing from the insertion of set speeches:
there is nothing necessarily rhetorical about it. It is
merely the vivid way of describing thought and
motive, the way natural to a simple age; and in the

---

[1] The story of the poet Sophocles defending the phrase ἐπὶ
πορφυρέαις παρῆσιν against the criticisms of a learned guest at a
supper-party in Chios. (Müller, *Fragm. Hist.* vol. ii. p. 46.) The
Ἐπιδημίαι, in which it occurred, seem to have been Ion's account
of his own "visits" to Athens and other cities. (*Ibid.* p. 45.)

case of a work meant to be heard rather than to be read, like the early Greek prose works, it has the obvious recommendation of helping to keep the attention alive. Even the longer speeches in Herodotus have usually the conversational tone rather than the rhetorical[1]. On the other hand, there are a few which may be considered as properly rhetorical, that is, as efforts by Herodotus to work up a vague tradition in the most effective form. The debate in the Persian cabinet on the invasion of Greece[2] is a case in point. The speeches of Xerxes, Mardonius, and Artabanus have been carefully elaborated, and have the elementary dramatic merit of expressing views which Persian speakers could conceivably have taken. Another example is the debate of the Persian conspirators after the death of the false Smerdis. Otanes argues for democracy,

---

[1] *E.g.* the speech in which Aristagoras of Miletus appeals for aid to Cleomenes, king of Sparta (Herod. v. 49), and that of Sosicles at Sparta (v. 92), which is simply a plain sketch of the Corinthian tyrannies, put into the mouth of a Corinthian speaker.

[2] Her. vii. 8—11. The council is called σύλλογος ἐπίκλητος Περσέων τῶν ἀρίστων: as in viii. 101 Xerxes ἐβουλεύετο ἅμα Περσέων τοῖσι ἐπικλήτοισι: *i.e.* with his "privy-councillors." Later writers went at least as far as Herodotus in reporting speeches made on occasions which presuppose privacy; as when Dionysius, Livy, and Plutarch give the expostulations of Veturia (or Volumnia) with Coriolanus,—when Sallust is present in imagination at a debate of Catiline's conspirators,—or when Livy transcribes the brilliant, but domestic, remonstrances of Pacuvius Calavius with his son Perolla, offered with a view of dissuading the young man from murdering Hannibal at Capua. Thucydides never violates dramatic probability in this particular way.

Megabyzus for oligarchy, Darius for monarchy ; but here the points of view seem purely Hellenic[1]. Herodotus prefaces his report of the discussion by saying, " Speeches were made which some of the Greeks refuse to credit; but made they were[2] ": and elsewhere[3] he remarks with triumph that " those Greeks who do not believe" in Otanes having advocated democracy will be surprised to hear that Mardonius established democracies in the Ionian cities. The ground of this dramatic episode, then, was a story current among the Greeks of Ionia, but rejected by some of them as manifestly inconsistent with Persian ideas. The spirit of rhetorical dialectic may be traced again very clearly in the conversation between Solon and Croesus, where Solon refines on the distinction between wealth, good fortune, and happiness[4]. Still, it cannot be said that Herodotus

[1] Her. iii. 80—82. Similarly in Her. iii. 36 the Lydian Croesus utters Hellenic thoughts.

[2] Her. iii. 80, ἐλέχθησαν λόγοι ἄπιστοι μὲν ἐνίοισι Ἑλλήνων, ἐλέχθησαν δ' ὦν.

[3] Her. vi. 43, ἐνθαῦτα μέγιστον θῶυμα ἐρέω τοῖσι μὴ ἀποδεκομένοισι Ἑλλήνων Περσέων τοῖσι ἑπτὰ Ὀτάνεα γνώμην ἀποδέξασθαι, ὡς χρεὼν εἴη δημοκρατέεσθαι Πέρσας: where μὴ ἀποδεκομένοισι implies more than μὴ πιστεύουσι would have implied,—viz. that the statement was offered for acceptance, not simply by Herodotus himself, but by a widely-spread rumour.

[4] Her. i. 32. The question of Croesus to Solon had been— τίνα ἤδη πάντων εἶδες ὀλβιώτατον; Solon answers, in effect, that πλοῦτος is certainly an element of ὄλβος, but that complete ὄλβος requires εὐτυχία also, and that a man's life cannot be called εὐτυχής unreservedly until we have seen it to the end. Dean Blakesley observes (on Her. i. 32), that this " might have proceeded from the mouth of Protagoras, or Hippias, or any other of the μεριμνηταὶ

had much love for set rhetorical display : his taste
was for conversation—lively, ingenious, argumenta-
tive it might be, but still mainly in the colloquial
key¹. A good instance of the way in which he
passes by an opportunity for oratory is his brief
notice of the speech made by Themistocles just
before the battle of Salamis² : " His theme was the
contrast between all that is worthy and all that is
base. He exhorted them to choose the better part
in all that men's nature and condition permit ; and
then, having wound up his discourse, he ordered
them to embark." The true rhetorician would have
developed the topic which Herodotus barely in-
dicates³. It may be noticed, too, that the ornament

λόγων alluded to by Euripides " (in *Medea* 1225 f.). If it has not
the matured subtlety of the rhetorical dialectic, it may certainly
be said to anticipate its spirit.

¹ Dionysius says most truly of Herodotus that he has almost
all the excellences of style except the ἐναγώνιοι ἀρεταί—the
combative excellences,—such as were afterwards developed by
strenuous controversy, political or forensic. οὐδὲ γὰρ δημηγορίαις
πολλαῖς ὁ ἀνὴρ οὐδ' ἐναγωνίοις κέχρηται λόγοις, οὐδ' ἐν τῷ παθαίνειν
καὶ δεινοποιεῖν τὰ πράγματα τὴν ἀλκὴν ἔχει (*de Thuc.* c. 23).

² Her. viii. 83, τὰ δὲ ἔπεα ἦν πάντα κρέσσω τοῖσι ἕσσοσι ἀντιτι-
θέμενα. ὅσα δὲ ἐν ἀνθρώπου φύσι καὶ καταστάσι ἐγγίνεται, παραινέσας
δὴ τούτων τὰ κρέσσω αἱρέεσθαι καὶ καταπλέξας τὴν ῥῆσιν ἐσβαίνειν
ἐκέλευε ἐς τὰς νῆας.

³ Cp. Plato, *Hippias Major*, p. 286, where the sophist Hippias
tells Socrates that he has composed " an admirable discourse " on
the theme of a question supposed to be put by Neoptolemus to
Nestor after the taking of Troy—What are καλὰ ἐπιτηδεύματα?
The phrase of Herodotus, καταπλέξας τὴν ῥῆσιν, reminds us of the
tone in which the speakers of Thucydides sometimes decline to
develop commonplaces.

of the speeches in Herodotus is sometimes distinctly
Homeric—illustrating his nearer affinity to epos
than to rhetoric. Thus the Corinthian Sosicles, in
the debate at Sparta, begins with truly epic force :
" Verily now the sky shall be under the earth, and
the earth shall hang above the sky, men shall have
their pastures in the sea, and fish upon land," if
Spartans become the friends of tyranny¹.

§ 3. Thucydides has stated the general principles on which he composed the speeches in his
History. The precise interpretation of that statement depends, however, partly on the question—
How far is it probable that Thucydides is there
instituting a tacit comparison between his own
method and that of Herodotus? So far as we know,
the work of Herodotus was the only prose work in
which Thucydides could have found a precedent for
dramatic treatment applied to history. If Thucydides
knew that work, it would naturally be present to his
mind at the moment when he was stating the rules
of his own practice. It can be shown almost
certainly that a period of at least twenty years must
have elapsed between the time at which Herodotus
ceased to write and the time at which the History of

¹ Her. v. 92, ἦ δὴ ὅ τε οὐρανὸς ἔσται ἔνερθε τῆς γῆς καὶ ἡ γῆ
μετέωρος ὑπὲρ τοῦ οὐρανοῦ καὶ οἱ ἄνθρωποι νομὸν ἐν θαλάσσῃ ἕξουσι
καὶ οἱ ἰχθύες τὸν πρότερον ἄνθρωποι, ὅτε γε ὑμεῖς, ὦ Λακεδαιμόνιοι,
ἰσοκρατίας καταλύοντες τυραννίδας ἐς τὰς πόλις κατάγειν παρασκευά-
ζεσθε. Compare the epic phrase which closes the spirited oration
of Dareius in the debate of the conspirators—οὐ γὰρ ἄμεινον
(Her. iii. 83; *Iliad* xxiv. 52, οὐ μήν οἱ τό γε κάλλιον οὐδέ τ' ἄμεινον,
etc.).

Thucydides received the form in which it has come down to us[1]. It was possible, then, for Thucydides to know the work of Herodotus; that he actually knew it, and that he pointedly alludes to it in

[1] Herodotus alludes to no event later than 425 B.C., the latest mark of time being a *doubtful* reference to the death of Artaxerxes in 425 (vi. 98). And there are instances in which his silence affords presumptive proof that later events were unknown to him. (1) In 437 B.C. Athenian colonists founded a city on the spot formerly called Ennea Hodoi, and their leader Hagnon named it Amphipolis, because the Strymon flowed on both sides of it. Herodotus mentions Ennea Hodoi (vii. 114), but nowhere speaks of Amphipolis. Had he been writing after the new colony had become important, he would naturally have mentioned it in this connection; he could scarcely have failed to do so after the battle of Amphipolis in 422 B.C. had made the place famous. (2) Demaratus tells Xerxes that Spartans never yield: it is their fixed law to conquer or die (Her. vii. 104; cf. 209). This passage would have been singularly infelicitous if it had been written after the surrender of the Lacedaemonians at Pylos in 425 B.C., when 120 Spartan prisoners were brought to Athens; an event which, as Thucydides expressly says (iv. 40), astounded the Greeks, precisely because their belief had been that which Herodotus expresses. (3) Demaratus advises Xerxes to detach 200 ships from his fleet, for the purpose of occupying the island of Cythera, and quotes the saying of Cheilon, that it would be well for Sparta if Cythera were sunk in the sea (Her. vii. 235). Xerxes neglected the advice. But in 424 B.C. the Athenians actually occupied Cythera, and the damage thence inflicted on Laconia was one of the causes which disposed the Spartans to conclude peace. Herodotus would not have omitted, if he had known, so forcible an illustration of Cheilon's saying. And there are indications that Herodotus did not live to give the last touches to his work: thus a promise made in vii. 213 is left unfulfilled. [The revolt of the Medes "from Dareius" (Her. i. 130), which Dahlmann identified with the revolt of 408 B.C. (Xen. *H.* i. 2. 19), has been shown

several places, cannot be doubted by any one who weighs the whole evidence[1].

In the view of Thucydides there had hitherto been two classes of writers concerned with the

by the Behistun inscription to belong to the reign of Dareius Hystaspes.]

F. W. Ullrich (*Beiträge zur Erklärung des Thukydides;* Hamburg, 1846) has ingeniously argued that Thucydides composed his first three Books, and Book iv. as far as ch. 48, in exile (about 421–413 B.C.); and the rest of the work, as a continuation, after the final close of the war. This view rests mainly on the alleged existence of passages in Books i.—iv. 48 which imply ignorance of later events. Classen has examined these passages in detail (*Einleitung,* xxxii.—liv.), and has, I think, shown that they are insufficient to support the theory built upon them. My opinion has not been altered by reading a learned essay in favour of Ullrich's hypothesis, which has appeared since Classen's Introduction was published (*Ueber die successive Entstehung des Thucydideischen Geschichtswerkes,* by Julius Helmbold; Colmar, 1876). But for the present purpose it is enough to assume, what even the supporters of Ullrich's view would allow, viz. that the whole work was at least revised by Thucydides after the end of the war. (See Thuc. i. 13. 18; ii. 65.) The probable influence of Herodotus is here being estimated in relation to those parts of the work of Thucydides which would have been the last to receive his finishing touches—the speeches.

[1] That Thucydides knew the work of Herodotus is assumed by Lucian (*de cons. hist.* § 42), Marcellinus (*vit. Thuc.* 54), Suidas s. v. ὀργᾶν), Photius (*cod.* 60), and the Scholiast on Thuc. i. 22, etc. In modern times it has been denied or questioned by F. C. Dahlmann (*Herodot.* p. 214), K. O. Müller (*Hist. Gk. Lit.* c. xxxiv. § 2, and *Dorians,* ii. 98, § 2), by J. C. F. Bähr (in his edition of Herodotus), and in an essay *De plurimis Thuc. Herodotique locis,* by H. Fütterer (Heiligenstadt, 1843). The proofs that Thucydides knew the works of Herodotus have been brought together by Mure (*Hist.*

recording of events. First, there were the poets, especially the epic poets, of whom Homer is the type, whose characteristic tendency, in the eyes of Thucydides, is to exaggerate the greatness or splendour of things past[1]. Secondly, there were the prose writers whom he calls chroniclers (λογογράφοι); and these he characterises by saying that they

Gk. Lit. Bk. iv. ch. 8), and more recently by H. Lemcke, in an essay entitled *Hat Thuc. das Werk des Herod. gekannt?* (Stettin, 1873). The crucial texts are (1) Thuc. i. 20, on the common errors regarding the vote of the Spartan kings and the Pitanate company, compared with Her. vi. 57 and ix. 53 ; (2) Thuc. ii. 97, on the Thracians and Scythians—tacitly correcting what Herodotus says of the Thracians (v. 3) and of the Scythians (iv. 46); (3) Thuc. i. 126, on Cylon's conspiracy, compared with Her. v. 71 ; Thuc. vi. 4 on Zankle (Messene) compared with Her. vi. 23 ; Thuc. ii. 8, on the earthquake at Delos (cf. i. 23) compared with Her. vi. 98. In view of all these passages, it seems impossible to doubt that in i. 97 Thucydides includes or specially designates Herodotus among those who ἢ τὰ πρὸ τῶν Μηδικῶν Ἑλληνικὰ ξυνετίθεσαν ἢ αὐτὰ τὰ Μηδικά.

I must add a word on the vexed interpretation of Her. vi. 57, τοὺς μάλιστά σφι τῶν γερόντων προσήκοντας ἔχειν τὰ τῶν βασιλέων γέρεα, δύο ψήφους τιθεμένους, τρίτην δὲ τὴν ἑωυτῶν. The question is, Does Herodotus mean τιθεμένους δύο ψήφους ἑκάτερον, τρίτην δὲ τὴν ἑωυτοῦ? Shilleto (Thuc. i. 20) thinks that this is not *certain*, suggesting that τοὺς προσήκοντας might mean τὸν ἀεὶ προσήκοντα, and comparing Her. iv. 62, τοῖσδε = τῷ ἐν ἑκάστῳ ἀρχηίῳ, but he sees the difficulty of supposing the same person to be nearest of kin to both kings. Failing this resource, we must surely allow that Herodotus means δύο ψήφους ἑκάτερον, for else how could he possibly have written τρίτην δὲ τὴν ἑωυτῶν? Would he not have written δευτέρας δὲ τὰς ἑωυτῶν?

[1] Thuc. i. 10, εἰκὸς ἐπὶ τὸ μεῖζον μὲν ποιητὴν ὄντα κοσμῆσαι: 21, ὡς ποιηταὶ ὑμνήκασιν ἐπὶ τὸ μεῖζον κοσμοῦντες.

"compiled[1]" their works with a view to attracting
audiences at a recitation, rather than to truth ; dealing largely, as they did, with traditions which could
no longer be verified, but had passed into the region
of myth. Now with such chroniclers Herodotus
was undoubtedly classed by Thucydides. The traits
common to Herodotus and the other chroniclers, as
Thucydides viewed them, were (1) the omission of
really accurate research—the tendency to take what
lay ready to the writer's hand ($\tau\grave{a}$ $\acute{\epsilon}\tau o\hat{\iota}\mu a$, i. 20) ;
(2) the mixture of a fabulous element with history ;
(3) the pursuit of effect in the first place, and of
truth only in the second. Probably Thucydides
would have said that Herodotus was more critically
painstaking and less indiscriminately tolerant of
fable than most of the other chroniclers, but that
his study of effect was more systematic and more
ambitious. The imaginary dialogues and speeches
in Herodotus would be the most conspicuous illustrations of this desire for effect. If they were not
absolute novelties in the chronicler's art, at least we
may be sure that they had never before been used in
such large measure, or with such success.

The first aim of Thucydides in his introduction
is to show that the Peloponnesian war is more
important than any event of which the Greeks have
record. He then states the principles on which his
History of the War has been composed. "As to
the various speeches made on the eve of the war, or

---

[1] Thuc. i. 21, $\xi\upsilon\nu\acute{\epsilon}\theta\epsilon\sigma a\nu$, as again 97, $\xi\upsilon\nu\epsilon\tau\acute{\iota}\theta\epsilon\sigma a\nu$, implying a
process more external and mechanical than $\xi\upsilon\gamma\gamma\rho\acute{a}\phi\epsilon\iota\nu$.

in its course, I have found it difficult to retain a memory of the precise words which I had heard spoken; and so it was with those who brought me reports. But I have made the persons say what it seemed to me most opportune for them to say in view of each situation; at the same time, I have adhered as closely as possible to the general sense of what was actually said. As to the deeds done in the war, I have not thought myself at liberty to record them on hearsay from the first informant, or on arbitrary conjecture. My account rests either on personal knowledge, or on the closest possible scrutiny of each statement made by others. The process of research was laborious, because conflicting accounts were given by those who had witnessed the several events, as partiality swayed or memory served them[1]."

The phenomena of the war, then, as materials for history, are classed by Thucydides under two heads —λόγοι, things said, and ἔργα, things done. These are the two elements of human agency[2]. As regards the ἔργα, the deeds, he is evidently contrasting his own practice with that of the chroniclers generally. He has not taken his facts, as they did, without careful sifting (ἀβασανίστως): he had formed a higher conception of his task (ἠξίωσα). In regard

---

[1] Thuc. i. 22.

[2] Shilleto remarks (on i. 21 § 2): "τὰ δ' ἔργα τῶν πραχθέντων is a somewhat bold expression for τὰ δ' ἔργα τὰ πραχθέντα." It may be added that the phrase has the special effect of bringing out the antithesis between *facts of speech* and *facts of action*.

to the words, the λόγοι, he is tacitly contrasting his own practice with that of Herodotus, the only conspicuous example in this department. If his statement were developed in this light, it might be paraphrased thus :—Thucydides says : (1) I have not introduced a speech except when I had reason to know that a speech was actually made : unlike Herodotus, when he reports the conversation between Croesus and Solon, the debate of the Persian conspirators, the discussion in the cabinet of Xerxes. (2) I do not pretend to give the exact form of the speeches made : as a writer implies that he does when, without warning the reader, he introduces a speech with the formula, "He said these things" (ἔλεγε τάδε)[1], instead of "He spoke to this effect" (ἔλεγε τοιάδε). (3) On the other hand, I have faithfully reproduced the speaker's general line of argument, the purport and substance of his speech, so far as it could be ascertained. Herodotus disregards this principle when he makes Otanes,

---

[1] Cp. Her. iii. 80, where the speeches of Otanes, Megabyzus and Dareius are introduced by λέγων τάδε . . . λέγων τάδε . . . ἔλεξε τάδε: so v. 91, ἔλεγον τάδε . . . εἶπον ταῦτα: 92, ἔλεξε τάδε (Sosicles): vii. 8, ἔλεξε Ξέρξης τάδε : and so usually. Thucydides nearly always has ἔλεξαν or ἔλεγον τοιάδε, with τοιαῦτα (or τοσαῦτα) at the end. In i. 85 (of Sthenelaidas), ἔλεξεν ὧδε ("in this manner," not = τάδε). In i. 58 the speech of Hermocrates is introduced by τοιούτους δὴ λόγους εἶπεν, where δή appears to mean "as we may presume"; i.e. he spoke "to this general effect"—the phrase intimating somewhat more plainly than the usual τοιάδε that Thucydides had only a very general notion of the ξύμπασα γνώμη.

Megabyzus and Dareius support democracy, oligarchy and monarchy by arguments which no Persian could have used. And in filling up such outlines, my aim has been to make the speaker say what, under the circumstances, seemed most opportune (τὰ δέοντα μάλιστα).

The last phrase is noticeable as marking a limit of dramatic purpose. According to the regular usage of the words[1] (τὰ δέοντα) in Thucydides, it can mean only " what the occasion required "—not necessarily what was most suitable to the character of the speaker. The latter idea would have been expressed by a different phrase (τὰ προσήκοντα). That is, in filling up the framework supplied by the reported "general sense" of a speech, Thucydides has freely exercised his own judgment on the situation. Suppose a report to have reached him in this shape : " Hermocrates spoke in the congress at Gela, urging the Sicilian cities to lay aside their feuds and unite against Athens." In composing on this theme, the first thought of Thucydides would be, " What were the best arguments available ? " rather than, " What arguments would Hermocrates have used ? " This general rule would, of course, be liable to various degrees of modification in cases where the speaker was well known to the historian as having marked traits of character, opinion or style.

---

[1] Thuc. i. 70, τὸ τὰ δέοντα πρᾶξαι : 138, αὐτοσχεδιάζειν τὰ δέοντα : ii. 43, γιγνώσκοντες τὰ δέοντα : ii. 60, γνῶναί τε τὰ δέοντα καὶ ἑρμηνεῦσαι ταῦτα.

§ 4. "Set speeches," says Voltaire, "are a sort of oratorical lie, which the historian used to allow himself in old times. He used to make his heroes say what they might have said....At the present day these fictions are no longer tolerated. If one put into the mouth of a prince a speech which he had never made, the historian would be regarded as a rhetorician[1]." How did it happen that Thucydides allowed himself this "oratorical lie,"—Thucydides, whose strongest characteristic is devotion to the truth, impatience of every inroad which fiction makes into the province of history, laborious persistence in the task of separating fact from fable; Thucydides, who was not constrained, like later writers of the old world, by an established literary tradition; who had no Greek predecessors in the field of history, except those chroniclers whom he despised precisely because they sacrificed truth to effect? Thucydides might rather have been expected to express himself on this wise: "The chroniclers have sometimes pleased their hearers by reporting the very words spoken. But, as I could not give the words, I have been content to give the substance, when I could learn it."

In order to find the point of view at which Thucydides stood, we must remember, first of all, the power which epic poetry had then for centuries exercised over the Greek mind. The same love of the concrete and comprehensible which moved the early Greeks to clothe abstract conceptions of a

---

[1] Preface to the *Hist. of Russia*, § 7.

superhuman power in the forms of men and women, "strangers to death and old age for ever," led them also to represent the energy of the human spirit as much as possible in the form of speech. The Homeric ideal of excellence is the man of brave deeds and wise words. The Homeric debates are not merely brilliant, but also thoroughly dramatic in their way of characterising the speakers[1]. The *Iliad* and *Odyssey* accustomed the Greeks to expect two elements in every vivid presentation of an action —first, the proofs of bodily prowess, the account of what men did; and then, as the image of their minds, a report of what they said. Political causes strengthened this feeling. Public speech played a much larger part in the affairs of States than it now does. Envoys spoke before an assembly or a council on business which would now be transacted by the written correspondence of statesmen or diplomatists. Every adult citizen of a Greek democracy had his vote in the assembly which finally decided great issues. To such a citizen the written history of political events would appear strangely insipid if it did not give at least some image of those debates which imparted the chief zest to civic life and by which political events were chiefly controlled. He was one who (in modern

---

[1] Sir G. C. Lewis, in illustrating this point, instances the embassies from Corcyra and Corinth to Athens (Thuc. i. 68), from Mitylene to Olympia (iii. 9), and from the Athenians and Syracusans to Camarina (vi. 76). (*Methods of Observation and Reasoning in Politics*, vol. i. p. 232.)

phrase) had held a safe seat in Parliament from the time when he came of age; who had lived in the atmosphere of political debate until it had become to him an almost indispensable excitement; and who would feel comparatively little interest in hearing the result of a Parliamentary division unless he was enabled to form some idea of the process by which the result had been reached. Such a man would not have been satisfied with the meagre information that the Athenian Ecclesia had discussed the fate of Mitylene, that Cleon had advocated a massacre, that Diodotus had opposed it, and that the view of Diodotus had prevailed by a narrow majority. His imagination would at once transport him to the scene of the parliamentary combat. He would listen in fancy, as he had so often listened in reality, to the eloquence of antagonistic orators, he would balance the possible arguments for severity or clemency, he would conceive himself present at the moment when one uplifted hand might incline the scale of life or death, and he would feel the thrill of relief with which those who supported Diodotus found that Athens was saved at the eleventh hour—saved, if the bearers of the respite, rowing night and day, could reach Lesbos in time—from the infamy of devoting a population to the sword. When Thucydides gave in full the speeches made by Cleon and Diodotus, he was helping his reader, the average citizen of a Greek republic, to do on more accurate lines that which the reader would otherwise have tried to do for himself. Thucydides was

writing for men who knew Greek politics from
within, and he knew that, if they were to follow him
with satisfied attention, he must place them at their
accustomed point of view.   The literary influences
of the age set in the same direction.   At the beginning of the war the Attic drama had been in vigour for
more than forty years.   The fame of Aeschylus was
a youthful memory to men who had passed middle
life ; Sophocles was sixty-four, Euripides was forty-
nine.   Each had given great works to Athens, and
was yet to give more.   An age of vivid energy had
found the poetry most congenial to it in the noblest
type of tragedy, and this, in turn, fed the Greek
desire to know character through deed and word.
In the hands of Euripides tragedy further became
the vehicle of dialectical subtleties and the dramatic
mirror of public debate.   At the same time Attic
oratory was being prepared by two currents of
influence which converged on Athens—the practical
culture of Ionia, represented by the Sophists, and
the Sicilian art of rhetoric[1].

§ 5.   If the speeches in Thucydides were brought
under a technical classification, the Funeral Oration
would be the only example of the "panegyrical" or
epideictic class ; the pleading of the Plataeans and
Thebans before the Spartan Commissioners might
possibly be called "forensic"; and all the other

---

[1] The early history of Greek oratory, and the various influences
which contributed to mould it during the fifth century B.C., have
been traced by the writer in the *Attic Orators from Antiphon to
Isaeos*, vol. i. Introduction, pp. xciii—cxxxvii.

speeches would be in some sense "deliberative[1]."
But such a classification, besides being rather forced,
does not correspond to any real differences of
structure or form. If the speeches are to be viewed
in their literary relation to the History, it is enough
to observe that the addresses of leaders to their
troops may be regarded as practically forming a
class apart[2].

The right of an adult citizen to attend the
debates of the Ecclesia must have been acquired by
Thucydides many years[3] before the war began.
From its very commencement, as he says, he had
formed the purpose of writing its history. There is
every probability that he had heard most or all of
the important discussions which took place in the
Ecclesia between 433 and 424 B.C. It was in
423 B.C., or at the end of the year before, that his
exile of twenty years from Athens began. Thence
we can name some at least of the speeches to which
he probably refers as heard by himself (αὐτὸς
ἤκουσα), and not merely reported to him. Such
would be the addresses of the Corcyrean and
Corinthian envoys, when they were rival suitors for
the Athenian alliance in 433 B.C.; the speeches of
Pericles; the debate on Mitylene in 427 B.C.; and

---

[1] *I.e.* in the largest sense of συμβουλευτικοί, under which the
addresses of leaders to troops would be included as προτρεπτικοί—
the speeches in political debate being δημηγορίαι in the proper
sense.

[2] See the table at the end; and below § 7.

[3] Probably from 451 B.C., if his birth may be placed in 471 B.C.
Cp. K. F. Hermann, *Antiq.* i. § 121; Xen. *Mem. Socr.* iii. 6. 1.

the speech of the Lacedaemonian envoys in 425 B.C., making overtures of peace to Athens. If he was not present on all these occasions, still, as a resident citizen, he would have exceptional facilities for obtaining a full and accurate account. Taking this group of speeches first, then, we may consider how far they are apparently historical in substance, or show traces of artificial treatment.

After giving the addresses of the envoys from Corcyra and Corinth in 433 B.C., Thucydides notices the course of the debate in the Ecclesia. Two sittings were held. At the first, he says, the Athenians inclined to the arguments of the Corcyreans, and were disposed to conclude an alliance both offensive and defensive; at the second they repented of this, but decided to conclude a defensive alliance. The considerations which prevailed with them were, that war was unavoidable in any case; that the Corcyrean navy must not be allowed to pass into the hands of the Corinthians; and that Corcyra was a useful station for coasting voyages[1]. These three arguments are just those on which the Corcyrean speech, as given by Thucydides, chiefly turns[2]. The circumstantial account of the debate in the Ecclesia cannot be treated as fictitious. Either, then, Thucydides has given the substance of the arguments really used by the Corcyreans, or he has ascribed to them arguments used on their side by Athenian speakers in the Ecclesia. Now the speech of the Corinthian envoys has at least one mark of

---

[1] Thuc. i. 44.   [2] i. 32—36.

substantial authenticity : the references to benefits conferred on Athens by Corinth in the matters of Samos and Aegina[1] would certainly have occurred to a Corinthian envoy more readily than to an Athenian writer. In both the Corcyrean and the Corinthian speech it seems probable that Thucydides has given the substance of what was really said, though he may have added touches from his recollections of the subsequent debate in the assembly. Similar is the case of the speech made by the Lacedaemonian envoys at Athens in 425 B.C.[2] The historian's comment on it is as follows : "The Lacedaemonians spoke at such length[3] [i.e. for Spartans], in the belief that the Athenians had previously desired a truce, and had been hindered only by Spartan opposition ; so that, when peace was offered, they would gladly accept it, and restore the men." This clearly implies that the speech ascribed to the envoys—which Thucydides may well have heard—is historical in substance.

The Thucydidean speeches of Pericles raise three distinct questions :—How far do they preserve the form and style of the statesman's oratory ? how far do they express the ruling ideas of his policy ? and how far do they severally represent what he said on the several occasions ?

---

[1] i. 42.   [2] Thuc. iv. 17—20.

[3] By τοσαῦτα in such a context Thucydides usually means "only thus much," as ii. 72, τοσαῦτα εἰπόντων Πλαταιῶν. But in iv. 21, τοσαῦτα εἶπον refers back to iv. 17 § 2, τοὺς δὲ λόγους μακροτέρους οὐ παρὰ τὸ εἰωθὸς μηκυνοῦμεν.

As Thucydides must have repeatedly heard Pericles[1]—whom he describes as the first of Athenians, most powerful in action and in speech[2],—it would be strange if he had not endeavoured to give at least some traits of the eloquence which so uniquely impressed contemporaries. Pericles is said to have left nothing written[3] : but Aristotle and Plutarch have preserved a few of the bold images or striking phrases which tradition attributed to him[4]. Several examples of such bold imagery occur in the Thucydidean speeches of Pericles[5], and it can hardly be doubted that they are phrases which have lived in the historian's memory. But the echo is not heard in single phrases only. Every reader of the

[1] See e.g. ii. 13, ἔλεγε δὲ καὶ ἄλλα οἷάπερ εἰώθει Περικλῆς.

[2] i. 139.

[3] Plutarch, Pericl. c. 8 : ἔγγραφον μὲν οὐδὲν ἀπολέλοιπε πλὴν τῶν ψηφισμάτων, ἀπομνημονεύεται δὲ ὀλίγα παντάπασιν.

[4] Arist. Rhet. iii. 10 § 7 : ὥσπερ Περικλῆς ἔφη τὴν νεότητα τὴν ἀπολομένην ἐν τῷ πολέμῳ οὕτως ἠφανίσθαι ἐκ τῆς πόλεως, ὥσπερ εἴ τις τὸ ἔαρ ἐκ τοῦ ἐνιαυτοῦ ἐξέλοι: ib. τὴν Αἴγιναν ἀφελεῖν ἐκέλευσε τὴν λήμην τοῦ Πειραιέως. Plut. Per. 8 § 5 quotes his saying, τὸν πόλεμον ἤδη καθορᾶν ἀπὸ Πελοποννήσου προσφερόμενον: and of those who fell at Samos, ἐγκωμιάζων ἐπὶ τοῦ βήματος ἀθανάτους ἔλεγε γεγονέναι καθάπερ τοὺς θεούς· οὐ γὰρ ἐκείνους αὐτοὺς ὁρῶμεν, ἀλλὰ ταῖς τιμαῖς ἃς ἔχουσι καὶ τοῖς ἀγαθοῖς ἃ παρέχουσιν ἀθανάτους εἶναι τεκμαιρόμεθα.

[5] E.g. ii. 43, τὸν ἀγήρων ἔπαινον κάλλιστον ἔρανον προϊέμενοι...: 41, μνημεῖα κακῶν κἀγαθῶν ἀίδια ξυγκατοικίσαντες...: 43, ἀνδρῶν ἐπιφανῶν πᾶσα γῆ τάφος..., and others passim in the ἐπιτάφιος : in ii. 62, κηπίον καὶ ἐγκαλλώπισμα πλούτου, and many more. Bold imagery of this kind was characteristic of the elder school of oratory, and generally of what Dionysius calls the αὐστηρὰ ἁρμονία: cp. Attic Orators, vol. i. p. 27.

Funeral Oration must be aware of a majesty in the rhythm of the whole, a certain union of impetuous movement with lofty grandeur, which Thucydides has given to Pericles alone. There is a large alloy, doubtless, of rhetorical ornament in the new manner of overstrained antithesis[1]: but the voice of the Olympian[2] Pericles is not wholly lost in it. There can be no question, again, that the speeches of Pericles in the Ecclesia accurately represent the characteristic features of his policy at the time[3]. But how far do they severally represent what Pericles said on the several occasions? Thucydides makes Pericles use different topics of encouragement at three successive stages.

In 432 B.C. Pericles emboldens the Athenians to

---

[1] The most glaring example is the reiterated contrast of "word" and "deed," which occurs some eighteen times in the Funeral Oration, and is parodied (as Mr H. M. Wilkins observes, *Introduction to the Speeches*, p. xxv) in the Platonic *Menexenus* [*Menex.* p. 236 D, Ἔργῳ μὲν ἡμῖν οἵδε ἔχουσι τὰ προσήκοντα σφίσιν αὐτοῖς, ὧν τυχόντες πορεύονται τὴν εἱμαρμένην πορείαν, προπεμφθέντες κοινῇ μὲν ὑπὸ τῆς πόλεως, ἰδίᾳ δὲ ὑπὸ τῶν οἰκείων · λόγῳ δὲ δή, κ.τ.λ. And immediately afterwards, ἔργων εὖ πραχθέντων . . . λόγῳ καλῶς ῥηθέντι.]

[2] Περικλῆς οὐλύμπιος, Ar. *Acharn.* 530. Eupolis notices the *rapidity*, the charm, and the *sting* of his eloquence (Δῆμοι, *Frag. Com.* i. 162); cp. *Attic Orators*, i. p. cxxx.

[3] Viz., to make no derogatory concessions, but to accept the war; to wage it, however, mainly on the defensive, allowing the enemy to ravage their lands, but guarding their possession of the city and the sea; to rely chiefly on their navy, and to retain a firm hold upon the allies, whose tribute gave the financial superiority to Athens.

reject the Peloponnesian demands by a general comparison of the resources and prospects on either side[1]. In 431 B.C., when Archidamus is about to invade Attica, Pericles repeats his former exhortations, but supplements them by a detailed exposition of Athenian resources, financial and military[2]. In 430 B.C., after the second invasion of Attica, when the land had been devastated and while the plague was raging, Pericles convened a special meeting of the Ecclesia[3], with the twofold purpose of reassuring his countrymen and of allaying their resentment against himself. "As to the prospects of the war, you may rest satisfied," he says, "with the arguments by which I have proved to you on many other occasions that you have no cause of uneasiness. But I must notice a special advantage which the scale of your empire confers,—one, I think, which has never occurred to you,—which I have not mentioned in addressing you before, and which I should not have noticed now—as the claim implied might seem too arrogant—did I not see you unreasonably dejected. You think that you rule your allies alone. I tell you that of the two fields open to human action, land and sea, the latter is under your absolute dominion, not merely to the extent of your actual empire, but as much further as you please. While you hold the sea in your present naval strength, you

---

[1] i. 140—144.　　　[2] ii. 13.

[3] ii. 59, ξύλλογον ποιήσας, i.e. ξύγκλητον ἐκκλησίαν, which Pericles could convene as one of the Ten Generals (ἔτι δ' ἐστρατήγει).

cannot be resisted by the Persian king, or by any nation on earth[1]." Thus, as the pressure on the Athenian spirit becomes more and more severe, the exhortations of Pericles go on from strength to strength, until, at the darkest hour of all, they culminate in a triumphant avowal that the naval empire of Athens is not relative but absolute, is not an empire over a limited confederacy but a boundless supremacy on the sea. If this ascending scale, so fitly graduated, was due to the invention or arrangement of Thucydides, it was a dramatic conception. But it seems more probable that the topics really used by Pericles on these three occasions were substantially those given by the historian. It is difficult otherwise to justify the emphatic clearness with which the special theme of the second speech is distinguished from that of the first, and that of the third, again, from both[2]. On the other hand, the first speech of Pericles betrays some remarkable traces of manipulation by the writer. Earlier in the same year the Corinthian envoy at the Peloponnesian congress had given several reasons for believing that the Peloponnesians were likely to prevail in the war. With help from the sacred treasuries of Delphi and Olympia, he had said, they might lure away the foreign seamen of Athens by offering

---

[1] ii. 62 § 2.

[2] Compare ii. 13 § 2, παρῄνει δὲ καὶ περὶ τῶν παρόντων ἅπερ καὶ πρότερον (referring to i. 140—144) . . . θαρσεῖν τε ἐκέλευε, κ.τ.λ. (introducing the special subject of the second speech), with ii. 62 § 1, introducing the special subject of the third.

higher pay. They could acquire naval skill by practice. And among the possibilities of the war he suggests the occupation of a fortress in the enemy's country[1]. The speech of Pericles answers these arguments point by point. But the correspondence is not merely in the topics. The very phrases of the Corinthian speech are repeated by Pericles in his reply[2]. Similar parallelisms may be traced between the Corinthian speech and that delivered by the Spartan Archidamus on the occasion of the former congress : one with which the Corinthians cannot be supposed to be acquainted in detail, since it was made to the Spartans only, after strangers had withdrawn[3]. The fact is that the eight[4] speeches recorded by Thucydides as delivered at Athens or Sparta before the commencement of the war form, for his purpose, a group by themselves. In these he has worked up the chief arguments and calculations which were current on either side. Collectively, they are his dramatic presentation of the motives at work, the grievances on each side, the hopes and fears, based on a comparison of resources, with

---

[1] i. 121 §§ 3—4; 122 § 1.

[2] Compare (1) Pericles, i. 143 § 1, εἴ τε καὶ κινήσαντες τῶν Ὀλυμπίασιν ἢ Δελφοῖς χρημάτων μισθῷ μείζονι . . . ὑπολαβεῖν τοὺς ξένους τῶν ναυτῶν, with the Corinthian speech, i. 121 § 3, ἀπὸ τῶν ἐν Δελφοῖς καὶ Ὀλυμπίᾳ χρημάτων . . . ὑπολαβεῖν μισθῷ μείζονι τοὺς ξένους αὐτῶν ναυβάτας: (2) Pericles, i. 142 § 6, with Corinthian, i. 121 § 4; (3) Pericles, i. 142 § 2, with Corinthian, i. 122 § 1.

[3] Compare i. 120—4 with i. 80—85.

[4] See the Table at the end of the Essay; cp. i. 21, ὅσα εἶπον μέλλοντες πολεμήσειν.

which the combatants entered on the struggle.   At
the .end of his first speech Pericles says : " I have
many other reasons to give for hoping that we shall
prevail; but these shall be given hereafter as the
events arise (ἄμα τοῖς ἔργοις)"—thus foreshadowing
the speech of which an abstract is given on a subsequent occasion[1].   In this particular case, as we have
seen, the disposition of topics may well be authentic
in the main. But the composer's phrase is significant.
It suggests the habit of selecting from a certain stock
of available material and disposing the extracts with
something of a dramatist's freedom.

In the Funeral Oration there is nothing, apart
from the diction, which distinctly shows the invention of Thucydides.   At first sight there is some
plausibility in the view that such an oration would
probably have contained allusions to the heroic
legends of Attica, and that the mind of Thucydides
is to be traced in their suppression[2].   But the
argument may be turned the other way.   The very
absence of mythical embellishment, it might be
urged, is rather a proof of the fidelity with which

---

[1] i. 144 § 2, ἀλλ᾽ ἐκεῖνα μὲν καὶ ἐν ἄλλῳ λόγῳ ἄμα τοῖς ἔργοις
δηλωθήσεται.   The promise is fulfilled by the speech of which an
abstract is given in ii. 13, and by that reported in the direct form
in ii. 60—64.

[2] The suggestion of F. C. Dahlmann (*Hist. Forschungen*, i. 23),
to which Grote justly opposes the μακρηγορεῖν ἐν εἰδόσιν οὐ βουλόμενος ἐάσω (Thuc. ii. 36).   The analogy of similar extant pieces
(the *Menexenus*, the ἐπιτάφιοι falsely ascribed to Lysias and
Demosthenes, the *Panathenaicus* of Isocrates, etc.) justifies
Dahlmann's major premiss, but does not support his conclusion.

Thucydides has reported a speaker who, regardless of the vulgar taste, was resolved to treat a well-worn theme in a new and higher strain. One or two passages, indeed, have been supposed to hint at the moral deterioration of the Athenian democracy in the years which followed the death of Pericles[1]; but the supposition seems gratuitous.

It remains to notice the debate in the Ecclesia on the punishment of Mitylene. Cleon urges a massacre, Diodotus opposes it. "These views," says Thucydides, "having been stated with nearly balanced effect, the assembly came after all to a division; and on a show of hands the parties proved nearly equal, but the view of Diodotus prevailed." The words can only mean that, in the speeches of Cleon and Diodotus, Thucydides has given the real substance of the arguments which were found to be so "nearly balanced," and which led to so close a division. Cleon's speech has one striking characteristic. In several places it echoes phrases which occur in the speeches of Pericles[2]. But, with these

---

[1] Viz. (1) ii. 37 § 3, the reference to a restraining δέος, and to those laws, ὅσοι ἄγραφοι ὄντες αἰσχύνην ὁμολογουμένην φέρουσι: (2) 40 § 1, φιλοκαλοῦμεν μετ᾽ εὐτελείας καὶ φιλοσοφοῦμεν ἄνευ μαλακίας. I cannot assume the allusions which Classen finds here to a subsequent and opposite state of society.

[2] Compare (1) Cleon, iii. 37 § 2, τυραννίδα ἔχετε τὴν ἀρχήν, with Pericles, ii. 63 § 2, ὡς τυραννίδα γὰρ ἤδη ἔχετε τὴν ἀρχήν: (2) Cleon, iii. 40 § 4, ἐκ τοῦ ἀκινδύνου ἀνδραγαθίζεσθαι, with Pericles, ii. 63 § 2, εἴ τις καὶ τόδε ἐν τῷ παρόντι δεδιὼς ἀπραγμοσύνῃ ἀνδραγαθίζεται: (3) Cleon, iii. 38 § 1, ἐγὼ μὲν οὖν ὁ αὐτός εἰμι τῇ γνώμῃ, with Pericles, ii. 61 § 2, καὶ ἐγὼ μὲν ὁ αὐτός εἰμι καὶ οὐκ ἐξίσταμαι. Compare also Cleon's notice (iii. 37 § 2) of τὸ καθ᾽ ἡμέραν ἀδεές in

verbal parallelisms, there is a pointed contrast of spirit. As Pericles describes the good side of the intellectual Athenian nature, Cleon brings out its weak side. As Pericles insists on the Athenian combination of intelligence with courage, Cleon declares that this intelligence leads men to despise the laws, and prefers ignorance combined with moderation[1]. Pericles is gone : Cleon echoes the words of the statesman as whose successor he poses, at the very moment when he is contradicting his principles. It may be observed that when Thucydides reports the speech of the Syracusan demagogue Athenagoras, he marks his manner by a certain violence of expression[2]. Cleon, whom Thucydides calls "most violent," has no violence of expression. Probably this abstention from vehemence of the

Athenian life, with what Pericles says of τὰ καθ' ἡμέραν ἐπιτηδεύματα, ii. 37 § 2.

[1] Cleon, iii. 37 § 3, ἀμαθία τε μετὰ σωφροσύνης ὠφελιμώτερον ἢ δεξιότης μετὰ ἀκολασίας, κ.τ.λ., contrasted with Pericles, ii. 40 § 2, οὐ τοὺς λόγους τοῖς ἔργοις βλάβην ἡγούμενοι, κ.τ.λ., and ii. 62 § 5, τὴν τόλμαν ... ἡ ξύνεσις ... ἐχυρωτέραν παρέχεται.

[2] E.g. vi. 40, ἀλλ' ἔτι καὶ νῦν, ὦ πάντων ἀξυνετώτατοι, εἰ μὴ μανθάνετε κακὰ σπεύδοντες, ἢ ἀμαθέστατοί ἐστε ὧν ἐγὼ οἶδα Ἑλλήνων, ἢ ἀδικώτατοι, εἰ εἰδότες τολμᾶτε.

In a *Mémoire sur Thucydide*, by M. Meierotto (in the Memoirs of the Berlin Academy for 1790–91, p. 530), the writer observes, with reference to the discrimination of character in the speeches : "Cléon et Athénagore parlent ordinairement d'un ton dur, offensant et grossier, dont pourtant ils s'écartent quelquefois." We have only one speech of Cleon and one of Athenagoras ; so far as these go, however, the striking thing, it seems to me, is not the resemblance, but the contrast.

demagogic type, this superficial imitation of Pericles, are traits in which the Cleon of Thucydides is historical.

˙ This closes the series of those seven speeches, delivered at Athens, for which Thucydides probably derived the "general sense" either from his own recollection or from the sources accessible to a resident citizen. The only one of these which exhibits distinct traces of artificial dealing with subject-matter is the first speech of Pericles. And in this the only traces are, first, a certain adjustment of the language to that of the Corinthian speech made earlier in the same year[1]; and, secondly, a phrase by which the composer prepares the reader for a subsequent speech of Pericles.

§ 6.   We now come to the speeches made elsewhere than at Athens from 432 B.C. onwards, or made at Athens later than 424 B.C.   In regard to all or most of these, Thucydides must have relied on reports of the "general sense" brought to him by others (τοῖς ἄλλοθέν ποθεν ἐμοὶ ἀπαγγέλλουσιν)[2].   The

---

[1] As the Corinthian speech contains a prophecy (after the event) of the occupation of Deceleia (ἐπιτειχισμός, i. 122 § 1), so the corresponding passage of Pericles contains what *may* be a reference to the Athenian occupation of Pylos and of Cythera (i. 140 § 3, ἐπιτειχίζειν . . . πλεύσαντας ἐς τὴν ἐκείνων).

[2] Thuc. v. 26: "It befell me to live in exile for twenty years [423–403 B.C., or nearly so] after my command at Amphipolis.   I thus became conversant with both parties—indeed, as an exile, I saw most of the Peloponnesians—and was enabled to study the events more at my leisure."   The phrase here—καὶ γενομένῳ παρ' ἀμφοτέροις τοῖς πράγμασι—certainly implies more than that

first general characteristic which claims notice is the occurrence of passages certainly, or almost certainly, written with a consciousness of later events. These passages may be cast into three groups, according as they relate to (I) the affairs of Sicily, (II) the Deceleian war, (III) the final defeat of Athens[1].

Thucydides was *in the countries* which were the theatre of the war. It implies that he was *in intercourse with the actors*. The words καθ' ἡσυχίαν denote the "ease" or "leisure" of one who had no official status, political or military. Hitherto Thucydides had been himself an actor in the war (in the Ecclesia or as στρατηγός) ; *now* he was only a thoughtful spectator. During his exile Thucydides certainly spent some time in Italy and Sicily. Marcellinus quotes (§ 25) the statement ὡς φυγὼν ᾤκησεν ἐν Ἰταλίᾳ, and there was even a tradition of his burial there (§ 33). There are traces, I think, of Thucydides' personal knowledge of Sicily in the speech of Alcibiades (vi. 17 § 3). Niebuhr conjectured, and E. Wölfflin has shown (*Antiochus v. Syrakus u. Coelius Antipater*, Winterthur, 1872), that Thucydides (vi. 2 ff.) used the Σικελιῶτις συγγραφή which Antiochus of Syracuse brought down to 424 B.C. These are the chief data for conjecturing the general nature of the materials which Thucydides may have had for the speeches subsequent to 425 B.C. In many cases, probably, he had good sources of information, though it is hardly likely that the words ὧν αὐτὸς ἤκουσα can include any speeches except those made at Athens before his exile.

[1] In the list of nine passages noticed here, I have not included any in which the suggestion of acquaintance with subsequent events did not seem to me tolerably strong and clear. Thus I have purposely omitted the passage in which Archidamus says (432 B.C.) of the war, δέδοικα δὲ μᾶλλον μὴ καὶ τοῖς παισὶν αὐτὸν ὑπολίπωμεν (i. 81 § 6), in which some find a knowledge of its actual duration ; a passage in vi. 11 (in the speech of Nicias), which might possibly be regarded as foreshadowing the aid actually lent by Sicily to Sparta at a later time (viii. 26) ; and

(I)　1.　Speaking in the congress at Gela in 424 B.C., Hermocrates warns his hearers against the designs of Athens. The Athenians, he says, are now on our coast with a few ships ; but some day they will come with a larger fleet, and endeavour to reduce the whole island[1]. The Athenian fleet on the Sicilian coast at this time must have numbered some fifty or sixty triremes[2]. Hermocrates, speaking in 424 B.C., certainly would not have spoken of these as "a few ships," least of all when it was his object to show that Athens was formidable[3]. But Thucydides, when he composed the speech, had in view the vast fleet—at least thrice as numerous[4]— sent to Sicily in 415 B.C.

2.　Nicias, in his second speech dissuading the Athenians from the expedition to Sicily, says that the only Sicilian cities likely to join the invaders are Naxos and Catana[5]. Both Naxos and Catana did, in fact, join the Athenians. But the Athenians, when they opened the campaign in Sicily, had hopes

a reference by Hermocrates to future feuds and reconciliations between the Sicilian cities (iv. 64).

Five of these passages have been noticed by previous writers, viz. Nos. 1, 5, 6, 7, 9; the others—Nos. 2, 3, 4, 8—have not, to my knowledge, been considered in this light before.

[1] iv. 60, ὀλίγαις ναυσὶ παρόντες . . . πλέονί ποτε στόλῳ ἐλθόντας.

[2] Twenty triremes had been sent in 427 B.C. under Laches (iii. 88), whom Pythodorus had superseded ; forty more were afterwards sent under Eurymedon (iii. 115), and these had now joined the first detachment (iv. 48).

[3] As Grote remarks, vii. 189, n.

[4] Thuc. vi. 31.　　　　　[5] vi. 20.

of other cities also. The alliance of Messene[1] was solicited by Alcibiades, though without success. Both Athenian and Syracusan envoys were sent to Camarina, and it was not without much hesitation that Camarina resolved to remain neutral[2]. The precision of the forecast made by Nicias betrays knowledge of the event.

3. Again, when the Athenian attack on Sicily is imminent, Hermocrates, in his speech at Syracuse, gives reasons for thinking that it will fail. Numerous as the Athenians are, he says, they cannot out-number the united forces of Sicily. "And if they should fail from want of supplies in a foreign country, they will still leave glory to those against whom their design was laid, even though they should be ruined mainly by their own errors[3]." Thucydides elsewhere expresses his own view of the Sicilian disaster. The primary cause of the failure was not, he thinks, a miscalculation of forces, but rather the neglect of the Athenians at home—distracted as they were by faction—to support the army in Sicily, a neglect which blunted the zeal of those engaged in the campaign[4]. The words ascribed to Hermocrates were written by Thucydides in retrospective view of the Athenian errors which had led to the Athenian defeat.

4. The speech of Euphemus, the Athenian envoy at Camarina, offers another example. Urging the people of Camarina to join the Athenians rather

---

[1] vi. 50.   [2] vi. 88.

[3] vi. 33.   [4] ii. 65.

than the Syracusans, he reminds them that they
will not often have an opportunity of securing such
powerful auxiliaries. And if, he says, you dismiss
them now, "one day yet you will long to see even
the least part of them, when their succour can no
more avail you[1]." A few years later (405 B.C.),
the Carthaginians, already victorious over Selinus,
Himera, and Agrigentum, advanced against Gela
and Camarina. Dionysius, who had become tyrant
of Syracuse, failed to relieve Gela. The inhabitants
of Camarina, like those of Gela, were forced to
abandon their city; and when the conclusion of
peace between Dionysius and the invaders allowed
them to return, they returned as tributaries of Carthage[2]. The protection of Syracuse, in which
Camarina had trusted, proved a broken reed. Thucydides must have been at work on his History for
some years after the end of the Peloponnesian war,
perhaps as late as 396 B.C.[3] When he put that

---

[1] vi. 86, ἢν εἰ τῷ ὑπόπτῳ ἢ ἄπρακτον ἐάσετε ἀπελθεῖν ἢ καὶ
σφαλεῖσαν, ἔτι βουλήσεσθε καὶ πολλοστὸν μόριον αὐτῆς ἰδεῖν, ὅτε
οὐδὲν ἔτι περανεῖ παραγενόμενον ὑμῖν. (For ἔτι thus used in menace
or presage, cf. Soph. *El.* 471. In Aesch. *Eum.* 812, Shilleto con-
jectured ὑμεῖς δ᾽ ἔτ᾽ [for ἐς] ἀλλόφυλον ἐλθοῦσαι χθόνα | γῆς τῆσδ᾽
ἐρασθήσεσθε.)

[2] Diod. xiii. 108—114; Xen. *Hellen.* ii. 3.

[3] Thucydides mentions an eruption of Aetna in 426 B.C. as
the third on record (iii. 116)—implying ignorance of that in
396 B.C., noticed by Diodorus, xiv. 59. On the probability that
Thucydides was at work on his History for at least some years
after 403, cp. Classen, *Einl.* xxx. I cannot, however, accept
Ullrich's ingenious suggestion that the reference to Antiphon—
ἄριστα τῶν μέχρι ἐμοῦ θανάτου δίκην ἀπολογησάμενος (viii. 68)—

emphatic menace into the mouth of Euphemus, the fate which actually overtook Camarina soon afterwards was surely present to his mind.

(II) 5. The Corinthian speaker at Sparta in 432 B.C. alludes to the establishment of a fort in Attica as one of the possibilities of the war[1]; and Pericles, in the parallel passage of his first speech, admits that the construction of a hostile fort might do harm by facilitating raids and by tempting slaves to desert[2].

6. Alcibiades, speaking at Sparta in 415 B.C., urges the occupation of Deceleia. " It will benefit you," he says, "and will embarrass the enemy in many ways. I will briefly notice the chief of these. Most of the property in the country will become yours by capture or surrender. The Athenians will forthwith lose their revenues from the silver mines of Laurium, and all their present gains from the land and the law-courts. Above all, they will suffer by the irregular transmission of tribute from their allies, who, when satisfied that you are making war in earnest, will slight their demands[3]." These predictions accurately correspond with the effects of the occupation as afterwards described in the historian's

points to a tacit comparison with the defence of Socrates (399 B.C.).

[1] Thuc. i. 122 § 1.   [2] i. 142 § 2.

[3] vi. 91 § 7. In the sentence, οἷς . . . ἡ χώρα κατεσκεύασται, τὰ πολλὰ πρὸς ὑμᾶς τὰ μὲν ληφθέντα, τὰ δ' αὐτόματα ἥξει, the word αὐτόματα, as commentators have seen, refers to the desertion of slaves, included in the κατασκευαί as household chattels or "live stock."

own words[1]. The temporary presence of the invading enemy had not hitherto hindered the Athenians from reaping the fruits of the soil; but now "they were deprived of their whole land"— including, of course, the mines at Laurium. "More than twenty thousand slaves had deserted to the enemy." All their sheep and oxen were lost. The whole number of adult male citizens was required for military duty on the walls or in the field, a necessity which would suspend the sitting of the law-courts and, as Alcibiades foretold, close that source of profit[2]. The expenses of the State were heavily increased, its revenues were perishing. Alcibiades might easily have foreseen the importance of occupying Deceleia. But the minute correspondence between the special results which he is made to predict and those which Thucydides relates in his own person indicates that the prophecy followed the event.

(III) 7. The Athenian speaker at Sparta in 432 B.C. says to the Spartans: "If you were to

---

[1] vii. 27—28. On the αὐτομολίαι of slaves, cf. viii. 40.

[2] The reference of Alcibiades in the words ὅσα ... ἀπὸ τῶν δικαστηρίων νῦν ὠφελοῦνται is to the income which the State derived from court-fees of various kinds, especially the deposits (πρυτανεῖα) made by parties to a law-suit, as well as from pecuniary fines, confiscations, etc. Böckh (*Publ. Econ.* i. 461) understands the passage thus, following the scholiast. Meineke (*Hermes* iii. 359) and Madvig (*Adv.* i. 328) conjecture δεκατευτηρίων, "places where public tithes and taxes were taken"—objecting, as against the vulgate, that it does not appear why even a virtual state of siege should suspend the sitting of the law-courts. Thucydides, vii. 28 § 2, gives the plain answer—all the citizens were required for military duty.

overthrow our empire and establish your own, you would soon alienate the good-will which you have gained because we are feared,—if you are to continue the policy of which you gave a specimen during your brief leadership of Greece against Persia. The usages of your community preclude intercourse with others, and moreover a Spartan citizen on foreign service observes these usages as little as those of Hellas at large[1]." There is a manifest reference here to the period after the close of the war, when the Spartan promises of "liberating Greece" were falsified. And the reference to the misconduct of the Spartan citizen abroad was certainly not suggested by the case of Pausanias alone. The war had furnished two signal instances. Gylippus had been convicted by the Ephors of appropriating part of the treasure taken after the capture of Athens[2]. Lysander—the first Greek who received divine honours from Greeks—had surpassed the arrogance of Pausanias[3].

8. The striking speech of Brasidas to the Acanthians (424 B.C.) deserves to be considered in this connection. It is throughout an emphatic assertion that the cause in which Sparta fights is the cause of Greek liberty. "I have not come," he says, "to support a party. I do not consider that I should be bringing you freedom in any real sense if I should disregard your constitution, and enslave the

---

[1] Thuc. i. 77 § 6.
[2] Plut. *Lys.* 16—17, *Nic.* 28, cf. Diod. xiii. 106.
[3] With Plut. *Lys.* 18 cf. Paus. vi. 3 §§ 14—15, Athen. xv. 696.

many to the few, or the few to the many. Such freedom would be harder than a foreign yoke: and we, the Lacedaemonians, should reap no thanks for our pains, but rather blame instead of honour and renown[1]." Now, what Brasidas protests that Sparta will not do, is precisely what Sparta actually did at the end of the war, with the result which he anticipates. Oligarchies of the narrowest type—boards of ten—were established by Lysander in most of the cities, with a Spartan governor and garrison in each to repress the popular party[2]. The many were literally enslaved to the few, and they found the freedom which Sparta had given them harder indeed than any foreign rule. It can scarcely be doubted that this speech of Brasidas—composed by Thucydides after the close of the war—was inserted by him here, just at the moment when Sparta was making the first advances to the democratic cities of Northern Greece, for the purpose of bringing out the glaring contrast between Spartan promise and Spartan performance.

9.   In the conference between the Athenian and

---

[1] Thuc. iv. 86 § 3.   In § 4 there is no doubt to my mind that οὐδ' ἂν σαφῆ [for οὐδὲ ἀσαφῆ] is the right reading, ἂν ἐπιφέρειν being the oblique of ἂν ἐπιφέροιμι.

[2] See Isocr. *Panegyricus*, §§ 110—114, where he denounces the partisans of the narrow Lacedaemonian oligarchies in the several States—οἱ τῶν δεκαρχιῶν κοινωνήσαντες—and speaks of the miseries which they inflicted on their own cities by "choosing to be enslaved to a Helot" (*i.e.* to the μόθαξ Lysander: ᾑροῦντο δὲ τῶν Εἱλώτων ἑνὶ δουλεύειν). The passage is a striking commentary on the Acanthian speech of Brasidas.

Melian negotiators, the Athenians remark that, in
the event of Athens being vanquished, they would
have less to fear from the vengeance of Sparta than
from the vindictiveness of smaller States[1]. The
reference here is unmistakable. After the surrender
of Athens in 404 B.C., a congress was held at Sparta
in which the destruction of the defeated city was
advocated, according to Xenophon, "by the Corinthians and Thebans chiefly, but by many other
Greeks too." It was by the Spartan vote that
Athens was saved[2].

The effect of such touches as these—suggested
by a knowledge of occurrences subsequent to the
dramatic date—may be compared with that produced
in a Greek tragedy when one of the persons uncon-
sciously utters a word or phrase which foreshadows
the catastrophe. The spectator who knows the
destined end of the drama is affected in the same
manner as the reader who knows the sequel of the
history. In using such touches, however, Thucydides
was probably thinking more of logical than of artistic
effect. His mind, with its strong concentration,
grasped the whole series of arguments or illustrations
which the experience of the war could yield; and he
brought the most forcible of these to bear on his
point without caring whether the facts which suggested them were earlier or later than the supposed
date.

§ 7.   It has already been remarked that the ad-

---

[1] Thuc. v. 91.
[2] Xen. *Hellen.* ii. 2, §§ 19—20.

dresses of leaders to their troops may be considered
as forming a class apart from the rest. These
military harangues, of which there are twelve in all,
are usually short. The object is always the same—to
bring out vividly the essential points of a strategical
situation ; and the historian has been less uniformly
attentive here to the details of dramatic probability¹.
A modern writer would have attained the object
by comments prefixed or added to his narrative of
the operations. Thus Archidamus, addressing the
Peloponnesian officers before the first invasion of
Attica, dwells on the certainty of the Athenians
being stung into giving battle when they see their
lands ravaged². This serves to heighten the reader's

¹ Thus (1) the harangue is sometimes ascribed to several
leaders collectively; e.g. vii. 65, παρεκελεύσαντο ἐκείνοις οἵ τε
στρατηγοὶ καὶ Γύλιππος καὶ ἔλεξαν τοιάδε. So ii. 86, ὁ Κνῆμος καὶ
ὁ Βρασίδας καὶ οἱ ἄλλοι τῶν Πελοποννησίων στρατηγοί . . παρεκελεύσαντο καὶ ἔλεξαν τοιάδε. In the case of the political speeches, the
only similar instance is when a single speech is given as made by
the two spokesmen of the Plataeans (προτάξαντες σφῶν αὐτῶν
Ἀστύμαχόν τε . . καὶ Λάκωνα). It is obviously a different case
when a speech is assigned to envoys collectively (i. 32, οἱ
Κερκυραῖοι ἔλεξαν τοιάδε, etc.), when one would speak for the
rest. (2) The military harangue is sometimes introduced in
words which imply that it was made several times over; thus
iv. 91 (Pagondas), προσκαλῶν ἑκάστους κατὰ λόχους, ὅπως μὴ ἀθρόοι
ἐκλίποιεν τὰ ὅπλα, ἔπειθε . . λέγων τοιάδε. Cf. vi 68 (Nicias), κατά
τε ἔθνη ἐπιπαριὼν ἕκαστα καὶ ξύμπασι τοιάδε παρεκελεύετο. (Cf.
ἐπιπαριὼν τὸ στρατόπεδον παρεκελεύετο, iv. 94.) In vii. 76 Nicias
ἐπιπαριὼν ἐθάρσυνέ τε καὶ παρεμυθεῖτο, βοῇ τε χρώμενος ἔτι μᾶλλον
ἑκάστοις καθ' οὓς γίγνοιτο, καὶ βουλόμενος ὡς ἐπὶ πλεῖστον
γεγωνίσκων ὠφελεῖν.
² Thuc. ii. 11.

sense of the provocation offered, and of the difficulty which Pericles must have had in restraining his fellow-citizens[1]. Sometimes the speech of the general on one side is as distinctly a reply to the general on the other as if it had been delivered in debate. The Peloponnesian captains, exhorting their men before the action in the Corinthian Gulf, tell them that, though naval skill is much, it cannot avail against courage[2]. Phormio, exhorting the Athenian crews, tells them, as if in retort, that though courage is invaluable, their decisive advantage is in their naval skill[3]. Pagondas, before the battle of Delium, tells the Boeotians that they must fight, even beyond their own border, for the safety of Boeotia, and reminds them that their fathers secured it for a time by defeating the Athenians at Coroneia[4]. Demosthenes tells the Athenians that they must fight, even on Boeotian ground, to protect Attica, and reminds them of the Athenian victory over the Boeotians at Oenophyta[5]. The speech of Brasidas to his men on his Illyrian expedition is intended to bring out the contrast between Hellenic and barbarian warfare[6]; his speech at Amphipolis serves to explain his tactics[7]. The harangue of Nicias before the last sea-fight at Syracuse marks the peculiar character of the action as "a land-battle on board ship" ($\pi\epsilon\zeta o\mu\alpha\chi\acute{\iota}\alpha$ $\dot{\alpha}\pi\grave{o}$ $\nu\epsilon\hat{\omega}\nu$), and at the same time sums up for the reader the whole meaning of that

[1] ii. 59 f.   [2] ii. 87.   [3] ii. 89.
[4] iv. 92.   [5] iv. 95.   [6] iv. 126.
[7] $\tau\grave{\eta}\nu$ $\dot{\epsilon}\pi\acute{\iota}\nu o\iota\alpha\nu$ $\phi\rho\acute{\alpha}\sigma\alpha\iota$, v. 9.

supreme crisis, when, as Nicias reminds the men about to embark, the fleet is all that remains of Athens and her great name[1]. This, and the corresponding speech of Gylippus on the Syracusan side[2], are in a high degree powerful and pathetic; so, above all, is the last speech of Nicias before the retreat[3]. Nowhere else, perhaps, has Thucydides given so free a scope to his own rhetorical power; yet even here it is strictly subordinated to his primary purpose—that of faithfully presenting the cardinal facts of the situation as he conceived them.

§ 8.   The expression of character in the Thucydidean speeches has the same kind of limitation which was generally observed in Attic tragedy.   It is rather typical than individual.   Thucydides seizes the broad and essential characteristics of the speaker, and is content with marking these.   We are sometimes reminded of the direct simplicity with which the epic or tragic heroes introduce themselves : " I am Odysseus, the marvel of men for all wiles, and my fame goes up to heaven."   " I am pious Aeneas, renowned above the stars[4]."   " You voted for war," says Pericles, "and now you are angry with me,—a man who deems himself second to none in discerning

---

[1] vii. 61—64, ἡ ὑπόλοιπος πόλις καὶ τὸ μέγα ὄνομα τῶν Ἀθηνῶν.

[2] vii. 65.

[3] vii. 76.   The two last military speeches of Nicias take something of the political character from the fact that, as he says in both, the army *is* now the city: ἄνδρες γὰρ πόλις—a striking illustration of Sophocles, *Oed. Tyr.* 56.

[4] *Od.* ix. 19; *Aen.* i. 379; cf. Soph. *Oed. Tyr.* 8, αὐτὸς ὧδ' ἐλήλυθα, | ὁ πᾶσι κλεινὸς Οἰδίπους καλούμενος.

and expounding the right course,—a man devoted to his country and proof against corruption[1]." These were salient points in the public character of Pericles as conceived by the historian[2], and accordingly Pericles is made to say so. The fate of Nicias seemed to Thucydides a signal example of unmerited misfortune, since Nicias had been remarkable throughout life for the practice of orthodox virtue[3]. And so, in his speech before the retreat from Syracuse, Nicias says, " The tenor of my life has been loyal to the gods, just and without offence among men[4]." In the debate at Athens on the Sicilian expedition Alcibiades is introduced by a prefatory sketch of his position and character. Thucydides notices his ambition, his magnificence,

---

[1] Thuc. ii. 60.   [2] ii. 65.

[3] vii. 86, ἥκιστα δὴ ἄξιος ὢν τῶν γε ἐπ' ἐμοῦ Ἑλλήνων ἐς τοῦτο δυστυχίας ἀφικέσθαι διὰ τὴν πᾶσαν ἐς ἀρετὴν νενομισμένην ἐπιτήδευσιν: i.e. lit., his whole course of life, regulated by law and tradition (νενομισμένη) in the direction of virtue. The ἀρετή of Nicias was that which consists in fidelity to the established observances of religion and to received notions of duty—as distinguished from the ἀρετή, less in conformity with popular conceptions, which Thucydides can still recognise in such a man as Antiphon (viii. 68).

[4] Thuc. vii. 77, πολλὰ μὲν ἐς θεοὺς νόμιμα δεδιῄτημαι, πολλὰ δὲ ἐς ἀνθρώπους δίκαια καὶ ἀνεπίφθονα. As to the Letter of Nicias (vii. 11—15), its *substantial* genuineness might perhaps be argued from the fact that, while it dwells on the wear and tear of the armament, there is no attempt to excuse his own delay and his failure to prepare for the coming of Gylippus ; but the manner of its introduction (δηλοῦσαν τοιάδε) seems to indicate the *composition* of Thucydides.

especially in the matter of horses and chariots, the licence of his private life, his insolence, his public efficiency, his personal unpopularity[1]. Then Alcibiades speaks, and begins by saying in so many words that he has a better right than others to high command; he boasts of having entered seven chariots at Olympia; he avows that he does not regard his fellow-citizens as his equals; he asks whether his personal unpopularity interferes with his administrative capacity[2]. The speech is merely the sketch developed. It is the character of Alcibiades, as Thucydides saw its salient points, condensed in a dramatic form; but it is not such a speech as Alcibiades could conceivably have made on this occasion, or indeed on any. Thucydides has given us distinct portraits of the chief actors in the Peloponnesian war, but these portraits are to be found in the clearly narrated actions of the men; the words ascribed to them rarely do more than mark the stronger lines of character; they seldom reveal new traits of a subtler kind. The tendency of Thucydides was less to analyse individual character than to study human nature in its general or typical phenomena. His observation was directed, first, towards motives and passions which may be considered, in regard to practical politics, as universal influences[3]: next, towards the collective attributes which distinguish whole communities from each

---

[1] vi. 15.   [2] vi. 16.

[3] iii. 82 § 2, γιγνόμενα μὲν καὶ ἀεὶ ἐσόμενα ἕως ἂν ἡ αὐτὴ φύσις τῶν ἀνθρώπων ᾖ.

other. Thus the normal Spartan character is exhibited in its merits and its defects[1]. The political character of the Athenians is arraigned and defended[2]; their intellectual character is illustrated in its strength and its weakness[3]. And Thucydides shows a desire to comprehend these conceptions of national character in formulas, which he gives as epigrams to his speakers. The Spartan disposition, says an Athenian, might be described as one which regards everything that is pleasant as honourable, and everything that is expedient as just[4]. The Athenians, says a Corinthian, are, in brief, men who will neither rest nor allow others to rest[5]. Athens, says Pericles, might be described as the school of Greece, and the Athenian nature as the most gracefully versatile in the world[6].

§ 9. Those cases in which Thucydides gives merely a brief summary[7] of a speech or debate suggest how slight the materials may often have

---

[1] i. 68—72, 80—85.   [2] i. 68—72, 73—78.

[3] ii. 37 f. ; iii. 37—40.

[4] v. 105.   [5] i. 70.

[6] ii. 41. I regard the Melian dialogue as neither less nor more historical than those speeches in which Thucydides had to rely on a slight knowledge of the ξύμπασα γνώμη. I cannot suppose, with Classen, that Thucydides had any written documents to go upon. The frankness of the Athenians, which Grcte finds startling, is Thucydidean: his wish to portray ruling motives is stronger than his regard for dramatic nicety.

[7] *E.g.* i. 72 (where the general lines of the discourse in 73—78 are indicated); iv. 21 (the general sense of Cleon's answer to the Spartan envoys); iv. 58 and vi. 32 (debates at Gela and Syracuse); viii. 53 (debate at Athens in 411 B.C.), etc.

been which he worked up in the oratorical form.
The political or ethical reflections with which the
meagre outlines were filled up were doubtless
supplied in large measure by Thucydides himself.
The speeches, taken altogether, are pervaded by
certain general conceptions, expressed in formulas
more or less constant, which indicate unity of
authorship. But it cannot be said, in the same
sense, that they bear the stamp of one mind. They
do, indeed, suggest certain intellectual habits, but
it is seldom possible to distinguish between opinions
or modes of thought which were in the air, and such
as may have been proper to Thucydides. Nor
would much be gained if we could. The real
interest of the speeches in this aspect is something
more than biographical; it is their interest as a contribution to the intellectual history of a transitional
period in an age of singular mental energy. The
age of faith was passing by, and a rational basis for
ethics—which were then included in politics—was
only in process of being sought. Thucydides is
here the representative of a time which, for the most
part, could no longer believe with Herodotus, but
which had not yet learned to bring a Socratic
method to bear on generalisations. He appears—
so far as he is revealed at all—as a thinker of
intense earnestness, with a firm and subtle apprehension of his chosen subject, alike in its widest
bearings and in its minutest details; and of profound
sensibility in regard to the larger practical aspects,
that is the political aspects, of human destiny. He has

neither a dogmatic religion nor a system of ethics. He cleaves to positive fact; his generalisations rarely involve a speculative element, but are usually confined to registering the aggregate results of observation upon human conduct in given circumstances. In the spirit of a sceptical age he makes his speakers debate questions of political or personal morality to which no definite answer is offered. In Plato's *Gorgias* Callicles distinguishes between "natural" and "conventional" justice, contending that "natural justice" entitles the strong to oppress the weak, and that "conventional justice" is merely a device of the weak for their own protection[1]. In the *Republic* Thrasymachus defends a similar doctrine, namely, that "justice is another's good and the interest of the stronger, and that injustice is a man's own profit and interest, though injurious to the weaker[2]." The sophist Hippias, in Xenophon's *Memorabilia*, argues in a like strain that justice and law are merely arbitrary and conventional[3]. This, no doubt, was one of the commonplaces of sophistical dialectic in the time of Thucydides. The Athenian speakers in his History defend the aggressive policy of Athens by arguments which rest on substantially the same basis as those of the Platonic Callicles and Thrasymachus[4]. But the historian is content to state their case from their own point of view; he does not challenge the doctrine—as the Platonic Socrates

---

[1] Plato, *Gorgias*, p. 482, c. 38.   [2] *Rep.* p. 367 c.
[3] Xen. *Mem.* iv. 4. 14.   [4] Thuc. v. 105; vi. 82—87.

does—by comments of his own. The victims of aggression, indeed, the Plataeans or Melians, appeal to a higher justice than the right of might, and Thucydides hints that his sympathies are with them[1]; but that is all. The abstention is characteristic. On the whole, it may be said that he evinces a personal liking for moral nobleness[2], but refrains from delivering moral judgments[3], as if these would imply laws which he was not prepared to affirm or deny. But he insists on discovering a rational basis for action. If a man or a State pursues a certain line of policy, there must be some intelligible reasons, he feels, which can be urged for it. This desire to enter into the mind of the actors—to find the motive behind the deed, and to state it with all possible logical force—is the mainspring of the oratory in Thucydides, in so far as this is his own creation. It is an element of dramatic vividness; sometimes also of dramatic untruth, when the reasonings supplied by the historian to his actors are subtler than would probably have occurred to the speakers or commended themselves to the

[1] Not expressly, but by the naked repulsiveness in which he exhibits the "right of might."

[2] As Professor Sellar says ("Characteristics of Thucydides," *Oxford Essays*, 1857): "His own feeling shines out in such expressions as this,—'Simple-mindedness, which is mostly an ingredient in noble natures' (iii. 83). The speeches attributed to Pericles are especially expressive of generous ideas of man."

[3] It is enough to instance the manner in which he relates without comment the treachery of Paches to Hippias (iii. 54), and the assassination of two thousand Helots by the Spartans (iv. 80).

hearers. Thucydides is a philosophical historian, in the sense that he wishes to record the exact truth, in a form which may be serviceable for the political instruction of mankind. But he has not, in the sense of Plato or Aristotle, a theory of ethics or politics. Thucydides groups the observed facts of practical politics, but without attempting to analyse their ultimate laws. It might be possible to piece together Thucydidean texts and, by filling up a few gaps, to form a tolerably coherent system of doctrine; but the process would be artificial and delusive. Possibly a Shakespeare might re-create Thucydides from the fragments of his personal thought, but the breath of life would be the poet's gift ; the broken lights are all that really remain. The paradoxes of one age are said to be the truisms of the next, but the violent contrast suggested by the epigram is hardly the important point to seize if we desire to trace the growth of opinion. There was a moment when the so-called paradoxes were neither paradoxes nor as yet truisms, but only rather new and intelligent opinions, seen to be such against the foil of notions which were decaying, but had not quite gone out. For instance, when Thucydides makes his speakers say, as he so often does, that the future is uncertain[1], we do more justice to the originality of the remark if we remember that in the time of Thucydides

---

[1] *E.g.* iv. 62, τὸ ἀστάθμητον τοῦ μέλλοντος ὡς ἐπὶ πλεῖστον κρατεῖ : vi. 9, περὶ τῶν ἀφανῶν καὶ μελλόντων κινδυνεύειν : ii. 42, τὸ ἀφανὲς τοῦ κατορθώματος : ii. 87, νομίσαι ταῖς τύχαις ἐνδέχεσθαι σφάλλεσθαι τοὺς ἀνθρώπους, etc.

there were those who thought that the future was
very frequently indicated, at great moments, by
signs from the gods. Herodotus, for example,
would have disputed the statement that the future
is uncertain, if it had been placed before him as
an unlimited proposition covering such crises as the
Peloponnesian war[1]. The same consideration applies
to many of the political or moral aphorisms, which
may be regarded as those of Thucydides himself.
They are in silent controversy with some unex-
pressed dissidence of contemporaries. The principle
of tacit contrast pervades the whole History, as in
the Funeral Oration the picture of Athens requires
to be supplemented by a mental picture of the
Sparta to which it is opposed[2]. This was of the
inmost nature of Thucydides: the reluctance "to
speak at superfluous length[3]" was deep in him. His
general views must be measured both by the credulity
and by the higher scepticism of a naïve age; so
gauged, they are never commonplaces, but, at the
least, hints for a part of the history which he has
not told in words, because he did not distinctly conceive that it could ever need to be told. "Fortune,"
τύχη, is the name by which he usually designates
the incalculable element in human life; but this

---

[1] See *e.g.* Her. i. 45, θεῶν τίς μοι . . . προεσήμαινε τὰ μέλλοντα
ἔσεσθαι: vi. 37, φιλέει δέ κως προσημαίνειν ὁ θεός, κ.τ.λ. On the
omens, prodigies, dreams, etc., in Herodotus, see Mure, Bk. iv.
ch. 6, § 3, and Rawlinson, i. 71 f.

[2] Esp. ii. 37 and 39.

[3] μακρηγορεῖν: i. 68, ii. 36, iv. 59.

"fortune" is no blind chance; it is, as he once explains it, "the fortune given by heaven" (ἡ τύχη ἐκ τοῦ θείου), the inscrutable dispensation of a divine Providence[1]. The course of this fortune not only baffles prediction, but is sometimes directly opposed to the reasonable beliefs of men concerning the source which dispenses it. Thrice only in the long tragedy of the war, as Thucydides unfolds it, do men appeal expressly to the gods, invoking the name of religion, in their agony, against tyrannous strength; thrice the power behind the veil is deaf, thrice the hand of the avenger is withheld, and the miserable suppliant is struck down by the secure malignity of man. The Plataeans appeal to the altars which had witnessed the consecration of Greek liberty[2], and the Spartans kill them in cold blood. The Melians are confident against the Athenians as the righteous against the unjust[3]; their city is sacked, their men are slain, their women and children enslaved. Nicias, after the great defeat at Syracuse, believes that the jealousy of the gods must now be exhausted, and has a firm hope, based on a good life, for himself and his followers[4]; but the wretched remnant of his defeated army are in great part butchered as they slake their thirst with the bloody water of the Assinarus; he himself is put to death lest he should tell tales under torture, and the

---

[1] v. 104.   [2] iii. 59 § 2.

[3] v. 104, ὅσιοι πρὸς οὐ δικαίους.

[4] vii. 77 § 4, καὶ ἡμᾶς εἰκὸς νῦν τά τε ἀπὸ τοῦ θεοῦ ἐλπίζειν ἠπιώτερα ἕξειν. οἴκτου γὰρ ἀπ᾽ αὐτῶν ἀξιώτεροι ἤδη ἐσμὲν ἢ φθόνου.

survivors pass into a horrible slavery. Thucydides feels that the ways of Heaven are hard to understand, but he does not complain of them ; they are matters not for reasoning but for resignation[1]. He regards the fear of the gods as a potent check on the bad impulses of men, and notices the loss of this fear[2] as a grave symptom of moral anarchy. As to omens, oracles, and similar modes of seeking miraculous light or aid, he nowhere denies the possibility of such light or aid being occasionally given, though his contempt is excited by the frequency of imposture[3]; this, however, he would affirm—that such resources are not to be tried until all resources within human control have been tried in vain[4]. There is one way only, Thucydides holds, by which man can certainly influence his own destiny, and that is by bringing an intelligent judgment (γνώμη) to bear on facts. Some have traced the influence of Anaxagoras in the prominence which Thucydides gives to the intellectual principle ; but no such prompting was needed by a strong understanding of sceptical bent, and it may be observed that Thucydides has at least not adopted the language of Anaxagoras[5]. It is the peculiar merit

---

[1] ii. 64, φέρειν τε χρὴ τά τε δαιμόνια ἀναγκαίως τά τε ἀπὸ τῶν πολεμίων ἀνδρείως.

[2] ii. 53; iii. 82.

[3] *E.g.* ii. 21; v. 26, 103; vii. 50 (of Nicias), ἦν καὶ ἄγαν θειασμῷ τε καὶ τῷ τοιούτῳ προσκείμενος.　　　　[4] v. 103.

[5] νοῦς, in Thucydides, occurs only in the phrases ἐν νῷ ἔχειν (to intend), τὸν νοῦν ἔχειν πρός τι, or προσέχειν, and κατὰ νοῦν, "to

of the Athenian character, as portrayed in Thucydides, to recognise intelligence as the true basis of
action and the true root of courage[1], instead of
regarding mental culture as adverse to civic loyalty
and warlike spirit[2]. If soothsayers cannot give us
prescience, reason well used can enable such a man
as Themistocles at least to conjecture the future[3].
In a trial of human forces the chances baffle prediction, but superiority in ideas (διάνοιαι) is a sure
ground of confidence[4]. Yet the man of sound
judgment will not presume on this confidence, for he
will remember that the other element, "fortune," is
beyond his control[5]. Justice, rightly understood, is
the "common good[6]," and is identical with true
self-interest[7]. As the remorseless exaction of an
extreme penalty, "justice" may be opposed to
"equity[8]"; or as a moral standard, it may be
opposed to "self-interest" in the lower sense[9].
And self-interest, when thus opposed to justice, can
appeal to "the immemorial usage[10]," believed to
obtain among the gods, and so certainly established

one's mind." The general term for the power of the intellect is
γνώμη, with which διάνοια and σύνεσις are sometimes nearly
synonymous.

[1] ii. 40 § 2 ; 62 § 5.

[2] As Archidamus does (i. 84), and Cleon (iii. 37).

[3] i. 138, τῶν μελλόντων ἐπὶ πλεῖστον τοῦ γενησομένου ἄριστος
εἰκαστής.   [4] i. 84 § 3; vi. 11 § 6.

[5] iv. 64.   [6] τὸ κοινὸν ἀγαθόν, v. 90.

[7] i. 41.   [8] iii. 40; iv. 19.

[9] i. 76, 79 ; iii. 56 ; v. 90 ; iv. 61.

[10] i. 76, τὸ ἀεὶ καθεστός.

among men that it may plausibly be called a sort of natural necessity[1],—that the stronger shall rule the weaker. No speaker in Thucydides goes quite so far as Callicles in the *Gorgias*, or proclaims this to be "natural" as distinguished from "conventional" justice. It is not said to be just, but only natural and not unreasonable[2]. The argument against capital punishment, which is put into the mouth of Diodotus, rests on the observation that no restraints have yet been devised which can be trusted to keep human passions in check. Legislators have gone through the whole list of possible penalties, and even the prospect of death is found insufficient to deter those who are goaded by want or ambition, and tempted by opportunity[3]. The friendship of men and of communities must be founded in the first place on a persuasion of mutual benevolence, and on some congeniality of character[4]; but in the long-run the only sure bond between States is identity of interests[5]. The Peloponnesian league is loose just because the interests diverge[6]. In default of a common interest, the only guarantee for an alliance is balanced fear[7]. Similarly, in the relation of the citizen to the State, patriotism is enforced by the dependence of private on public welfare[8]. Pericles even says that no fair

---

[1] v. 105, ἡγούμεθα γὰρ τό τε θεῖον δόξῃ τὸ ἀνθρώπειόν τε σαφῶς διὰ παντὸς ὑπὸ φύσεως ἀναγκαίας, οὗ ἂν κρατῇ, ἄρχειν. Cf. iv. 61, vi. 87.   [2] vi. 85, οὐδὲν ἄλογον ὅτι καὶ ξυμφέρον.

[3] iii. 45 § 3.   [4] iii. 10.   [5] i. 124.

[6] i. 141.   [7] τὸ ἀντίπαλον δέος, iii. 11; cf. iv. 92.

[8] ii. 60.

or just legislation can be expected from citizens who
have not such a stake in the country as is represented
by the lives of children[1]. The distinctive merits of
an oligarchy—always provided that it is constitutional, and not of the narrow type which Thucydides
calls a "dynasty[2]"—are fairly recognised in the
History. Archidamus and Brasidas claim stability,
moderation and disciplined loyalty for the Spartan
State[3]. A true democracy is pictured as one in
which three elements work together for the common
good : the rich are the guardians of property, the
able men offer counsel, and the mass of the citizens
decide on the opinions laid before them[4]. Democracy
was the form of government under which Athens
had been greatest and most free[5]: and the best
phase of the Athenian democracy in his recollection,
Thucydides says, was just after the Revolution of
the Four Hundred, since then the oligarchic and
popular elements were judiciously tempered[6]. Destiny
may alter the part which a State is called upon to
perform, and its institutions may require to be
modified accordingly. Thus the Corinthians say to
the Spartans, "Your system is out of date if you
are to cope with Athens. In politics, as in art,

---

[1] ii. 44.

[2] The δυναστεία (οὐ μετὰ νόμων, unconstitutional) of Thebes in
the Persian wars is opposed to the later ὀλιγαρχία ἰσόνομος, iii. 62.

[3] i. 84; iv. 126 § 4.

[4] vi. 39 (Hermocrates); cf. ii. 37 (Pericles). It is only
Alcibiades (at Sparta) who uses δημοκρατία in a narrow and bad
sense, as a synonym for ἀκολασία πλήθους (vi. 89).

[5] vi. 89 § 6.   [6] viii. 97.

improvements must prevail.   Fixed institutions are best for a city at peace.   But the call to manifold enterprise imposes the need of manifold development.   Hence—owing to their varied experience—the Athenians have been greater innovators than you[1]."   The analogy suggested here between politics and a progressive art[2] is the more significant when it is remembered what the historian's age had seen accomplished in sculpture, architecture and drama. It is also worthy of remark that the only unqualified censures of democracy which occur in Thucydides, and the only protests against change as such, are ascribed to the "violent" Cleon and the "licentious" Alcibiades[3].

§ 10.   The choice of moments for the introduction of speeches is not, with Thucydides, a matter of rhetorical caprice, but has an intelligible relation to the general plan of his work.   A speech or debate reported in the direct form always signalises a noteworthy point in the inner or mental history of the war, as distinguished from the narrative of its external facts: it announces thoughts and arguments which exercised an important influence, and which therefore require to be apprehended with the utmost possible distinctness.   The event which furnishes

---

[1] i. 71.

[2] "Among early inquirers into the nature of human action the arts helped to fill up the void of speculation." (Prof. Jowett, Introduction to *Plato's Republic*.)

[3] iii. 37 § 3; vi. 18 § 7. Thucydides speaks of the οὐ δημοτικὴ παρανομία of Alcibiades in vi. 28; cf. vi. 15, where the same term is applied to him as in i. 132 to Pausanias.

the occasion for inserting a speech need not be of
first-rate importance in itself, if only it is typical of
its kind, and therefore suitable for the dramatic
exhibition of reasonings which applied to several
similar cases. The destruction of Plataea by Sparta
was an impressive event; but its effect on the
general course of the war would scarcely have
warranted the amount of space devoted to the
Plataean and Theban pleadings[1], if the occasion had
not been a typical illustration of Spartan and Theban
policy. Such, again, is the case of Mitylene, viewed
as exemplifying the relation between Athens and
her subject allies; and the dramatic form is given
accordingly, not merely to the Athenian debate on
Mitylene, but also to the appeal of the Mityleneans
at Olympia[2]. The speech of Brasidas at Acanthus
is given in the direct form as a specimen of his
persuasive diplomacy in dealing with the cities of
the Chalcidic peninsula[3]. The rival overtures of
Athens and Syracuse to Camarina have a similarly
representative character in relation to the wavering
neutrality of the Sicilian cities, and accordingly the
direct form is given to the arguments of Euphemus
and of Hermocrates[4]. The absence of speeches in
the Eighth Book has been reckoned among the
proofs that this book had not received the author's
last touches. There can be no doubt that Thucydides
was prevented by death from completing or revising

---

[1] iii. 53—59, 61—67.   [2] iii. 9—14.

[3] iv. 85—87.   [4] v. 76—80; 82—86.

the Eighth Book[1]: but if his general practice is con
sidered, the argument from the absence of speeches
will appear questionable. Much of the Eighth Book
is occupied with negotiations, either clandestine or
indecisive, or both ; and in a period of similar
character which fills the greater part of the Fifth
Book Thucydides nowhere employs the dramatic
form[2]. It cannot surprise us that Thucydides has
not given a dramatic emphasis to the mere mis-
representations by which Alcibiades and Chalcideus
prevailed on the Chians to revolt[3]. The Revolution
of the Four Hundred certainly afforded opportunities
for the insertion of speeches made in debate. But
that Revolution was primarily concerned with the

[1] Classen examines the evidence in his *Vorbemerkungen* to
Book viii., with these results :—(1) Book viii. was left unrevised,
owing to the author's death while he was engaged upon it, and
hence several inaccuracies of expression or statement remain
[cf. *e.g.* c. 8 § 3—4: the notice of the βραχεῖα ναυμαχία in c. 80,
compared with c. 102 : c. 89 § 2 (τῶν πάνυ στρατηγῶν, κ.τ.λ.) :
c. 90 § 1, where σφῶν recurs four times in a few lines : c. 101 § 3,
where the geographical details are obscure]. (2) Such defects of
the text were early recognised, but for a long time no attempt
was made to remedy them. (3) In the Alexandrian or Roman
age a recension of the whole History was made, of which codex
Vaticanus 126 is the representative. For Books i.—vi. the cases
in which the codex Vaticanus *alone* has the true reading are not
numerous : in vii. they are more so : in viii. they are so frequent
that here the Vaticanus, as compared with all the other MSS.,
assumes the character of a revised text.

[2] Thuc. v. 14—83 (422—416 B.C.). In Book v. the direct
form of speech occurs only in the harangue of Brasidas (v. 9) and
the Melian dialogue (85—116).

[3] viii. 14.

form of the Athenian constitution ; its special importance for the history of the war lay in the use
which Alcibiades was making of it to procure his
own recall. This is perhaps the only point in the
extant part of the Eighth Book at which the usual
practice of Thucydides would lead us to expect
the dramatic emphasis ; and just here it is found.
Peisander brings his opponents to admit that the
case of Athens is desperate without the help of
Persia. " This, then," he says, " we cannot get,
unless we adopt a more temperate policy, and concentrate the administration in fewer hands, so as
to secure the confidence of the king, . . . and recall
Alcibiades, the only man living who can gain our
end[1]." In a revision of the book Thucydides would
possibly have worked up the speech of Peisander at
greater length[2].

§ 11. As regards the language of the speeches,
Thucydides plainly avows that it is chiefly or wholly
his own[3]. The dramatic truth, so far as it goes, is
in the matter, not in the form. He may sometimes
indicate such broad characteristics as the curt blunt-

---

[1] viii. 53.

[2] The absence of military harangues, too, in Book viii. is
sufficiently explained by the absence of any good occasion for
them. The sea-fights at Euboea (95) and Cyzicus were hardly
such : and the narrative breaks off before the more decisive
actions of Cynossema and Aegospotami. The question has been
discussed lately in an essay, *De Thucydidei Operis Libri viii.
indole ac natura*, by Paul Hellwig (Halle, 1876).

[3] i. 22, where the ἀκρίβεια αὐτὴ τῶν λεχθέντων is opposed to
the ξύμπασα γνώμη.

ness of the ephor Sthenelaidas[1] or the insolent
vehemence of Alcibiades[2]. But, as a rule, there is
little discrimination of style. In all that concerns
expression, the speeches are essentially the oratorical
essays of the historian himself. At the end of the
war, when he composed or revised them, the art of
Rhetoric was thoroughly established at Athens. The
popular dialectic of the Sophists had been combined
with lessons in the minute proprieties of language.
Protagoras taught correctness in grammatical forms[3],
Prodicus in the use of synonyms[4]. The Sicilian
Rhetoric had familiarised Athenian speakers with
principles of division and arrangement[5]. Gorgias,
with his brilliant gift of expression[6], had for a while
set the fashion of strained antithesis and tawdry
splendour. It might have been expected from the
character of his mind that Thucydides would be
keenly alive to what was hollow and false in the new
rhetoric. Several touches in the History show that

---

[1] i. 86, τοὺς μὲν λόγους τοὺς πολλοὺς τῶν Ἀθηναίων οὐ γιγνώσκω,
κ.τ.λ.

[2] vi. 18 § 3, ταμιεύεσθαι ἐς ὅσον βουλόμεθα ἄρχειν: § 4,
στορέσωμεν τὸ φρόνημα, etc., where the scholiast remarks that
this is the harshest (σκληρότατον) of the metaphors in Thucydides,
ἀλλὰ κατὰ Ἀλκιβιάδην.

[3] ὀρθοέπεια, Plat. *Phaedr.* 267 c.

[4] ὀρθότης ὀνομάτων, Plat. *Euthyd.* p. 277 E.

[5] The two things which the early Sicilian Rhetoric most
sought to teach were skill in marshalling facts and skill in
arguing probabilities: cp. *Attic Orators*, vol. i. p. cxviii f.

[6] Cp. *ib.* i. cxxiii. Gorgias was not properly either a student
of technical rhetoric or a sophist.

he was so. Citizens in grave debate are contrasted with men who play audience to the empty displays of sophists[1]. A contempt for rhetorical commonplace is frequently indicated. Thus Pericles declines to dilate on the legendary glories of Athens[2] or on the advantages of patriotic fortitude[3], and Hermocrates begs to be excused from enlarging on the hardships of war[4] or the blessings of peace[5]. On the technical side, however, Thucydides shows the influence of the new art. This often appears in his method of marshalling topics and in his organisation of the more elaborate speeches[6]. It is seen still more clearly if his style is compared with that of the orator Antiphon. The extant work of Antiphon as a writer of speeches for the law-courts falls in the

---

[1] Thuc. iii. 38 § 7. σοφιστῶν [the word only here in Thuc.] θεαταῖς ἐοικότες καθημένοις μᾶλλον ἢ περὶ πόλεως βουλευομένοις. Cf. § 5, μετὰ καινότητος λόγου ἀπατᾶσθαι ἄριστοι. Thucydides thrice uses ἐπίδειξις, but only once in reference to oratory, and then in a general, not in a technical sense (iii. 42). The regular speakers in the Ecclesia are thrice spoken of as ῥήτορες, and always in a more or less unfavourable tone (iii. 40; vi. 29; viii. 1).

[2] ii. 36.   [3] ii. 43.   [4] iv. 59.

[5] iv. 62. Compare what Alcibiades says at Sparta in declining to dwell on the evils of democracy—ἀλλὰ περὶ ὁμολογουμένης ἀνοίας οὐδὲν ἂν καινὸν λέγοιτο.

[6] As in the Plataean and Theban speeches to the Spartan judges (iii. 53—59, 61—67), in the speeches of Hermocrates and Athenagoras to the Syracusan assembly (vi. 33—34, 36—40), and in the Funeral Oration. We can recognise a conscious partition, more or less complete, into προοίμιον, πρόθεσις (or προκατασκευή), διήγησις, πίστεις, ἐπίλογος. Cp. Attic Orators, vol. i. pp. 36, 181; ii. 422.

years 421—411 B.C.[1] The warmth of the terms in
which Thucydides describes him as "a master of
device and of expression[2],"—a phase identical with
that which is ascribed, as a definition of statesman-
like ability, to Pericles—testifies at least to an intellectual sympathy. There is, however, no evidence
for the ancient tradition that the historian was the
pupil of the orator[3]. Thucydides and Antiphon
belong to the same rhetorical school, and represent
the same early stage in the development of Attic
prose. Both writers admit words of an antique or
a decidedly poetical cast[4]. Both delight in verbal
contrasts, pointed by insisting on the precise difference between terms of similar import[5]. Both use

---

[1] Of his extant works, *Or.* v., περὶ τοῦ Ἡρώδου φόνου, may be
referred to about 417 B.C., and *Or.* vi., περὶ τοῦ χορευτοῦ, to about
412 B.C. Cp. *Attic Orators*, i. 34, 58, 63.

[2] viii. 68, κράτιστος ἐνθυμηθῆναι . . . καὶ ἃ γνοίη εἰπεῖν. Cf. ii.
60, ὃς οὐδενὸς οἴομαι ἥσσων εἶναι γνῶναί τε τὰ δέοντα καὶ ἑρμηνεῦσαι
ταῦτα.

[3] Caecilius of Calacte, in the Augustan age, conjectured that
Thucydides had been the pupil of Antiphon (*Vitt. x. Oratt.*);
Hermogenes (περὶ ἰδ. ii. 497) notices the belief as current, but
rejects it. It seems to have been a mere guess, resting on resemblance of style. See *Attic Orators*, i. p. 4.

[4] *E.g.* Antiphon : ἀλιτήριος—ποινή—προστρόπαιος—ἐνθύμιος—
ἀσπαίρω (ii. δ. 5)—ἀνθρώπινον φῦλον (iv. α. 2)—εὐδία (ii. β. 1)—
χωροφιλεῖν (v. 78)—φιλοθύτης (ii. β. 12). Thucydides : περιωπή
(= σκοπία, iv. 86)—ἀχθηδών (ii. 37)—ναυβάτης (i. 121 ; cf. Pollux
i. 95, τὸ ναυβάτας ὀνομάζειν (τοὺς ναύτας) τραγικώτερον—ἐσθήματα
(iii. 58)—ἑσσαμένων (= ἱδρυσαμένων, *ib.*)—κεκμηῶτες (iii. 59)—
περίρρυτος (iv. 64)—φυλοκρινεῖν (vi. 18)—ἐπηλυγάζεσθαι (vi. 36),
and many more.

[5] *E.g.* Antiphon : γνωρισταί—δικασταί—δοξασταί—κριταί (v.

metaphors rather bolder than Greek prose easily tolerated in its riper age[1]. On the other hand, there are three respects in which the composition of Thucydides may be contrasted with that of Antiphon. First, Thucydides has a pregnant brevity which would not have been possible in such measure for a practical orator, since no ordinary hearer could have followed his meaning with full comprehension[2]. Secondly, Thucydides often departs not only from the natural but from the rhetorical order of words, in

94): the πράκτορες τῶν ἀκουσίων distinguished from the αἴτιοι τῶν παθημάτων (ii. β. § 6): τὰ παρῳχημένα σημείοις πιστώσαι, τὰ δὲ μέλλοντα τεκμηρίοις (ap. Ammon. 127). Thucydides: αἰτία—κατηγορία (i. 68): φρόνημα—καταφρόνημα—αὔχημα—καταφρόνησις (ii. 62): ἐπανέστησαν—ἀπέστησαν (iii. 39)—οὐκ ἀξυνετωτέρου, κακοξυνετωτέρου δέ (vi. 76): κατοικίσαι—ἐξοικίσαι (ib.)—παραίνεσις—ἀξίωσις (i. 41)—δοκοῦσα—φαινομένη (i. 32)—προεπιβουλεύειν—ἀντεπιβουλεύειν (i. 33): δικασταί . . . σωφρονισταί (vi. 87).

[1] E.g. Antiphon : τὰ ἴχνη τῆς ὑποψίας εἰς τοῦτον φέροντα (ii. γ. 10): ἰατροὺς τῆς ἀτυχίας (ii. β. 13); cf. i. γ. 1 and ii. β. 10. Thucydides : ἡ ἐπιστήμη ἐγγηράσεται (vi. 18)—ἰατρὸς τῆς πόλεως (vi. 14)—δουλοῖ τὸ φρόνημα τὸ αἰφνίδιον (ii. 61)—πόλεμος βίαιος διδάσκαλος (iii. 82)—ἐπικλασθῆναι (iii. 59), etc.

[2] This brevity appears (1) in such constructions as γυναικείας ἀρετῆς, ὅσαι . . . ἔσονται (ii. 45), or τῶν μὲν ἄρχειν τῶν δὲ διανοεῖσθαι (sc. ἄρχειν, i. 124); (2) in the suppression of a clause which can be supplied mentally, as often before a sentence introduced by γάρ (cf. i. 120 ad init.) : (3) in the pregnant use of words, as vi. 11, ὅπερ ἡμᾶς ἐκφοβοῦσι (= ἐκφοβοῦντες λέγουσι). Cic. de Orat. ii. 22, sententiis magis abundat quam verbis . . . ; 13, ita verbis aptus et pressus est, etc. Quint. x. 1, densus et brevis et semper sibi instans. Dionys., p. 792, says that it belongs to Thucydides πειρᾶσθαι δι᾽ ἐλαχίστων ὀνομάτων πλεῖστα σημαίνειν, and Marcellinus, § 50, speaks of his θαυμασταὶ βραχύτητες.

order to throw a stronger emphasis on the word which is the key-note to the thought; and in this again he is seen to be writing for readers, not for hearers[1]. Thirdly, the strings of clauses, forming periods of a somewhat loose and inartistic kind, are longer with Thucydides than with Antiphon, and this because Thucydides is striving to express ideas of a more complex nature[2]. The originality and the striking interest of the historian's style consists, in fact, in this, that we see a vigorous mind in the very act of struggling to mould a language of magnificent but immature capabilities. Sometimes the direction of the thought changes in the moment that it is being uttered[3]. Then arise obscurities which have their source in the intense effort of Thucydides to be clear at each successive moment— to say exactly what he means at that moment. The strong consciousness of logical coherence then makes him heedless of formal coherence. The student of

---

[1] *E.g.* iii. 39, μετὰ τῶν πολεμιωτάτων ἡμᾶς στάντες διαφθεῖραι: i. 33, γενήσεται δὲ ... καλὴ ἡ ξυντυχία κατὰ πολλὰ τῆς ἡμετέρας χρείας: vi. 82, οὓς ξυγγενεῖς φασιν ὄντας ἡμᾶς Συρακόσιοι δεδουλῶσθαι: v. 91, ἐπὶ σωτηρίᾳ νῦν τοὺς λόγους ἐροῦμεν τῆς ὑμετέρας πόλεως.

[2] *E.g.* such a sentence as that in Antiphon v. 21, ἡ μὲν πρόφασις ἑκατέρῳ—ἀποθανεῖν αὐτὸν τὸν Ἡρώδην, may be compared in general structure with Thuc. vi. 82, ἡμεῖς γὰρ Ἴωνες ὄντες ... Συρακόσιοι δεδουλῶσθαι, but the latter has a much longer series of clauses. In Thucydides the transition from a simple string of clauses to a period properly so called is commonly made by the insertion of explanatory parentheses introduced with γάρ.

[3] *E.g.* vii. 42, τοῖς Συρακουσίοις ... κατάπληξις ἐγένετο ... ὁρῶντες, κ.τ.λ. Cp. iii. 36, vi. 24, iv. 108, etc.

Thucydides has one consolation which is not always present to the student of a difficult writer. He knows that he is not engaged in the hopeless or thankless task of unravelling a mere rhetorical tangle. Every new light on the thought is sure to be a new light on the words[1].

§ 12. The practice of introducing speeches was continued through the whole series of Greek and Roman historians, and, owing to its classical prestige, even maintained itself for a time in modern literature. But it is curious to trace the process by which it was gradually estranged from the spirit and significance of its origin. For Xenophon, the idea of portraying character in deed and in word was as natural as for Thucydides. Herodotus, Thucydides, and Xenophon, with all their differences, alike belong to an age in which the historian draws from life and for life, setting forth what has been done and said, but rarely theorising or commenting. In the political life which Thucydides and Xenophon represent, public speech

---

[1] Jelf (following Kühner) rightly classes Thucydides with those writers who, "engrossed with the subject, were overpowered by their flow of thought, and endeavouring to concentrate these notions in all their fulness in as few words as possible, passed from thought to thought, without taking much care that the several parts of the whole sentence should be connected together with a strict grammatical accuracy." The constructions of Thucydides, he adds, "in spite of, or perhaps because of, their grammatical inaccuracy, have a power and depth of expression which perhaps no other prose writer ever attained." (*Greek Grammar*, ii. 593.)—Thucydides wishes his *thought* to be what Aristotle requires in the period (*Rhet.* iii. 9)—εὐσύνοπτον. Cp. *Attic Orators*, i. 35.

wielded the decisive force; but while the main
purpose of Thucydides is political, that of Xenophon
is rather ethical. Xenophon introduces direct speech
or dialogue chiefly to enforce the moral lessons of
individual character. The colloquial tone prevails
even in political debate[1], and there is rarely any
attempt at condensed reasoning of the Thucydidean
type. In the course of the fourth century B.C. the
school of Isocrates developed a normal literary prose,
and such writers as Ephorus and Theopompus applied
a rhetoric more florid than their master's to the mis-
placed embellishment of history[2]. At the same time
the political life of Greece was decaying, and with it
the instinct which in earlier days would have been
offended by the obtrusion of false ornament on a
narrative of civic action. Then came the age of
the Alexandrian erudition, and history was made a
province of learned research. Polybius is a learned
historian with a theory, but he is also a practical
statesman and soldier. He is utterly opposed to
the rhetorical treatment of historical subjects. He
expressly condemns the sensational writers who
confound the scope of history with that of tragedy.
Tragedy, he says, may stir the emotions by any
fiction which is not too improbable: the part of

---

[1] See *e.g.* the speeches of Critias and Theramenes in Xen.
Hellen. ii. 3. This colloquial tone is one element of the quality
in Xenophon which Quintilian (x. 1) calls "iucunditas inaffec-
tata."

[2] On the rhetorical historians of the Isocratic school, see *Attic
Orators*, ii. 48 and 427.

history is to teach lessons of permanent worth "by
means of real deeds and words¹." At the same
time, he is keenly alive to the power of oratory.
He observes how a single weighty speaker may turn
the tide at a crisis², and he apparently feels bound
to make some attempt at representing oratorical
effect. When he makes his persons speak, he does
so much in the spirit of Thucydides, though less
elaborately : that is, he has some definite points or
arguments which he wishes to present in the most
vivid form at a critical moment. Like Thucydides,
he sometimes balances the harangues of generals on
opposite sides³. Sometimes he begins to give merely
the purport of what was said, and then passes
from the oblique to direct speech⁴, as Thucydides
occasionally does. And it may be concluded that,
like Thucydides, he gave the "general sense" faithfully whenever it could be ascertained⁵. But Polybius
stands alone in this respect among the historical
writers after Xenophon. In the period between

----

¹ Polyb. ii. 56 : ἐκεῖ μὲν γὰρ (*i.e.* in Tragedy) δεῖ διὰ τῶν
πιθανωτάτων λόγων ἐκπλῆξαι καὶ ψυχαγωγῆσαι κατὰ τὸ παρὸν τοὺς
ἀκούοντας, ἐνθάδε δὲ (in History) διὰ τῶν ἀληθινῶν ἔργων καὶ λόγων
εἰς τὸν πάντα χρόνον διδάξαι καὶ πεῖσαι τοὺς φιλομαθοῦντας.

² Polyb. xi. 10 : οὕτως εἷς λόγος, εὐκαίρως ῥηθεὶς ὑπ᾽ ἀνδρὸς
ἀξιοπίστου, πολλάκις οὐ μόνον ἀποτρέπει τῶν χειρίστων ἀλλὰ καὶ
παρορμᾷ πρὸς τὰ κάλλιστα τοὺς ἀνθρώπους.

³ *E.g.* of Hannibal and Scipio, Polyb. iii. 108—111.

⁴ Polyb. xi. 28 ; xxii. 14.

⁵ See Polyb. xxx. 4 : ἦν δ᾽ ὁ νοῦς τῆς ἀποκρίσεως τοιοῦτος,—
the ξύμπασα γνώμη of Thuc. i. 22.

Alexander and Augustus the rhetorical school of history prevailed. Diodorus Siculus and Dionysius of Halicarnassus[1] are both rhetoricians, the rhetoric of Diodorus being combined with a quasi-philosophical bent, and that of Dionysius with æsthetic criticism. Diodorus, indeed, has some quaintly judicious remarks on the introduction of long speeches into history. They interrupt the story, he says, and distract the reader: writers who wish to show their eloquence should do so somewhere else. A history should be an organic whole; a speech which is inserted amiss cannot have vital grace[2]. Still, speeches are sometimes desirable, Diodorus adds, for the sake of variety ($\pi o \iota \kappa \iota \lambda \iota a$). When circumstances require that an envoy or senator should speak, the historian must gallantly accompany his personages into the arena of debate[3]. Diodorus appears to recognise, as he certainly used, the free licence of invention[4]. His view is substantially that

---

[1] I have purposely abstained from examining the criticisms of Dionysius on the speeches in Thucydides, since he regards them exclusively from the point of view of contemporary rhetoric, not at all from the historian's. His criticisms on Thucydides are, for this very reason, immeasurably inferior to those in his excellent essays on the orators. The lengthy speech of Veturia to Coriolanus (Dionys. *Ant. Rom.* viii. 46—53) is a fair specimen of his own practice in the rhetorical embellishment of history.

[2] ἐστέρηται τῆς ψυχικῆς χάριτος, Diod. xx. 2.

[3] Diod. xx. 2, ὁ μὴ τεθαρρηκότως συγκαταβαίνων πρὸς τοὺς ἐν τοῖς λόγοις ἀγῶνας καὶ αὐτὸς ὑπαίτιος ἂν εἴη.

[4] Thus he says, *ib.*, μεγάλων καὶ λαμπρῶν τῶν ὑποθέσεων οὐσῶν, οὐ περιορατέον ἐλάττονα τῶν ἔργων φανῆναι τὸν λόγον.

of Plutarch[1] and Lucian[2]. They demand that the speech shall be appropriate to the speaker and to the occasion, but the same conditions are equally binding on an epic poet. Among the Roman historians of the first rank, Livy is the one who has made the largest use of this freedom. He once says, in reference to a speech of Cato's, that, as the real text is extant in Cato's *Origines*, he will not give the reader a pale copy of that rich eloquence[3]. It might have been inferred that Livy was careful in his speeches to represent individual character and manner[4]. But the inference is scarcely supported by the extant portion of his work, though it is possible that his portraits may have become more accurate in this respect as he came to later times and ampler materials. The speeches are sometimes of great power and beauty, but the rhetorical colour is uniform, and there is sometimes an absolute

---

[1] Plut., *praecept. ger. Reipubl.* 6, where he objects to long speeches before battles as out of place. The speeches, often happily dramatic, in his own biographies are the best comment on his remark (*de glor. Athen.* p. 346), τῶν ἱστορικῶν κράτιστος ὁ τὴν διήγησιν ὥσπερ γραφὴν πάθεσι καὶ προσώποις εἰδωλοποιήσας.

[2] Lucian, *de conscrib. hist.* 58, ἢν δέ ποτε . . . δεινότητα : "And if it should ever be necessary to introduce a person speaking, first of all let the speech be suitable to the person and the matter ; next let it be as clear as possible : then, however, you are at liberty to declaim (ῥητορεῦσαι) and to show your oratorical power."

[3] "Simulacrum viri copiosi," Liv. xlv. 25.

[4] As Quintilian says of Livy, "ita dicuntur omnia, cum rebus tum personis accommodata," x. 1.

disregard of dramatic probability[1]. Sallust has higher merit in this department. The war of Jugurtha and the conspiracy of Catiline were, when Sallust wrote, events of recent memory, and each had been illustrated by striking contrasts of character. According to Plutarch, the employment of shorthand writers[2] to report debates in the Roman Senate began in 63 B.C.; it was certainly well established in the closing years of the Republic. Sallust had some advantages for the presentation of character in a manner at once dramatic and historical, and he seems to have used them well. There is no reason to doubt that Caesar's speech in the debate on the punishment of the conspirators was substantially such as Sallust reports[3]; and his way of introducing a discourse of Memmius in the Jugurthine War implies that it is true not only to

[1] *E.g.* Liv. ii. 40 ; xxiii. 8, 9. Livy seems sometimes to have taken hints from Polybius or Thucydides; cp. xxx. 30 with Polyb. xv. 6, and vii. 30 with Thuc. i. 32.

[2] Plut. (*Cat. min.* 23) says that the speech of Cato in the debate on the conspiracy of Catiline is believed to be the only one of his preserved—Cicero having taught some of the most rapid writers the use of a shorthand (σημεῖα προδιδάξαντος ἐν μικροῖς καὶ βραχέσι τύποις πολλῶν γραμμάτων ἔχοντα δύναμιν), and having distributed these writers through the Senate-house. For the Romans, Plutarch adds, did not yet possess τοὺς καλουμένους σημειογράφους: this was the beginning of it. Suetonius mentions a speech of Julius Cæsar which, Augustus thought, must have been imperfectly taken down by the *actuarii* (*Caes.* 55). The usual Roman word was *notarius.* Martial has an epigram on a shorthand writer, xiv. 208.

[3] Sallust, *Catil.* 51, 52.

the substance but to the manner[1]. Tacitus uses the dramatic form more variously than Sallust, but with a stricter historical conscience than Livy. He resembles Thucydides and Polybius in never introducing a speech merely for oratorical effect, but always for the purpose of illustrating a political situation or character[2]. There is a well-known instance—the only one in ancient literature—in which the discourse given by the historian can be compared with an official record of the discourse really delivered. In the Eleventh Book of the *Annals* the Emperor Claudius addresses the Senate in support of a proposal for imparting the Roman franchise to the provincials of Gallia Comata[3]. The bronze tablets found at Lyons in the sixteenth century, and now in the Museum there, give what purports to be the real speech of Claudius on this occasion. Tacitus and the tablets disagree hopelessly in language and in nearly all the detail, but agree in the general line of argument[4]. Knowing

---

[1] *Bellum Jugurth.* 31—a striking illustration of the Roman feeling that oratory, for its own sake, deserved a place in history.

[2] Ulrici, indeed (*Charakteristik der antiken Historiographie*, p. 148), regards some of the speeches in Tacitus as inserted merely for dramatic ornament; *e.g. Ann.* i. 17, 22, 42, 43, 58, 59; ii. 14, 45, 46; iii. 16, 61; iv. 34, 35; xii. 10. But in all such cases, I think, it will be found that a more serious motive is also present.

[3] Tac. *Ann.* xi. 24.

[4] The text of the two bronze tablets, found in 1524, has been edited by A. de Boissieu in his *Inscriptions antiques de Lyon.* It is printed in Orelli's edition of Tacitus at the end of Book xi. of the *Annals*, p. 342.

the antiquarian turn of Claudius, Tacitus might easily have concluded that the Emperor's speech would dwell largely on historical precedents; but it seems more likely that he knew, from oral or written report, the substance of what Claudius had said, and worked up this in his own way. Here, then, is a rough gauge of the approximation which might be made to the truth by a historian who composed a speech based on "the general sense of what was really said." Thucydides and Polybius, Sallust and Tacitus, are widely removed from writers who introduce harangues merely as opportunities of display[1]. The latter tendency prevailed in what Gibbon calls "the elaborate and often empty speeches of the Byzantine historians[2]." The Latin chroniclers of the middle ages rarely ventured on such ambitious efforts. But at the revival of letters the classical practice of inserting speeches was revived by historical writers, whether they wrote in Latin[3]

---

[1] As they are introduced, for example, by Quintus Curtius, who gives the speech of the Scythian ambassadors to Alexander (vii. 8), and an impossible harangue of Dareius to his army before the battle of Arbela (iv. 14).

[2] *Decline and Fall*, ch. 43. It is difficult to believe, with Gibbon, that the speech of Attila to his soldiers before the battle of Chalons—as given in Cassiodorus—can rest on any basis of fact (ch. 35); however it may be with the letter of Belisarius to Justinian given by Procopius, which Gibbon thinks "genuine and original" (ch. 43).

[3] *E.g.* Paulus Aemilius, Strada Mariana, Buchanan, Grotius, De Thou.

or in their vernacular[1]. M. Daunou[2] quotes some
curious examples from the French literature of the
three centuries before our own. Thus Vertot, in
his *Révolutions romaines*, entered into competition
with Dionysius, Livy and Plutarch, by inventing a
fourth version of the appeal made to Coriolanus by
his mother in the Volscian camp. Mézerai could
make Joan of Arc address her executioners in a
harangue full of violent invective and sinister prediction; and this when the contemporary record of
her trial existed, with its notice of the rare and
broken utterances which belonged to her last hours[3].
By degrees a controversy arose on the question
whether a historian is entitled to invent speeches for
his persons, and the literary world was long divided
upon it. Isaac Voss[4] and Mably[5] were among
the more distinguished champions of the oratorical
licence; among its opponents were Voltaire—whose

---

[1] *E.g.* Machiavelli, Guicciardini, Mézerai.

[2] *Cours d'Études Historiques*, vol. vii. p. 466 ff.

[3] As M. Daunou gravely observes : " La plus simple réflexion
suffit pour concevoir que les Anglais, tenant en leur pouvoir la
malheureuse Jeanne, ne lui auraient pas permis, à sa dernière
heure, de débiter publiquement toutes ces sottises" (p. 476). The
authentic records of her trial and execution are contained, he
adds, in vol. iii. of the *Notices et Extraits des Manuscrits de la
Bibliothèque du Roi.* It is an extraordinary example of the
rhetorical taste of the age that Mézerai should have preferred to
declaim, when he might have told a true story of the deepest
pathos.

[4] *Ars Historica*, 20.

[5] *De la manière d'écrire l'Histoire*, Works, vol. xii. 452—461.

opinion has been quoted already—and D'Alembert.
The latter declared, in 1761, that a historian who
filled his work with speeches would be sent back
to college[1]. But the practice lingered on a little
longer, being commonly defended by the plea that
it was enlivening, and that it could not be really
deceptive[2]. The spirit of scientific criticism has
now banished it for ever from history, and has
relegated it to its proper sphere in the province of
historical romance.

§ 13. Thucydides set the first great example of
making historical persons say what they might have
said. The basis of his conception was common to
the whole ancient world : it was the sovereign im-

---

[1] "Tranchons le mot, aujourd'hui l'on renverrait aux amplifications de collége un historien qui remplirait son ouvrage de
harangues": quoted by Daunou (vii. 472) from a paper on the
art of writing history, read by D'Alembert to the French Academy
(*ib.* p. 115).

[2] Thus Gaillard, in his History of Francis I., published in
1766, answers the charge of a "petite infidélité" by saying :
"Je réponds que je ne puis voir une infidélité réelle où d'un côté
personne ne veut tromper, et où d'un autre côté personne ne
peut être trompé" (Daunou, p. 458). This is much the same as
the apology for Livy's speeches made by Crevier in the preface to
his edition : "Quasi vero cuiquam innocens ille dolus imponat."
Botta's History of Italy from 1780 to 1814 contains one of the
latest examples, perhaps, of the licence, when he gives (Book iii.)
the speeches of Pesaro and Vallaresso in the debate of the
Venetian Senate on the French invasion of Italy (1793), and
(Book v.) a debate in the Piedmontese Council. The practice
was thoroughly suited to the Italian genius, and maintained itself
longest in Italy.

portance of speech in political and civic life. But
in Thucydides the use of the licence is dramatic—
that is, conducive to the truthful and vivid presentment of action. In most of the later Greek and
Roman historians it is either rhetorical—that is,
subservient to the display of the writer's style—or
partly dramatic and partly rhetorical. The art of
rhetoric passed through two stages of educational
significance in the ancient world. In the first stage,
with which Thucydides was contemporary, rhetoric
meant a training for real debate in the assembly or
the law-courts. Then, as Greek political life died
down, rhetoric came to mean the art of writing or
declaiming[1]. The speeches in Thucydides have
the dramatic spirit, and not the rhetorical, because,
although the art of rhetoric has helped to make
them, they are in direct relation with real action and
real life. The rhetorical historians of the ancient
world represent the second stage of rhetoric : their
speeches are only more or less possible declamations.
The modern writers who attempted to revive the
practice were in a lower deep still, since for them
rhetoric was not even a living element of culture[2].
But it may be well to consider a little more closely

[1] The process of this change has been sketched in the *Attic
Orators*, vol. ii. ch. xxiv.

[2] The Roman historical writers of the Empire were under the
influence of the recitations (cp. Mayor on Juvenal iii. ; and
Heitland and Raven, in the Introduction to their extracts from
Quintus Curtius, in the Pitt Press Series, p. 12). Prejudicial to
history as this influence was, it yet gave a special interest to the
speeches, regarded as exercises in a familiar art.

how far and in what sense Thucydides can be called
dramatic. The epithet "dramatic" is sometimes
applied to narrative when no more is apparently
meant than that it is vivid or graphic. In the proper
sense, however, a narrative is dramatic only when
it elicits the inherent eloquence of facts. Thucydides
is dramatic, for instance, when he places the Melian
dialogue[1] immediately before the Sicilian expedition.
The simple juxtaposition of insolence and ruin is
more effective than comment. The bare recital,
thus ordered, makes the same kind of impression
which the actions themselves would have made if
one had immediately succeeded the other before our
eyes. It might not be difficult, with a little adroit-
ness, to represent Thucydides as a conscious dramatic
artist throughout his work ; and an ingenious writer
has actually shown how his History may be conceived
as a tragedy cast into five acts[2]. But it would perhaps

---

[1] In the remarkable speech of the Athenian envoy Euphemus
at Camarina (vi. 82—86, 415 B.C.), the dramatic purpose of the
Melian dialogue is continued and completed. The plain avowal
of Athenian motives is reiterated, and their bearing on the Sicilian
expedition is explicitly stated. See vi. 83, τήν τε γὰρ ἐκεῖ ἀρχὴν
(in Greece) εἰρήκαμεν διὰ δέος ἔχειν, καὶ τὰ ἐνθάδε (in Sicily) διὰ τὸ
αὐτὸ ἥκειν μετὰ τῶν φίλων ἀσφαλῶς καταστησόμενοι. 85, ὥστε
καὶ τἀνθάδε εἰκὸς πρὸς τὸ λυσιτελοῦν καί, ὃ λέγομεν, ἐς Συρακοσίους
δέος καθίστασθαι.

[2] Ulrici, *Charakteristik der antiken Historiographie*, p. 313.
Book i. is a prologue, he says, which acquaints the reader with
the immediate antecedents of the drama and the relative positions
of the chief actors. The First Act comprises the plague at
Athens, the supreme efforts of Pericles and his death, the destruction of Plataea by Sparta, the overthrow of Mitylene by

be truer to say that the war itself presented striking contrasts, analogous to those which a dramatic poet contrives : the dullest writer could not have wholly missed these contrasts ; and if Diodorus had been the historian, his work, too, might have revealed the five acts ; but Thucydides was peculiarly well fitted to bring out these contrasts with the most complete effect. He was so, because he felt the whole moment and pathos of the events themselves ; because he saw them with the distinctness of intense concentration ; and because, partly under the influence of language[1], he had even more than the ordinary Greek love of antithesis. It is obvious that the Peloponnesian war, as a subject for history, may be

Athens (ii. 1—iii. 68). The Second Act presents the typical party-strife at Corcyra ; fortune wavers; the Athenians are defeated by the Aetolians, but blockade the Spartans in Sphacteria (iii. 69—iv. 36). The Third Act opens with the surrender of the Spartans; the Athenians occupy Cythera ; both sides are weary of the struggle, and at length a peace is concluded. But there are signs that it cannot last, and now Alcibiades comes forward to advocate the Sicilian expedition (iv. 37—vi. 23). The Fourth Act is the crisis—the Sicilian expedition, ending in the Athenian defeat (vi. 24—vii.). In the Fifth Act the catastrophe is delayed for a moment by the recall of Alcibiades. He brings back a gleam of prosperity with him. But he is again dismissed ; and then comes the final ruin of Athens (viii.).

[1] The Greek instinct for symmetry and just measure sharpened the perception of contrast, and the desire of vividly expressing contrast helped to mould the language. Thus when it is said of Antigone, πασῶν γυναικῶν ὡς ἀναξιωτάτη | κάκιστ' ἀπ' ἔργων εὐκλεεστάτων φθίνει (694), it is the keenly felt opposition of things that is striving to utter itself in the forcible opposition of words. Then Rhetoric arose, with its opposition of words even where

said to have dramatic unity in the sense that it is a single great action : as, by an analogous metaphor, the subject of Herodotus may be said to have epic unity, because the various parts, though they cannot be brought within the compass of one action[1], can be brought within the compass of one narrative. And, apart from this rudimentary dramatic unity, the Peloponnesian war has a further analogy to a drama in presenting a definite moment at which the cardinal situation is decisively reversed—as it is reversed in the *Oedipus Tyrannus*, for instance, when the king discovers that he is an incestuous parricide. That moment is the Sicilian expedition. The supreme test of "dramatic" quality in a history of the Peloponnesian war must be the power with which the historian has marked the significance of the Sicilian expedition as the tragic "revolution" (*peripeteia*), the climax of pity and terror, the decisive reversal. Thucydides has devoted the whole of his Sixth and Seventh Books to the events of those two years, thus at once marking the significance of the expedition as the turning-point of the war. And every reader knows with what tremendous effect he has traced its course, from the moment when the whole population of Athens was gathered at the

there was no commensurate opposition of things. Thucydides was partly under this influence of Rhetoric: witness his ἔργον and λόγος, etc.; but, by a reversal of the natural process, the very habit of verbal antithesis tended to quicken the observation of opportunities for its effective employment.

[1] *I.e.* no drama on the Persian wars could have included (*e.g.*) the Egyptian and Scythian episodes of Herodotus.

Peiraeus in the early midsummer morning to see
the splendid fleet sail for Sicily, and the trumpet
commanded silence while the whole multitude joined
in prayer, and wine was poured from vessels of
silver and gold as the pæan[1] arose, down to that
overthrow of which he writes that they were destroyed with utter destruction, and that few out of
many came home[2]. Here, at the point in his story
which supplies the crucial test, Thucydides shows
that he possesses true dramatic power. By the
direct presentment of the facts, not by reflections
upon them, he makes us feel all that is tragic in the
Sicilian disaster itself, and also all that it means in
relation to the larger tragedy of the war. The same
power is seen in many particular episodes of the
History : for example, in the self-restrained majesty
of Pericles, the great protagonist of the opening
war, whose courage, amidst havoc and pestilence,
ever rises as the Athenian courage declines ; or in
the first appearance of Alcibiades on the scene,
with his brilliant versatility and his profound lack
of loyalty, with his unmeasured possibilities for good
or evil, just when the Sicilian project is trembling in
the balance. Without pressing the parallel between
the History and a work of dramatic art to any
fanciful length, it may be said with a definite meaning that Thucydides has not merely the inspiration
of action, but often also the spirit of the noblest
tragic drama.

It is natural to regret his silence in regard to the

[1] vi. 30. [2] vii. 87.

social and intellectual life of his age[1]. The simplest
explanation of it is that he did not conceive such
details as requisite for the illustration of his purely
political subject. The art and poetry of the day,
the philosophy and the society, were perhaps in his
view merely the decorations of the theatre in which
the great tragedy of the war was being played.
Though he wrote for all time, he did not conceive
of an audience who would have to reconstruct this
theatre before they could fully comprehend his
drama[2]. No writer has ever been at once so

---

[1] The names of Aeschylus, Sophocles (the poet), Euripides
(the poet), Aristophanes, Pheidias, Ictinus, Anaxagoras, Socrates,
are among those which Thucydides nowhere mentions. In addition
to Helen (i. 9) and Procne (ii. 29), only four women are named in
the whole History, and not one of them has the slightest human
interest in reference to the war—Chrysis and Phaeinis, succes-
sively priestesses of the Argive Hera (ii. 1, iv. 133); Stratonice,
the sister of Perdiccas (ii. 101); and Archedice, the daughter of
Hippias (vi. 59). The Parthenon is alluded to as a treasury; and
the Propylaea are noticed—as a work which had reduced the
balance in it (ii. 13 § 3, where ἐν τῇ ἀκροπόλει = ἐν τῷ ὀπισθοδόμῳ).

[2] Thucydides can, indeed, imagine a time when Sparta shall
be desolate, and only the ruins of Athens shall remain; i. 10 § 2,
Λακεδαιμονίων γὰρ εἰ ἡ πόλις ἐρημωθείη . . . 'Αθηναίων δὲ τὸ αὐτὸ
τοῦτο παθόντων, κ.τ.λ. But he has no conception of a time when
the Hellenic civilisation that he knew should have passed away.
Thus Pericles says that Athens (unlike Troy or Mycenae, he
means) needs no Homer to persuade posterity of her greatness:
she has established on every shore *imperishable monuments* of
her power for evil or good, where the ἀίδια μνημεῖα are the
Athenian settlements on conquered or on friendly soil. Cf. ii. 64,
ἢν καὶ νῦν ὑπενδῶμέν ποτε . . . μνήμη καταλελείψεται, κ.τ.λ.—where
the μνήμη assumes a purely Hellenic standard.

anxiously careful and so haughtily improvident of the future. His characteristic dislike of superfluous detail seems to have been allied with a certain hardness of temperament, such as is indicated by the tone of his reference to the poets[1]. His banishment may also have infused something of bitterness[2] into his recollections of the Athenian life, with all its gracious surroundings, with all its social and intellectual delights, from which he was suddenly cut off, so that he should know them no more until he came back in his old age and found them changed.

[1] He cites them simply as authorities for facts, whose statements often require to be modified : i. 21 § 1. Thus he makes a sort of apology for quoting so equivocal an authority as Homer respecting the power of Agamemnon (i. 9 § 4), and the size of the Greek fleet (10 § 3). His extracts from the fine passage in the Hymn to the Delian Apollo are the briefest which could establish his two points—that there *was* an Ionian festival at Delos, and that it included a musical contest (iii. 104).

[2] There is a singular suggestiveness in the speech which the exile Thucydides attributes to the exile Alcibiades (at Sparta in 415 B.C., vi. 92). It is the historian's way of showing how the pain which he himself had known might work in a disloyal character. "My patriotism," says Alcibiades, "is not for a country that wrongs me ; it was given to a country that protected my rights . . . The true patriot is not he who abstains from moving against the country from which he has been unjustly banished, but he who, in his passionate love for her, strives by all means to regain her."

May not these words—καὶ φιλόπολις οὗτος ὀρθῶς, οὐχ ὃς ἂν τὴν ἑαυτοῦ ἀδίκως ἀπολέσας μὴ ἐπίῃ—have a reference to Thrasybulus and the patriotic exiles who marched from Phyle upon Athens? Just after the restoration of the democracy the point would have been peculiarly effective.

No one can tell now how the memories of early
sympathies may have grouped themselves in his
mind as he looked out in later years from his home
in Thrace on the sea over which he had sailed on
the long-past day when he failed to save Amphipolis;
but at least there is a twofold suggestiveness in those
passages[1] which touch on the glories of Athens.
There is the feeling of the man who has never lost
his love and admiration for the Athenian ideal; and
there is also a certain reluctance to translate this
ideal into concrete images[2], as if, in the words of
Oedipus after his ruin, it were sweet for thought to
dwell beyond the sphere of griefs[3]. Perhaps in this
very reticence the modern world may find a gain

---

[1] Most striking of all these, perhaps, is one in the speech of
Nicias to the army before the retreat from Syracuse (vii. 63 § 3),
where, addressing the *non*-Athenians, he reminds them of the
pleasure (ἡδονή) which they have derived from *passing for*
Athenians—through their knowledge of the Attic dialect, and
their imitation of Attic manners—and so being admired throughout Greece: Ἀθηναῖοι νομιζόμενοι καὶ μὴ ὄντες ... τῆς τε φωνῆς
ἐπιστήμη καὶ τῶν τρόπων τῇ μιμήσει ἐθαυμάζεσθε κατὰ τὴν Ἑλλάδα.
Among Peloponnesians, Italians or Siceliots, the Athenian exile
had ever carried about with him the consciousness of belonging
to that city which was the παίδευσις Ἑλλάδος.

[2] Even in the Funeral Oration—that splendid monument of
his grave enthusiasm for Athens—Thucydides has been restrained,
whether by fidelity to the original or by his own feeling, from ex-
ceeding the limit of such abstract expressions as τὰ καθ' ἡμέραν
ἐπιτηδεύματα, πόνων ἀναπαύλαι, ἀγῶνες, θυσίαι, φιλοκαλεῖν, φιλο-
σοφεῖν.

[3] τὸ γὰρ | τὴν φροντίδ' ἔξω τῶν κακῶν οἰκεῖν γλυκύ, *Oed.
Tyr.* 1390.

when it views his work from the artistic side.
Thucydides must always hold his fame by a double
right; not only as a thinker who, in an age of
transitional scepticism, clearly apprehended the value
of disciplined intelligence as a permanent force in
practical politics, but also as a writer who knew how
to make great events tell their own story greatly;
and the dramatic power of the immortal History is
heightened by its dramatic reserve.

TABLE OF THE SPEECHES.

[Asterisks mark those delivered at Athens before the exile of Thucydides.]

Book.   Date B.C.

VII. 61–64   413   Nicias to the Athenian troops ⎱ before the last
„   66–68   „   Gylippus to the Syracusan troops ⎰   sea-fight.
„   77   „   Nicias to his troops before the retreat from
                   Syracuse.

The short speech of the Elean Teutiaplus to Alcidas and the Peloponnesian leaders at Embaton (iii. 30, 427 B.C.) is virtually of this class.

From the set speeches are to be distinguished a few shorter utterances in the direct form, but of a more colloquial character, viz. the dialogue between Archidamus and the Plataeans (ii. 71–74, 429 B.C.); the conversation with the Ambracian herald and an Athenian (iii. 113, 426 B.C.); and the words of Peisander in the Athenian Ecclesia (viii. 53, 411 B.C.). The letter of Nicias (vii. 11–15, 414 B.C.) would be classed by some with the speeches composed by Thucydides, by others as an authentic document. Cp. p. 403, note 4.

Appendix B
Intellectual Background
John H. Finley, Jr.

IN THE preceding chapter we saw something of the political events which shaped the life and, to a considerable degree, the thought of Thucydides. Yet obviously no man's thought, not even a historian's, is in the main directly molded by events themselves. Rather, events, by altering the conditions of life, demand new assumptions and create new habits of mind which in turn, as they become accepted, constitute what is called the intellectual atmosphere of an age. And since it is this atmosphere which influences men most constantly and most directly, we may well go on in this chapter to inquire what were the intellectual forces of Thucydides' day and how he was affected by them. For only by so doing shall we recapture something of the outlook and of the standards of judgment with which he entered upon his *History*. But there exists a still more important reason for making such an inquiry. Of the many problems presented by the *History*, undoubtedly the most important to ourselves is whether or not it offers, especially in the speeches, a reasonably authentic picture of men's minds in the period when, purportedly at least, the speeches were delivered — or (to put the matter in another way) whether the general cast of style

Reprinted from John H. Finley, Jr., *Thucydides*, Cambridge, Mass. (Harvard University Press), 1942, pp. 37-73. Reprinted by permission of the publishers, Harvard University Press, Copyright, 1942, by the President and Fellows of Harvard College; 1970 by John Huston Finley, Jr.

and thought in the speeches must be imagined as widespread in the early period of the war or, on the contrary, peculiar to Thucydides at the end of the war and thus fundamentally misleading for the earlier period. The value of the *History* will evidently be quite different depending on which of these alternatives is correct. In the one case it will contain for us an invaluable picture of Athens, and to some extent of Greece, at this crucial period of their existence. In the other it will present, to be sure, the impressions of an extremely acute contemporary observer, but will lack the former far more representative scope. Now in no part of his work are Thucydides' characteristic rationalism and his profound powers of political analysis more evident than in the speeches of the first four books covering the period before his exile; indeed, these books contain some two-thirds of the more than forty speeches in the *History*. An understanding of Athenian political thought and oratory in these years should therefore serve a double purpose. It should not only suggest something of the atmosphere in which the *History* was conceived but provide a means of judging how far we should see in these speeches the authentic voice of the later Periclean age.

It is obvious at the start that the sophistic movement is the great central fact with which we shall now be dealing. For the sophists as a class were not merely teachers of oratory; they led the way in that sweeping development by which prose supplanted verse as the vehicle of serious thought and acquired numberless new uses in the investigation of all individual and social problems. They, in short, fashioned both a vehicle and a field of inquiry suited to the realistic temper of the later fifth century.

But in order to understand the exact character of their influence, it may be useful, as often, to go back. It is self-evident that all peoples, from the time when they begin to think consciously of their way of life, find some characteristic means of expressing the standards by which they live. When, as among the ancient Jews, belief in the guidance of a single God is strongly felt, then men express themselves theologically and point to God's acts as an explanation of the world and to his commandments as the basis of society. But the Greeks, on the other hand, who lacked any such overpowering belief in divine guidance, were inevitably driven to find other than theological explanations for their life and past, and it is significant that even in Homer the emphasis is not on the gods but on man. What happens in the *Iliad* and *Odyssey* happens because the characters are what they are.

It is not easy to describe all the ways by which this essentially secular outlook on life found expression: it did so partly in myths, partly in gnomic rules and observations, and partly in broad generic pictures of human behavior. This last method is for the present purpose the most important. When Homer portrayed opposite types of women in Helen and Andromache, opposite types of men in Achilles and Hector, different ages and attitudes of mind in the keen Odysseus, the wise Nestor, the haughty Agamemnon, and the simple Ajax, he not only rested his poems on the lasting foundation of human experience; he also established for the

Greeks that tradition of generic portraiture and broad
analysis which, perhaps more than anything else, lies
at the root of the term "classic." But what is chiefly
important here is to realize that this capacity for generalization, this insistence on the typical, remained characteristic of the Greek mind, because, being secular, it was
compelled to draw its leading ideas almost entirely from
observation. One must remember that the Greeks had
no organized priesthood and no accepted theology, and
that through the formative centuries of their development they further lacked any such sense of scientific law
as in modern times supplies the basis of thought. The
poets rather, as Aristophanes says,[1] were the teachers of
Greece — a fact which shows once more how thoroughly
the national mind was formed on broad truths of the
sort that wisdom and observation can supply. For, bar-
ring theology or science as the foundation of thought,
such insights into the nature of social and individual life
necessarily remained the chief means whereby men saw
themselves in relation to the world. There is no need
here to follow the subject in detail or to see how, even
during the more religious era that intervened between
Homer and the writers of the fifth century, the poets
remained true to their calling as interpreters of civic
standards and human experience to the people. It is
essential merely to recognize that, when after the middle
of the fifth century the sophists to some degree took
over the poets' earlier function in society, they could not
and did not abandon the latter's essential attitude of
mind. The Greeks still relied not on scientific or reli-

[1] *Frogs* 1054.

gious truths but on truths drawn from human observation, and, however novel the precise views of the sophists
may have been, the character of those views was inevitably generic, inevitably more concerned with the law
than the occurrence, the type than the individual.

The reasons for the appearance and success of the
sophists are on the whole clear. The growth of democracy at Athens and the establishment of the empire,
sketched in the last chapter, vastly altered the ways of
life evolved in simpler ages. Shaken from their security
and faced with the demands of a more complicated and
competitive world, the aristocrats had to learn new arts
of oratory and statecraft if they were to maintain their
position, while the middle classes now had access to
leadership if they could command the means to attain
it. To describe adequately the change in outlook that
resulted from these changed circumstances is of course
extremely difficult. Something of it appears if one recall, for instance, the aristocratic ideal presented by
Pindar. He praises, on the one hand, the physical
strength and beauty of the victors and, on the other,
their moral courage and self-restraint, qualities which
he believes have descended from semi-divine ancestors
and which he illustrates by the famous legends of the
latter's feats. What is striking in this ideal is its
extreme localism: in celebrating an Aeginetan victor
Pindar points to the heroes of Aegina, in praising an Argive to the heroes of Argos. At the same time, the ideal
rested on the assumption of innate personal virtue
($\dot{\alpha}\rho\epsilon\tau\dot{\eta}$), the development of which a man owed to himself, to his class, and to his ancestors — that is, to the

standards implicit in his local associations. But there is
a diverting story in Herodotus which tells what happens
to such standards in a time of growing intercommunica-
tion.[2] It is the story of how certain Greeks and Indians
were talking about each other's burial customs and were
each profoundly shocked: the Indians to learn that the
Greeks burned their fathers, and the Greeks to discover
that the Indians devoured theirs. Herodotus does not
say that the standards of each were thereafter weakened,
but that is inevitably the case, since the sanctity of
standards is in their seeming universality. It is apparent then that, when the developments of the fifth century immensely broadened men's knowledge of each
other and created in Athens at least a metropolis where,
as Pericles says,[3] the produce of all the world was familiar, the sanctity of local custom could hardly survive.
In its place men sought a wider and more objective
knowledge of mankind and were prepared to base their
ideals of conduct upon these broader findings. The
sophists, then, though they inherited the poets' function
as classifiers and interpreters of experience, expounded
a view of life far less local than theirs and standards of
behavior derived from far more naturalistic sanctions.
When Protagoras said that he did not know whether
the gods existed or not,[4] he clearly left no place for any
standards other than those based on the observed workings of human nature.

It would be false to assume that the sophists were
alone responsible for so profound a change of outlook

---

[2] III 38. 3–4.   [3] II 38. 2.
[4] Diels-Kranz, *Vorsokratiker* [5], II, fg. 4.

or that it became universal among their contemporaries. Their realism and objectivity would be unthinkable without the concept of fixed natural law first given currency by the Ionian physicists of the sixth century. One of the readiest and most fruitful ways of understanding the sophists is in fact to realize that they merely applied to human behavior those principles of mechanistic causation which the Ionian physicists had applied to the cosmos. Then again, Simonides, for example, anticipated their scepticism when he asked how far the standards of personal ἀρετή, in which Pindar saw the authority of the gods themselves, could be thought of as in any sense universal. Man, he said, is largely the creature of circumstance. "He is good if his luck is good and bad if it is bad." [5] On the other hand, even during the period of the sophists' greatest influence, Sophocles resisted both their agnosticism and their tendency to regard human conduct as merely the result of natural forces. For, though more aware than Pindar of the dangerousness of life, he clung to the belief that the gods oversee the world and that human conduct ultimately has meaning in their eyes. But such amplifications and limitations do not alter the central fact before us: that the sophists as a class came into existence and won continuing success because they explained, or seemed to explain, the more complicated world evoked by Attic imperialism and Attic democracy.

What, then, were their teachings? In answering this question, it is necessary to remember that though the minor interests of individual sophists were extremely

[5] Fg. 4, 10–11 (Diehl).

diverse (Protagoras, for instance, concerning himself among much else with grammar, mathematics, and dialectic, Hippias with mathematics and history, Antiphon with mathematics and physics, Prodicus with physics and mythology), they had one great purpose in common, the teaching of argument and oratory. For ability to speak, with all it implies of practical knowledge and power of analysis, was the chief instrument by which their pupils hoped to win success in active life. In Plato's *Protagoras* [6] the great sophist is made to state the fact clearly when he says that he instructs his pupils in the intelligent administration of their own and the city's business, an art which Socrates calls the "political art." Evidently, then, the essential teachings of the sophists, as well as the underlying outlook which those teachings embodied, will appear most clearly in the methods of argumentation that they introduced. The fact is important; for it is often assumed that the few extant fragments of the early sophists constitute our main evidence on the movement, and, since these are in many cases harmless, it has even been argued that the sophists were simply rhetoricians exerting no profound effect on the thought of the day. When, however, one seeks their major influence in the methods of reasoning which became widespread in Athens after their arrival, not only are the implications of that reasoning quite clear, but even the date of its acceptance is relatively certain. For the sophistic arguments emerge suddenly in many works of the period, notably the plays of Euripides, the tract of the Old Oligarch, the long frag-

[6] 319a.

ments of the sophist Antiphon, and the speeches of the like-named orator, even in Herodotus, Sophocles, and Aristophanes. These authors in turn permit us to reconstruct to some extent the intellectual currents of the Athens which Thucydides knew and thus to achieve what it was stated at the start we should ideally possess: namely, some insight into why the *History* was conceived when and as it was and some means of appraising its basic truthfulness of tone.[7]

The form evolved for his instruction by the first and greatest of the sophists, Protagoras, was the so-called antilogy, that is, opposite arguments, known as the ἥττων and the κρείττων λόγος, on either side of a question. By training his pupils in this way, Protagoras acquainted them with alternative lines of reasoning to be used as the case demanded, and that these arguments set forth fundamentally opposed attitudes towards a given subject and were thus of very wide application follows from the fact that they furnished a general preparation for speaking. It is significant that almost all the authors of the period, Thucydides not least, used pairs of arguments for exactly this purpose of expounding some basic contrast of attitudes. We know little about Protagoras' actual works except that many of them were political in character, but it is clear, at least, when his influence was felt at Athens. He was sufficiently known to be sent as lawgiver to the colony of Thurii founded in 443,[8] and the earliest of Sophocles' extant plays, the

---

[7] The subject is discussed in much greater detail in the first of the articles mentioned in the Foreword.

[8] Diogenes Laertius, IX 50, on the authority of Heraclides Ponticus.

Ajax and *Antigone*, both almost certainly produced in the forties, contain pairs of arguments of the kind that Protagoras had introduced. These debates not only embody the essential questions of the plays, but in the *Ajax*, at least, the end of each speech in a given pair so markedly echoes that of the opposite speech as to create an almost statuesque contrast.[9] The same is true of the *Medea* of 431,[10] where, as one might expect, Euripides' argumentation is even more developed than that of Sophocles. Aeschylus, on the other hand, had made no use of such debates, even in the *Eumenides*, where the conflict of the old religion with the new forms the essence of the play. Evidently, then, Sophocles was affected as early as the forties by the new fashions of oratory — a fact further confirmed by the political content of his speeches. Menelaus in the *Ajax* and Creon in the *Antigone* expound the premises of oligarchy in words strikingly similar to those of Archidamus in the first book of Thucydides.[11] We have already seen that Protagoras was much concerned with government and his influence is usually found in the amusing debate in Herodotus in which Darius and certain other Persians discuss with truly superb inappropriateness the relative merits of monarchy, democracy, and oligarchy.[12] But in Greece, and particularly in Athens, as the characteristics and consequences of Attic democracy were becoming clear, such questions were not inappropriate. On the contrary, they must have been canvassed now as

[9] Cf. ll. 479–480 and 523–524.
[10] Cf. ll. 516–519 and 569–575.
[11] I 84. 3–4. *Ajax* 1081–1086, *Antigone* 666–676.   [12] III 80–82.

never before, and it is not too much to say that political questions, phrased by the method of searching antithesis introduced by Protagoras, must have formed the essence of Thucydides' early training. Nothing else can explain the profundity with which the habit of grasping ideas by pairs and in contrast was fixed in his mind. It showed itself later not only in the paired speeches of his *History*, but more pervasively in almost any given paragraph or sentence, being, as it were, the most instinctive, necessary clothing of his thought.

Of the lines of argument developed by the early sophists, the most striking perhaps is the argument from likelihood, εἰκός. Its most obvious use — and the one which, we are told, led to its perfection by the Sicilian Corax — was in the courtroom. A man accused, for instance, of murder could argue that it was unlikely that he, a small man, would attack a much larger man. The argument appears in this form in Antiphon's first Tetralogy and in a closely similar form in the *Hippolytus* and *Oedipus Rex*,[13] the former produced in 428, the latter possibly a year earlier. But if this use of the argument was mild enough, that is not the case as one sees it in the tract of the Old Oligarch, usually dated at 424.[14] The author is there discussing the character of democracy, and bases his whole argument on how it is

[13] Respectively, ll. 994–1007 and 584–602.

[14] Pseudo-Xenophon, *Constitution of Athens*. A somewhat later date has, to be sure, been urged by A. W. Gomme, *Athenian Studies* (*Harv. Stud. in Class. Philol.*, Suppl. Vol. I, 1940), pp. 211–245. The extremely numerous parallels between this work and the speeches of the *History*, particularly those of Pericles, are listed in the first of the articles mentioned in the Foreword, p. 25, n. 2. These parallels are one more proof that Thucydides attributes to his speakers ideas current in their times.

likely that a common man, given his nature and interest, will act politically. Without describing the argument in detail, it is enough to say that, from the premise that the masses are ill-educated and solely interested in their material advantage, the author deduces most of the actual practices of the Athenian state: distribution of offices by lot, prominence of litigation, harshness towards the subject allies, reliance on the lower classes as sailors rather than on the upper classes as hoplites. The extreme materialism of the point of view is obvious; in fact, though hostile to the masses, it closely resembles the materialist dialectic of our own times. For it assumes that a man's conduct is predictable from his interest, and that government is necessarily created for the material advantage of one class.

Of more immediate present concern, however, is the tremendous scope of the argument from likelihood when it is thus applied, not to the individual, but to the class. If one can say that it is natural for a large or small man to act in a certain way, it is equally possible to say that a democrat or oligarch and hence a democracy or oligarchy will tend to act in a certain way. In the eighth book of the *Republic*, Plato follows this line of reasoning when he derives the various forms of government from the various tendencies of human nature, and, since the method is already developed in the tract of the Old Oligarch, one concludes that it was evolved even earlier. At least, Aristotle's pupil Aristoxenus stated that much of the *Republic* was anticipated by Protagoras,[15] and it seems not unreasonable to believe

[15] Diels-Kranz, *Vorsokratiker*⁵, II, fg. 5.

that the great sophist discussed the different forms of government in much this same way. But however that may be, the reasoning of the Old Oligarch clearly illustrates two points made earlier: that sophistic thought, inevitably based on observation, was concerned with the generic and the typical, and that in its essential materialism it left no place for ideals drawn from the social and religious sanctions of earlier times. It was based rather on the mechanistic view that behavior is simply the result of natural stresses. And since these stresses applied not to the individual but to the class and were therefore conceived as operating uniformly, it is easy to see what a formidable weapon of analysis was thus put in men's hands. As will be made clear in the next chapter, Thucydides unquestionably thought that he possessed an absolutely new and absolutely reliable means of appraising the forces at work in his own day. He was convinced that these forces would operate similarly in similar eras of the future and for that reason predicted undying usefulness for his book. There can be little doubt that he came to these opinions largely because the idea had already become widespread that a given class of people will react uniformly to given conditions and hence that their behavior is subject to analysis and even to prediction. A strong reason why he undertook his work as a young man at the start of the war must have been that he felt the enormous pertinence of such reasoning to the writing of history.

Example after example could be given to show how Thucydides follows the pattern of thought underlying the argument from likelihood, but one or two instances will perhaps suffice. In the first chapters of the work comprising the so-called Archaeology, he justifies his early prescience of the magnitude of the war by contrasting contemporary economic conditions with those of Greece at the time of the Trojan War. In so doing, he reasons that, since in backward regions in his own day certain practices still obtained — for instance, piracy and the carrying of arms — which Homer described as prevalent in the heroic world, then the general cast of heroic life must have resembled that in these contemporary backward regions.[13] Given social traits evidently postulated to him a given type of society and government. The one followed naturally from the other. Again, his famous analysis of the effects of revolution on the public mind [17] draws its unrivalled power from his habit of seeing the typical consequences of a given condition. Calamities then took place, he says, "which occur and always will occur while human nature remains the same," and he goes on to enumerate the sharp changes in behavior and outlook which, so he thought, inevitably attend the dislocations of war.

These passages perhaps sufficiently illustrate how thoroughly Thucydides had learned to reason along the same materialistic and observational lines which were noted in the tract of the Old Oligarch, but one other use of the argument from likelihood is worth mentioning because of its extreme importance in the *History*. Aristotle makes a distinction between courtroom speaking, which looks to the past, and parliamentary speaking,

[16] I 5–6.
[17] III 82–83.

which is concerned with the future.[18] Just as the lawyer Antiphon argues how a certain type of man would probably have acted, so the various speakers in the *History* are constantly predicting the probable outcome of policies and the future course of events. Now to Thucydides the supreme requisite of a politician is his πρόγνωσις — his ability to foresee — and the *History* itself is, in essence, a manual for future statesmen, instructing them in the outcome of conditions destined to be repeated. Inevitably, therefore, he attributes to his speakers these same methods of deducing the typical results of given circumstances. But though no genuine political speech has come down to us from the early — indeed (except for a brief fragment of Thrasymachus) from any — period of the war, and we thus cannot prove how accurately Thucydides catches the oratory of the time, there is no good reason to doubt his essential truthfulness. The period which saw, in Antiphon and in the speeches of tragedy, such broad arguments directed to past events and, in the tract of the Old Oligarch, such sweeping deductions regarding contemporary conditions could hardly have produced speeches on policy of quite a different cast. As was argued earlier, one of the greatest traits of the Greek mind — a trait never better exemplified than in the fifth century — was its concern for the generic, and when Thucydides' speeches are supremely marked by this trait, one should not explain the fact merely by his genius but by his actual experience, doubtless somewhat idealized in retrospect, of the Attic oratory of his youth.

[18] *Rhetoric* I 8. 4, 1858b 14.

Another line of sophistic argument which, though different from the preceding, often accompanies it, is that from expedience — τὸ συμφέρον. The statement, "men tend to do what profits them," illustrates how easily the two arguments coalesce, and in fact any such general assertion necessarily implies a judgment of how men as a class are likely to act. In itself, however, the concept that men are primarily moved by their advantage forms the obvious antithesis to the ideals of justice and honor, τὸ δίκαιον and τὸ καλόν, which had been the wellspring of Greek literature since Homer's time, and is used to refute these. Thus, in the *Medea*,[19] when the heroine has stated her rightful claims on her husband Jason, he replies harshly that, the world being what it is, he is acting for her and their children's best interests by finding a richer wife. There are similar arguments in the *Oedipus* and *Hippolytus*.[20] Again, as we have seen, the tract of the Old Oligarch is based on the assumption that the Athenian demos acts wholly and simply for its own interest. Now it could be said that this is nothing more than a very ancient and permanent human attitude exemplified, for instance, in the speech of Odysseus in the ninth *Iliad* or, even more, by that of Thersites in the second. But one must remember that we are dealing here with lines of argument formally taught and consciously adopted in the late Periclean age as the basis of successful pleading. The careful symmetry of the debate in the *Medea* has already been noted. No better example could be found of the fashion of reasoning on

[19] Lines 545–567.
[20] Respectively, ll. 594–595 and 462–465.

opposite lines which Protagoras had introduced and which profoundly affected Thucydides. But if so, then the argument from advantage is more than a mere trick of pleading; it offers a searching commentary on the temper of the day. For that it was perfected for practical use means that speakers expected to make, and audiences to hear, realistic estimates of human motives and public policy. It was noted in the last chapter that, when Pericles in the fifteen years before the war consciously substituted outright control of the Delian Confederacy for the dangers and strains of a common war against Persia, a new hardening of mood is to be felt in Athens, as if men's estimate of human nature, their own included, was subtly darkening. The change is to be felt, for instance, in the opening scene of the *Medea* where the old servant, on being told by the shocked chorus that Jason is preparing to desert Medea, replies:

> Have you just realized this,
> That each man loves himself beyond all others? [21]

It is equally to be felt in the fragments of the sophist Antiphon, to be discussed presently, and in the tract of the Old Oligarch. More than anything else, this new insistence on the concept of advantage, τὸ συμφέρον, epitomizes the curious disillusionment which now, as at other times in history, darkened men's outlook in the period of their greatest material achievement.

It is not therefore surprising that the argument and the underlying attitude which it implies appear prominently in the *History*. As contrasted with Herodotus,

[21] Lines 85–86.

Thucydides devotes his whole work to analyzing the actual, and therefore often the material, aspects of the war, and Sophocles' remark about Euripides could as well have been made by the older about the younger historian, "I make men as they should be, he makes them as they are." [22] More specifically, the first debate in the *History*,[23] that between the Corcyreans and Corinthians, turns on the same conflict between expedience and justice that has been noted in the *Medea*. The question at issue is whether Athens should ally herself with Corcyra, a colony of Corinth then at odds with the mother city. The Corcyreans point to the great advantage that their navy would be to Athens in the event of war, while the Corinthians have nothing to offer except evidences of past decency, alike towards Athens and towards Corcyra. It is significant of Thucydides' attitude towards events that the arguments of the Corcyreans prevail, and not less significant of his method that the issue is put exactly in this way. The close parallel presented by the debate in the *Medea* offers striking proof that these were the methods of argument in use at the time in Athens, and, though that fact might be taken to prove merely that Thucydides was influenced as a writer by the tragedians, surely it proves more than that. For the whole development of Attic tragedy was towards a greater naturalism, and Euripides in 431 would hardly have made his characters speak in this way unless the sophistic arguments were generally known and practised. In sum, though other such parallels could be adduced, this one is

[22] *Poetics* 25, 1460b 32.
[23] I 32–43.

perhaps sufficient to indicate both the mood of conscious realism which was prevalent in Athens during Thucydides' earlier years and the faithfulness with which he portrayed that mood in the *History*. He was the child of an age that had seen the ideal vision of a great movement of liberation fade into the consciousness of mere struggle for power — which is to say that he lived in an age of growing imperialism when man had become jealously aware of their local advantages. This fact had called forth the attitudes of mind phrased by the sophists, and this fact both explains and validates the essential picture of the times which emerges from the speeches of the *History*.

Finally, there is an argument of transcendent importance for the thought of the period, that from φύσις, human nature. Though obviously related to the concept of likelihood (with which it is grouped by later writers on rhetoric), it nevertheless seems to stand by itself in the writings of this era as a fresh and profoundly cogent idea. In the *Medea*,[24] after the heroine has recalled to Jason what she has done for him, he replies that these acts signify no merit on her part and demand no requital on his, since she was acting under the sway of passion. The poet evidently conceives of human nature as so subject to overmastering impulses as to be almost powerless before them, as is made doubly clear later in the play [25] when Medea cries out that she knows the evil that she contemplates towards her children but cannot keep from it. Similarly in the *Hippolytus*,[26] when Phae-

[24] Lines 526–531.
[25] Lines 1078–1080.   [26] Lines 437–476.

dra has said that she will die before revealing her passion, the Nurse answers that there is no call for shame, since passion is a natural instinct governing human beings as it does all creatures. One must therefore accept it, she goes on, making what outward adjustments are necessary to the purely artificial standards of society.

These passages, which are quite central to these peculiarly bitter, because hopeless, plays, might have been thought to express merely the despairing insight of one tragedian, were it not for the discovery some years ago of fragments of the 'Aλήθεια, *Truth*, of the sophist Antiphon [27] which express views almost identical with those of the Nurse in the *Hippolytus* and are thus evidently of about the same period. Broadly speaking, Antiphon is interested in showing that the laws of nature govern human behavior far more forcibly than the shallow and inconsistent laws of society, his argument being that if you break the former you are instantaneously punished by being made less able to survive, whereas if you break the latter you may or may not come to harm. The fragments are doubly interesting because they reveal an early stage in the famous dispute on the relative authority of nature and convention, which finds its ultimate expression in the *Gorgias* and *Republic* of Plato. By the end of the century, men argued, as Callicles does in the *Gorgias*, that the strong individual is justified by nature in pursuing his advantage unchecked. But that extreme view probably first arose in reactionary circles at the time of the democracy's worst excesses, and An-

[27] Diels-Kranz, *Vorsokratiker*[5], II, fg. 44, pp. 346–355.

tiphon knows nothing of it.[28] He only asserts the existence of the natural laws. His tone is in general that of a
scientist (in fact, the lost first book of the ’Αλήθεια dealt
with the mathematical and physical constitution of the
world), and he may therefore exemplify for ourselves
the class of teachers who during Thucydides’ early manhood were expounding in Athens a new and objective
concept of society based on their new understanding of
man’s place in nature.

That such was a common function of sophists at the
time appears from Aristophanes’ portrait of Socrates in
the *Clouds*, a portrait not so much of the individual as
of a typical sophist concerned partly with public speaking, partly with novel views on society, and partly with
physical investigation. Antiphon well illustrates the
kind of teacher that Aristophanes had in mind. It is
further evidence on how widespread the interest in
natural law then was that the famous debate in the
Clouds [29] between the Old and the New Education turns
on this same question of social restraint as opposed to
natural impulse which we have already seen in Euripides
and Antiphon. By the outbreak of the war many phi-
losophers, notably Anaxagoras, had long been in Athens,
and, though their direct teachings on the physical make-
up of the universe could hardly have reached a wide
circle, it is not surprising that men were generally recep-
tive to similar, if more popular, views. The sophists, who
were themselves versed in the higher philosophy of the
time, merely applied its inherent materialism to the

[28] W. W. Jaeger, *Paideia* (Eng. trans. by G. Highet, New York, 1939),
pp. 321–326.   [29] Lines 889–1104.

problems of society, and, if the effect of the new doc-
trines of natural law was to undermine men's faith in
earlier standards, that was not so much the fault of the
sophists as of the times. For the immense growth of
Athens inevitably produced more materialistic and universal standards, and the sophists simply phrased what
the Athenians as a people had come to feel by experience.

How deeply Thucydides was affected by this new
sense of man as the creature of natural forces seems
hardly necessary to say, particularly after what has been
said already about the argument from likelihood. The
idea that human life, like the life of the cosmos, follows
observable laws is clearly only another and stronger way
of stating what men as a class are likely to do, and therefore of establishing that uniformity and even predict-
ability of human conduct which, as we saw, provides the
very foundation of the *History*. But, as is evident from
the passages referred to in the last paragraph, the doctrine of φύσις has a somewhat special connotation: that
of exposing the real, as opposed to the artificial, springs
of human action. Euripides and Antiphon make it quite
clear that, even during Thucydides' earlier years in
Athens, men were casting away the reasons formerly
given for behavior and substituting what seemed truer,
if less moral, explanations. Thucydides' own outlook is
much affected by that attitude, and herein one sees again
how his early acquaintance with politics in this period of
frank imperialism coalesced, as it were, with the harsher
theories then in the air. The purpose of the *History* will
be considered in the next chapter, but it is evidently

directed in some measure to future politicians, men whose business it is to see in this way the real, rather than the apparent, reasons for things, and it is impossible that this purpose was absent from Thucydides' mind when he conceived his work.

His speakers also appeal to the authority of the laws of nature. Thus in the first book the Athenian ambassadors at Sparta justify the empire in the following words: "It follows that it is nothing surprising or unusual if, moved by three of the strongest motives — fear, honor, and interest — we originally accepted and later refused to give up the empire that was offered us. We did not set the example; it has always been the law that the weaker should be subject to the stronger." [30] Pericles, too, in his third speech, describes the empire as a tyranny and justifies it by the eternal necessity of ruling or being ruled.[31] The idea appears again in the famous debate in the third book between Cleon and Diodotus on the punishment proper for the revolting Mytileneans. Cleon urges summary execution on the ground that rebellion constituted an accepted offense and that death was therefore justified by Greek precedent. Diodotus, in answering him, relies chiefly on the argument from expedience, urging that Athens should do nothing that is not in her own best interests, but he also states that it is impossible to talk of criminal disobedience in the present connection, since in recorded history human beings have never been checked by any law from doing what they really wished to do. "Either, then, some fear stronger than death must be found or it must be admitted

[30] I 76. 2.   [31] II 63.

that this restraint is useless, and that as long as poverty
forces men to courage, or power gives them the ambitions natural to the confident and proud, and the other
conditions of life all remain subject to some dominating
passion, even so long will men be driven into danger." [32]

The contrast in positions between Cleon and Diodotus, it will be observed, is exactly the same as that
between Phaedra and the Nurse in the *Hippolytus*,
produced the year before this debate was held. Like
Phaedra, Cleon urges what is considered just by Greek
practice, and, like the Nurse, Diodotus counters by the
expedient, reinforcing his views, as she does hers, by
reference to the amoral promptings of natural law.
Now, as was said earlier, we have no actual speeches of
the period which will permit us to judge how faithful
the speeches in the *History* are. Moreover, as we have
just seen, Thucydides himself was a strong rationalist
with his own views about history and his own purposes
for his work, and it may well be that this bias colored his
work, making the speeches in particular more searching
and profound than the originals would have been. Nevertheless, this close similarity between the debate in the
Hippolytus and the Mytilenean speeches, like the similar parallel between the *Medea* and the Corcyrean debate, leaves no room for doubt that the ideas which
Thucydides attributes to his speakers were in fact the
fresh and moving ideas of the period. His own mind was
formed on these ideas and he inevitably pondered them
throughout his exile during the long years before he
wrote his *History*. But the popularity of the sophists is

[32] III 45. 4.

sufficient proof that many others in Athens besides himself thought in these new ways, and the fundamental reason for believing in the truthfulness of the speeches is that the oratory and thought of these years before his exile was all that he knew from his own experience, and he inevitably kept it before him, perhaps with all the greater clarity, throughout the rest of his life.

There is perhaps no need to speak further of the argumentation introduced by the sophists or to give more examples of how Thucydides reflects it. His style will be considered in a later chapter, and the question how far it too derives from the style common in his youth will be discussed then. But it may be useful to bring together the points hitherto made about the sophistic movement in order to achieve a more general picture of it, not merely as an historical force but, more broadly, as embodying certain long-standing attitudes of the Greek mind.

At the start of the chapter, it was pointed out that the Greeks, because of the secular nature of their thought, relied more than other peoples on observation, and that since, further, this observation was long dissociated from purely scientific inquiry, it expressed itself in delineations of human types, in myths that portrayed basic relationships, and in gnomic statements of social and moral truths. On the other hand, the Ionian physicists and, even more, the medical writers of the fifth century were very largely moved by the spirit of detailed, specific inquiry familiar in modern times. And since Thucydides, as we have seen, was evidently much concerned with the generic and the typical but at the same time was at equal pains to trace specific events with utmost accuracy, it is of interest to see how these two opposite tendencies — the one towards the typical, the other towards the specific — revealed themselves in the thought of his time. For this larger aspect of his inheritance is clearly of final importance for his work.

To begin with what has been called the tendency to the typical, it was observed in Homer's great delineations of the kinds and conditions of men. Certainly it is not less apparent in Pindar's descriptions of the heroes as prototypes of the different virtues, or in Aeschylus' half-symbolic figures, his Prometheus and Xerxes, his Furies and Apollo. Such characters as these, however, are not purely symbolic. The Greeks' sense of reality permitted them to simplify and generalize, but never to desert experience for abstraction. The marvel of Greek literature resides not a little in this fact, that its characters somehow possess a clear generic significance without, at the same time, losing reality as creatures of flesh and blood. And if one seek to explain this achievement, one inevitably returns to the fact that it was the poets of Greece, not priests or scientists, who chiefly explained and clarified experience to the people. Hence it can be said of Greek thought that it derived on the one hand from observation, not from dogma, but on the other hand from the observation of experience, not from scientific observation. That this process, moreover, involved generalization must be evident from the fact that, if a people is to possess a body of thought at all, that thought must rest on general ideas and broadly applicable truths. Thus it is no accident that in the wide field of legend of which the poets wrote, they discovered not primarily individuals but persons of representative lives and lasting attitudes. As was suggested earlier, that is part of the meaning of the word classic. It is humane observation broadened and tested until it achieves almost — though it never fully can — the objective validity possessed in another domain by scientific thought.

If one examine the sophistic movement in the light of this tradition, it is evident that the arguments from the likely, the expedient, and the law of nature possess in a slightly different sense this same generic quality. That is equally true of the opposite arguments from the noble and just, though these illustrate less well the new naturalism of sophistic thought. What therefore must be emphasized at the risk of repetition is that neither the sophists nor their pupils can be expected to have thought in those specific and concrete lines familiar to the modern mind. We have seen the Old Oligarch expounding the underlying tendencies of Athenian democracy and, only in the light of these, touching upon the actual institutions and policies of Athens. Similarly, the sophist Antiphon sets forth the doctrine of natural law with only occasional instances of its specific application, and in the debates of the *Medea* and *Hippolytus* the immediate, personal conflict rises to a truly representative conflict of opposing attitudes. Other examples would merely reinforce the same conclusion that the sophists did not diminish, but probably even increased, the long-standing Greek concern for the typical. People still demanded from these new interpreters of life, as from the poets, those broad statements of men's relationship to each other and to the outside world which were the main avenues of truth to the humanistic Greek mind.

But if this is the case, then one or two conclusions of some importance for the *History* follow. The first concerns the rhetoric on which Thucydides and his contemporaries were educated. We are accustomed to think of rhetoric as decoration, something which glozes and adorns an unrelated subject. Even Aristotle a century later calls it a derivative art which takes its method from the science of logic and its substance from the findings of ethics and politics.[33] But it is clear from what has been said that in the fifth century these latter subjects could have had no existence as apart from the art of speaking. To be sure, as was said earlier, the sophists pursued subsidiary lines of investigation. Nevertheless because, like the poets, these men existed to set forth general ideas actively by the spoken word, all their minor studies were only parts or instruments of rhetoric. That is doubly clear because, as was said, the reason why the sophists arose was that they might teach men to face the altered conditions of the latter half of the fifth century, and their views on ethics and government which gave rise to the later study of these subjects were integral parts of that teaching and designed for active use. Evidently, then, the pupils of the sophists acquired from them more than the mere art of speaking, more than rhetoric in the modern sense. In learning to speak, they learned to analyze the nature of government and to appraise the older ethical standards, precisely because these subjects were

[33] *Rhetoric* I 2. 7, 1356a 25.

at the very heart of what they had come to learn. This wide concept of rhetoric as embracing and making effective all other humane studies was reaffirmed by Isocrates, Cicero, and Quintilian, and remained perhaps the greatest single force in ancient education. But even this vast legacy of the sophists is of less importance here than to realize that, if what has been said of the generalizing character of Greek thought is true, one cannot think of the oratory of the later fifth century as in any sense narrow in its aims. When in the *History* Pericles analyzes the nature of democracy or the Athenian ambassadors at Sparta state the principles of imperial power, one can only believe that these very searching speeches do in fact reflect the contemporary manner of speaking. Thucydides' speeches, it is true, are compressed and therefore more abstract than actual speeches would have been, but in their absorption with the general principles of ethics and politics they essentially reflect a period in which these new studies were a living part of rhetoric.

It might be replied that the mass of the people could not have followed speeches of so general a character, but to make such an objection is to misunderstand the mind of the fifth century, indeed of any great period. The plays of Shakespeare and the sermons of early Protestantism give proof enough of the capacity assumed in an ordinary audience or congregation. It could be argued that any era which offers the ordinary man vast horizons of opportunity demands and receives from him a fresh comprehension proportionate to his fresh self-respect. Attic tragedy, even the philosophic and political subjects treated by Aristophanes, cannot be explained on any other assumption. If, therefore, one keep in mind the character both of Greek thought and of the age, the breadth of Thucydides' speeches becomes not only explicable but expected. They are great partly because a keen observer trained himself to distil the inner meaning from the events of his age. But they are great also because they reflect the first ambitious flowering of rhetoric in a great period.

The other conclusion has been in part expressed already. It concerns the new abstraction of sophistic thought as compared with that of the past. We have seen that Homer chiefly portrayed the kinds and conditions of human beings. He was not, it is true, unfamiliar with more general ideas, as the fables of the Prayers and of the Jars of Zeus well show.[34] Hesiod had a greater interest in such ideas, and in later ages this interest increased still further. Solon's Εὐνομία, Tyrtaeus' portrait of the true Spartan, and many passages of Pindar and Aeschylus are concerned not so much with man himself as with his ethical standards and political relationships. Nevertheless, it is in the sophistic age that one first encounters a truly widespread absorption with ideas rather than persons. The Old Oligarch has no interest in human beings as such, but only in that part of them that shows itself in government; he is concerned, in sum, with the idea of democracy. Similarly, both the sophist Antiphon and Euripides treat the tendencies of the human mind with a new breadth of conception. Even the debates of the *Ajax* and the *Antigone*, previously

[34] *Iliad* IX 502–512; XXIV 527–533.

cited as showing the influence of Protagoras, reveal
something of this same spirit. Though Sophocles'
rounded vision, it need hardly be said, saw much more
than a conflict of ideas in the tragic clash of personalties,
it is nevertheless true that the *Antigone* treats a great
social problem with a bareness and concentration quite
unknown to earlier verse. To be sure, Aeschylus in his
Prometheus and *Eumenides* had typified great social
problems. But the writers of this age see such questions
more theoretically, abandoning Aeschylus' lofty symbolism for more analytical methods. Now we have seen
that such a capacity for theory strongly marks both the
speeches of the *History* and Thucydides' direct exposition. Pericles' analysis of democracy in the Funeral
Oration and the author's own train of reasoning in the
Archaeology provide examples of what is meant, though
great numbers of other passages would serve as well.
But it follows from what has just been said that the
rhetoric introduced by the sophists must not only have
embraced wider fields of study, such as ethics and politics, but have done so with a more conscious emphasis
on theory. The contemporary world was so complex
that any other method would have been impossible. The
older symbolism drawn from mythology no longer
served, and therein lies much of the reason why prose
now rapidly replaced verse as the main vehicle of
thought. We return therefore to the conclusions reached
earlier regarding the origins of Thucydides' own thought
and the basic veracity of his speeches. However individually prone to abstraction Thucydides may have been
or may have come to be through his long exile, such a
capacity for abstraction is nevertheless the very hall-

mark of the period and particularly of that rhetoric in which the changed conditions of the period find their fullest expression.

This much will perhaps suffice to suggest what was called earlier the tendency to the typical in Greek thought and in that of Thucydides. It has been emphasized to such an extent not merely because of its importance for any judgment of his work but because it has been too often neglected. Thucydides' contrary feeling for the specific, manifested in his rigid and detailed standards of accuracy, is without doubt imposing. But, since this latter aspect of his thought is far more comprehensible to the modern mind, it has too often been represented as the whole of this thought, as if Thucydides were chiefly remarkable for being, so to speak, a modern historian born before his time. But to think of the *History* as notable merely for its accuracy is to miss its essence, to forget that its author was a Greek, and to neglect that profoundest of Greek abilities, apparent alike in their literature and in their art, the ability to convey the generic without falsifying the unique. No other trait of the Greek mind more clearly reveals the humanistic character of their civilization, and none is more to be admired by an age that relies more heavily on the postulates of science than on those of social insight and tested experience. Thucydides himself expressly valued his work not for its accuracy (important as he thought accuracy to be) but for its exposition of recurrent social forces,[35] and his judgment sets the order in which we too should appraise it.

But to say a few words, finally, of what was called

[35] I 22. 4.

the tendency to the specific, it is revealed in his extreme care in verifying the exact nature of events, in the precision of his chronology, and in the detailed information which he gives about a multitude of matters bearing on the progress of the war. More will be said on these points in the next chapter, but it may be useful now to consider whether these rigorous standards, differing as they do from those of Herodotus, were peculiar to himself or whether they too reflect currents of contemporary thought. Not many years ago an able and interesting book was written to show that Thucydides formulated his ideas of historical proof under the influence of the Hippocratic school of medicine.[36] The reasons for so thinking are: first, that he applies to the causes of the war the same word πρόφασις by which the medical writers commonly denote the cause or, more literally, the "explanation" of disease; and second, that by his own words the *History* as a whole is to fulfil the same prognostic function — namely, the function of enabling men to recognize recurrent phenomena — that underlies many medical writings of the period and, particularly, his own account of the plague. Others, he says in the latter passage, may debate the causes of the plague, but, "as for myself, I shall simply describe its progress, setting down the symptoms that one should look for in order to be able to recognize it if it should recur." [37] The idea that by describing events exactly and refraining from unverifiable theories regarding their origins you can establish a pattern which will be valid for the future

[36] C. N. Cochrane, *Thucydides and the Science of History*, Oxford, 1929.
[37] II 48. 3.

is an idea which has a close bearing on the *History*.

To be sure, Thucydides is concerned with the causes of the war, as the medical writers likewise treat the immediate origins of disease. What he rejects appears to be purely philosophic or religious speculation in regard to causes, and herein is perhaps his closest tie with the best medical thought of the time. For without going into that interesting subject here, it can be said that the identifying mark of a body of writings from the late fifth century usually called Hippocratic — notably the *Prognostic, Regimen in Acute Diseases*, and *Epidemics* I and III — is that they substitute alike for religious dogma and philosophic theory an exclusive regard for the symptoms and circumstances of disease. The theory on which these writings were based is that all disease is marked by periods of crisis and that painstaking clinical study will therefore enable the physician to appraise the probable severity of these periods, his function being not to prevent them (which would be impossible) or generally to expect a successful issue but simply to assist as he can the patient's powers of resistance. It is natural that the adherents of the school should have taken stock also of local and atmospheric conditions. This practice, particularly marked in the *Epidemics*, as in an earlier work possibly by the same hand, the famous *Airs, Waters and Places*, has given rise to the name "meteorologische Medizin" as a designation for the whole school,[38] and, like the practice of noting periods of crisis, is strongly observable in Thucydides' description of the

[38] K. Deichgräber, "Die Epidemien und das Corpus Hippocraticum," *Abhandl. d. Berl. Akad.*, Phil.-Hist. kl., 1933, no. 3.

plague. If the scientific mind is one which is strictly governed in its conclusions by the data of observation, then the mind revealed in this group of writings has every claim to be called scientific, and the author's cool impersonal tone is in keeping with his method. From Thucydides' description of the plague, there can be no doubt that he was thoroughly acquainted with this school of thought, and the kinship of tone between the *History* and the tracts of the Hippocratic group, particularly the *Epidemics*, has struck more than one observer. It is difficult therefore to escape the conclusion that he was to some extent influenced by medical theory, both in his standards of accuracy and in the prognostic intention of his work. It even seems possible that his clear emphasis on the crucial stages of the war, which he normally marks by speeches, reflects some feeling on his part that the social, like the individual, organism is subject to periods of crisis.

Nevertheless, it would be false to overstress this influence. The arguments of the sophists, as we saw, assume a stable world in which men respond uniformly to given circumstances, and this mechanistic reasoning was valued because it permitted men, they thought, to understand and thus in part to foretell human behavior. The statesman, quite as much as the physician, needed this power of prediction, and it is of statesmanship that Thucydides wrote. It seems rather that, in the latter half of the fifth century, similar tendencies appeared at the same time in different fields of investigation and that the ideas proper to one subject proved fruitful in another, just as in recent times the concept of relativism

has come to have a wide application outside of Ein-
steinian physics. The fact can be observed not only as
regards the ideal of prognosis but also in respect to
Thucydides' standards of accuracy, which exemplify
what was called earlier the tendency to the specific in
his thought. He certainly did not share this tendency
with the medical writers alone. On the contrary, notices
exist of many contemporary writings of a specialized
nature: for instance, Sophocles on the Chorus (that is,
probably on tragedy as a whole), Ictinus on the Parthenon, Polyclitus on symmetry, Meton on the calendar,
Hippodamus on city-planning. Developments in all
the practical arts were also taking place very rapidly
throughout the period, and those advances necessarily
imply a more exact understanding of a given subject
and more thorough standards of accuracy. Indeed, one
class of contemporary prose, the so-called ὑπόμνημα, defi-
nitely bore the character of a scientific tract, the medical
writings being one subdivision of the larger category.
It is impossible to think of the great material progress
of the fifth century without realizing the new importance that came to be attached to technique. But the
same fact is hardly less apparent in the realms of
thought and literature. In such characters as his Pheres
or his Electra, Euripides notably departed from precedent to portray human beings as he knew them. He,
moreover, makes much the same criticisms of Aeschylus'
unrealistic art [39] as Thucydides makes of that of his own
predecessors; both reflect the more exacting spirit of
the age. Even Socrates' manner of thought, directed

[39] *Suppliants* 846–857, *Electra* 524–544, *Phoenissae* 751–752.

though it was towards ideal aims, tells much of the same methods. He was strikingly unwilling to accept any previous hypotheses on the nature of man but constantly examined particular instances of behavior in the hope that he might inductively reach some new and valid conclusions. Clearly he had this in common with the medical writers and with Thucydides, that he believed general conclusions possible only through a detailed study of particulars.

These instances of the current trend towards careful observation do not, it is true, make clear exactly how far Thucydides was influenced in his standards of accuracy by the medical writers. But they at least show that that influence, whatever it may have been, was only part of a more general contemporary influence — what has been called the tendency to the specific, existing side by side with the more peculiarly Greek tendency to the typical. But from what has been said of this double aspect of Thucydides' inheritance, one is perhaps justified in making a final judgment of him: namely, that he, more than any of his contemporaries, succeeded in allying standards of detailed accuracy with a deep and compelling sense of the generic. Socrates ironically stated that he could reach no general conclusions; the best medical thought, as was seen, was by its own theories confined to the specific; even Euripides, in spite of his striking realism and his equally great ability to portray the inward and fundamental conflicts between his characters, rarely so blended the one capacity with the other as to leave a clear and unified interpretation of life. On the other hand, such sophistic theorists as the Old Oligarch and, even more, the sophist Antiphon were so absorbed with general ideas as to neglect or to distort the specific instances on which those ideas were based. Only Thucydides is able to mount consistently and with even flight from events in themselves to their larger bearing. It is true that he rarely gives his own judgment of events, but commonly reserves such judgments for the speeches. Nevertheless, the narrative and speeches taken together do effect a union, as rare as it is imposing, between detailed fact and broad deduction. If the previous argument has any merit, then it will follow that he could not have risen to such heights of achievement merely because he was a gifted man or because he had had military and political experience or because during his exile he had leisure to ponder on all that he had seen, but because, as an Athenian of the fifth century, he was reared in a long tradition of broad generic insight, now fortified by a new feeling for objective fact. In short, the peculiar quality of his greatness reveals the quality of the fifth-century Attic mind.

Appendix C
A Chronology of Principal Events

A. Greece and the Peloponnesian War

Periods B.C.

478-477 Confederacy of Delos founded.
478-445 Growth of the Athenian Empire, at height 457.
499-429 Pericles — in power 469-429, at height 442.
459-456 Athens at war with Peloponnesian Alliance.
450-445 Five years truce between Athens and Sparta.
445-404 Decline of the Athenian Empire.
431-404 Peloponnesian War.
421-415 Peace of Nicias.
457-456 Long Walls Built.
430-429 Plague at Athens.
429-427 Siege of Plataea.
415-413 Sicilian Expedition.
404-371 Sparta supreme in Greece.

Events by years B.C.

455 Thucydides probably born; made general 424; probably died 400.
450 Peace with Persia. Athens sends 60 ships to help Amyrtaeos in Egypt.
449 Siege of Citium in Cyprus by Cimon. His death. Athenian victory at the Cyprian Salamis.
447 Colonization of the Chersonese. Athenians under Tolmides defeated by Boeotians at Coroneia. Athenians evacuate Boeotia.
445 Euboea and Megara revolt from Athens. Thirty years truce between Athens and Sparta.
444 Athenian relations with Sicily begin. Foundation of Thurii on the site of Sybaris.
440 Revolt of Samos from Athens. Andocides and Sophocles command with Pericles against Samos. Samos surrenders and congress at Sparta.
436 Citizens of Epidamnos seek help from their metropolis Corcyra. On refusal they turn to Corinth.
435 Corinthian army enters Epidamnos: sea-battle between Corinthians and Corcyraeans. Epidamnos capitulates to Corcyraeans.

433 Congress at Lacedaemon. Embassies to Athens from Corcyra and from Corinth. Athens makes a defensive alliance with Corcyra. Ten Athenian ships sent to Corcyra under Lacedaemonios.

432 Corcyraeans, supported by Athenians, defeated in sea-battle by Corinthians in spring. Athenians blockade Pydna and Potidaea. Congress at Sparta in autumn. Large majority of allies vote for war with Athens.

431 *Year 1 of War.* Peloponnesian demands rejected by Athens. War begins. Theban attempt to invade Plataea. Archidamus invades Attica. Brasidas rescues Methone from Athenians.

430 *Year 2 of War.* Second invasion of Attica. Plague begins in Athens. Pericles becomes unpopular, is fined 15 talents, but re-elected *strategos.*

429 *Year 3 of War.* Potidaea surrenders on conditions. Phormio won two naval victories in the Corinthian Gulf. Pericles dies. Siege of Plataea begins.

428 *Year 4 of War.* Lesbos except Methymna revolts. Athenians siege Mytilene. Cleomenes begins third invasion of Attica.

427 *Year 5 of War.* Plataea destroyed by Sparta. Fourth invasion of Attica by Cleomenes. Mytilene taken by Athens. Massacre proposed by Cleon and averted by Diodotos. Strife at Corcyra between oligarchs and demos in summer. Athens sends aid to Leontini.

426 *Year 6 of War.* Athenians purify Delos and restore the Panionic festival, to be held there every four years. Demosthenes in Actolia. 41 ships from Athens to Sicily.

425 *Year 7 of War.* Corcyraean demos, helped by Eurymedon and Athenians, attack Istone. Massacre of oligarchs. Fifth invasion of Attica led by Agis II. Demosthenes occupies Pylos. Spartan hoplites blockaded in Sphacteria. Cleon takes the island and returns with Spartan prisoners to Athens. Cleon flourished 425-422.

424 *Year 8 of War.* Thebans defeat Athenians at Delium. Brasidas campaigns in Thrace: captures Acanthos, Amphipolis, Stageiros, Torone. Congress of Sicilian Greeks at Gela. Hermocrates denounces Athenian aggression. Alcibiades flourished 415-413 and 411-404.

423 *Year 9 of War.* Thucydides banished from Athens for failure to save Amphipolis. Returns to Athens in 403. Brasidas in Thrace. Skione and Mende revolt from Athens. One year's truce declared.

422 *Year 10 of War.* Torone recaptured by Cleon. Battle of Amphipolis: Cleon and Brasidas killed. Population data on Athens: total

including aliens and slaves approx. 82,000; males above age of 20
— 20,000; Average attendance in Ecclesia 5,000.

421 *Year 11 of War.* Peace of Nicias for 50 years. Nominally valid
down to 414, but not recognized by Boeotians, Corinthians, or
Megarians.

420 *Year 12 of War.* Separate treaty of Sparta with (1) Boeotians,
(2) Argives. Alcibiades manages to alienate Argives from Sparta:
defensive alliance among Athens, Argos, Elis, and Mantineia.

419 *Year 13 of War.* Alcibiades becomes *strategos.* Progresses through
Achaia. The Argives invade Epidauros. Peloponnesian War
resumed.

418 *Year 14 of War.* Spartans invade Argos. Argives with Alcibiades
attack Orchomenos. Spartans come to rescue of Tegea. Battle at
Mantineia. Complete victory of Spartans over Argives and Athenians. Oligarchical conspiracy of the Thousand at Argos.

417 *Year 15 of War.* Rising of Argives demos against oligarchs. Athens
sends expedition to get back Amphipolis. Perdiccas of Macedon
breaks faith, and plan fails.

416 *Year 16 of War.* Athenians seize Melos. Alcibiades at Argos. Victories of Alcibiades at Olympia. Embassy to Athens from Egesta
requesting help against Selinus. Athens sends envoys to Egesta.

415 *Year 17 of War.* Envoys return from Egesta. Sicilian expedition
voted. Mutilation of the Hermae, just as fleet prepares to sail for
Sicily in May. Alcibiades accused of profaning mysteries. Sicilian
expedition sails under command of Nicias, Lamachos, Alcibiades.
Excitement caused at Athens by disclosures of Dioceides and
Andocides. Alcibiades condemned to death in his absence. Nicias
fails to take Syracuse.

414 *Year 18 of War.* Second campaign in Sicily. Siege of Syracuse.
Lamachos killed. Gylippus enters Syracuse as Spartan commander. Nicias sends letter to Athens for more help.

413 *Year 19 of War.* Decelea in Attica fortified by Lacedaemonians
under Agis who ravages Attica. Formal end of truce of 421.
Beginning of the second phase of the War, called the Δεκελειχὸς
or Ἰώνιος Πόλεμος (to 404 B.C.). Third campaign in Sicily. Sea-
battle at Syracuse. Athenian fleet destroyed. Death of Nicias and
of Demosthenes. Death of Peridiccas, King of Macedonia
(454 B.C.-). Accession of Archelaos (-399 B.C.).

412 *Year 20 of War.* Revolt of Lesbos from Athens. Revolt of Euboea.
Revolt of Chios. Peridatos commands Spartan troops there.

Revolt of Miletos. Boeotians seize Oropos. Athenians lose sea-battle off Cnidos, Samian demos, loyal to Athens, rises against the oligarchs. Athenian fleet at Samos: Spartan Astyochos defeats Charminos. Alcibiades takes refuge from Spartans with Tissaphernes: his overtures to Athenian leaders.

411 *Year 21 of War.* Government of the 400 at Athens (March-June). Eratosthenes active at Hellespont for the oligarchs. Athenian victory at Cynossema. Evagoras begins his reign. Thrasybulus with Athenian fleet.

410 *Year 22 of War. History* of Thucydides breaks off after battle of Cyzikos. Thrasyllos commands on coast of Asia Minor. Second form of Trierarchy brought in from partners fitting out triremes. Athenians attack and recover Cyzikos. Athens rejects Spartan offers of peace.

409 *Year 23 of War.* Athenian campaign in Lydia under Thrasyllos. Messenians in Pylos surrender to Sparta. Megara recovers Nisaea.

408 *Year 24 of War.* Alcibiades recovers Selymbria and Byzantium for Athens. Troops under Thrasyllos defeated at Ephesos.

407 *Year 25 of War.* Alcibiades returns to Athens, is elected *strategos* and leads the procession to Eleusis. Antiochos, the pilot of Alcibiades, defeated by Lysander off Notion. Alcibiades plunders; Relieved as *strategos.* Ten new Generals elected.

406 *Year 26 of War.* Dionysius I becomes tyrant of Syracuse. Callicratidas (successor of Lysander) storms Methymna and blockades Conon in Mytilene. Complete victory of Athenians at Arginusae. Death of Callitratidas. Theramenes accuses the Generals; six are executed, Socrates protesting.

405 *Year 27 of War.* Battle of Aegospotami (late autumn). Downfall of the Athenian Empire, followed (in 404) by the rulê of the Thirty Tyrants.

404 Theramenes brings the terms of peace from Sparta. Agoratos informs. Athens surrenders to Lysander. Critias and Eratosthenes are among the five ephors, and then among the Thirty. Death of Alcibiades.

403 Democracy restored at Athens in September. Expedition from Athens to Eleusis to dislodge the Thirty.

B. Sicily, Asia, Africa

498	Persia recovers Cyprus.
492	Mardonius subdues Macedonia.
485-465	Carthaginians in Sicily. Xerxes I reigns.
485-477	Gelon in Syracuse.
480	Persian invasion of Greece under Xerxes. Battle of Himera; Greek victory at Salamis.
488-472	Theron at Agrigentum.
478-475	Hiero I at Syracuse.
477	Delian League for defense against Persia. Pausanius at Byzantium.
476	Victories of Cimon.
474	Naval victory of Hiero over Tuscans.
466-405	Syracuse free.
465-447	Themistocles in Persia.
460-455	Egyptian War with Persia.
460	Athenians in Egypt.
454	Treasury of Delian League transferred to Athens; members pay tribute to Athens.
470-405	Agrigentum is powerful.
449	Athenian victory at Salamis in Cyprus.
446	Syracuse subdues Agrigentum.
446	Syracuse defeats Etruscans.
441	Athenian colony to Thurii.
440-439	The Samian War.
431	Carthaginians in Sicily.
428	Revolt of Lesbos.
427	Fall of Mytilene.
426	Congress of Sicilians at Gela.
422	Athenians at Delos.
415	Alcibiades and Nicias off Sicily.
415	Athenian fleet anchors at Naxos and Catana for winter.
413	Gylippus arrives at Syracuse.
412-411	Athenian allies revolt.
412-411	Persian treaties with Peloponnesus.
412-411	Revolt at Samos.
411	Battle of Cynossema.
406	Siege of Agrigentum.
405-439	Artaxerxes II reigns.
401	Expedition of Cyrus the Younger. March of the 10,000.

C. Rhetoric, Oratory, Literature, Art

495-406 Sophocles — wrote 125 plays.
487 Simonides of Ceos flourishes.
485 Gorgias, Protagoras, and Tisias born about this year.
484 Aeschylus (525-455) begins his tragedies. Herodotus born.
488-430 Aristophanes.
480 Antiphon born (480-411). Euripides born (480-406). Aeschylus (525-456) was now 45 and Sophocles 15.
480-406 Euripides — wrote 80-90 plays.
470 Empedocles of Agrigentum.

Era of the Sophists
460 Corax.
444 Protagoras.
444 Prodicus.
430 Gorgias.
429 Hippias of Elis.
415 Thrasymachus.

469-399 Socrates — see Plato's *Apology* for his trial.
470 Parmenides (philosopher) flourished.
460 Zeno of Elea (philosopher) flourished.
420 Democritus (philosopher) flourished.
480-425 Herodotus.
458 Approximate date of birth of the orator Lysias.
440 Approximate date of birth of the orator Andocides.
460 Approximate date of birth of Hippocrates.

427-348 Plato — believed spoken word superior to the written.
348-322 Aristotle — founder of the Lyceum (c. 335); creator of the syllogism and of formal logic.

438 Parthenon completed and dedicated.
432 Pheidias and Aspasia prosecuted for impiety.
431 Pericles speaks Epitaphios for those who had fallen in first year of the war. Euripides' *Medea* produced.
429 Damon the musician flourished. Death of Pericles.
427 Gorgias visits Athens as chief ambassador of Leontini. Tisias accompanies him. Aristophanes begins to satirize the New Culture.

426	Aristophanes' *Babylonians* (lost) played soon after the reduction of Mytilene and its bare escape from the massacre of its male inhabitants as urged by Cleon.
425	Aristophanes' *The Knights* ridicules Cleon and satirizes the defects of democracy. Thucydides banished.
423-421	*The Clouds, Wasps, The Peace.*
415	Agathon flourished. His house the setting of Plato's *Symposium*. Socrates flourished — age 53. Plato now 14, Alcibiades 34, Xenophon about 16.
405	Dramatic date of Plato's *Gorgias.*
404	Isocrates leaves Athens for Chios.
403	Lysias speaks. Isocrates returns.
402	Final return of Andocides to Athens.
401	Sophocles' *Oedipus the King.*
399	Death of Socrates. Plato withdraws to Megara.

This three-part Chronology is compiled from Jebb's *Attic Orators* Vol. I, Harvey's *Oxford Companion to Classical Literature,* Blakeney's *Smaller Classical Dictionary,* Kennedy's *The Art of Persuasion in Greece,* and other sources.

Appendix D
A List of References

The translations, books, and articles listed below have been useful in preparing this edition of *The Speeches of Thucydides*. Every hour spent in trying to understand Athenian life in the Age of Pericles will enable the reader to interpret the speeches far more sympathetically. The following topics, if pursued in some of these references, will be most rewarding: Early Rhetoric in Sicily (Gorgias and Tisias), The Sophists, The Athenian Ecclesia, Pericles and Aspasia, Alcibiades and the Hermae Affair, Athenian Naval Warfare, Democracy according to Peµicles, Why Thucydides Lost his Command, The Attic Orators, Herodotus as Historian, Slavery in Athens, The Role of Women in Athens, Athens according to Plato, The Athenian Playwrights of about 431-404 B.C., The Gorgianic Figures, Anaxagoras, Socrates, The Role of the *Strategos*, The Parthenon, The Written and the Spoken Word, The Peace of Nicias, Was Thucydides "a Scientific Historian?", Socrates and Alcibiades — Friends or Actors?, Herodotus and Thucydides, Were the Teachings of the Sophists Harmful or Good?, Why Did Athens Fail as an Empire?, The Place of Speeches in Historical Writing.

Translations

Richard Crawley, translator, *History of the Peloponnesian War* by Thucydides. Introduction by John Warrington. Everyman's Library. New York: E.P. Dutton & Co., Inc., 1903.

John H. Finley, Jr., editor, *The Complete Writings of Thucydides: The Peloponnesian War*. (Crawley translation). New York: Random House (Modern Library), 1954.

Benjamin Jowett, translator, *Thucydides, The Peloponnesian War*, with introductory essays by Hanson Baldwin and Moses Hadas. New York: Bantam Books, Inc., 1960.

Sir R.W. Livingstone, editor, *Thucydides, The History of the Peloponnesian War*. (Crawley-Feetham translation). London: Oxford University Press, World's Classics, 1951.

George Rawlinson, translator, *Herodotus: The Persian Wars*. Introduction by Francis R.B. Godolphin. New York: Modern Library, 1941.

Charles Forster Smith, translator, *Thucydides, History of the Peloponnesian War*, 4 vols., Loeb series. London and New York: Heinemann and G.P. Putnam's Sons, 1919-1923.

Rex Warner, translator, *Thucydides: History of the Peloponnesian War.* Baltimore: Penguin Books, 1954.

Books

F.E. Adcock, *The Greek and Macedonian Art of War.* Berkeley and Los Angeles: University of California Press, 1967.

Friedrich Blass, *Die Attische Beredsamkeit von Gorgias bes zu Lysias.* Leipzig: Teubner, 1868.

S.F. Bonner, *The Literary Treatises of Dionysius of Halicarnassus.* Cambridge: Cambridge University Press, 1939.

C.M. Bowra, *Periclean Athens,* London: Weidenfeld and Nicolson, 1971.

Donald C. Bryant and others, editors, *Ancient Greek and Roman Rhetoricians.* Columbia, Mo.: The Artcraft Press, 1968.

J.B. Bury, *The Ancient Greek Historians.* London: Macmillan, 1909.

————, *A History of Greece.* New York: Modern Library, 1937.

S.H. Butcher, *Some Aspects of the Greek Genius* [esp. ch. 5 on "The Written and the Spoken Word"]. London: Macmillan, 1893.

Donald L. Clark, *Rhetoric in Greco-Roman Education.* New York: Columbia University Press, 1957.

Sir Edward S. Creasy, *The Fifteen Decisive Battles of the World* [ch. II deals with the Battle of Syracuse]. New York: Everyman's Library, Dutton, 1962.

J.F. Dobson, *The Greek Orators.* London: Methuen and Co. Ltd., 1919.

John H. Finley, Jr., *Four Stages in Greek Thought.* Stanford: Stanford University Press, 1966.

————, *Three Essays on Thucydides.* Cambridge: Harvard University Press, 1967.

————, *Thucydides.* Cambridge: Harvard University Press, 1942. London: Oxford University Press, 1947. Also, Ann Arbor paperback, Ann Arbor: University of Michigan Press, 1963.

M.I. Finley, *The Greek Historians.* New York: Viking Press, 1959.

A.W. Gomme, *Essays in Greek History,* Oxford: Blackwell, 1937.

————, *Greece.* Oxford: Oxford University Press, 1945.

————, *The Greek Attitude to Poetry and History.* Berkeley and Los Angeles: University of California Press, 1954.

————, *A Historical Commentary on Thucydides.* Oxford: Oxford University Press, 3 vols., 1956.

Peter Green, *Achilles and His Armour,* New York: Doubleday and Company, 1967.

David Grene, *Greek Political Theory, The Image of Man in Thucydides and Plato.* Chicago: University of Chicago Press, 1965.

G.M.A. Grube, *The Greek and Roman Critics.* Toronto: The University of Toronto Press, 1965.

G.B. Grundy, *Thucydides and the History of His Age.* London: Murray, 1911. Second edition, Oxford: Blackwell, 1948.

Edith Hamilton, *The Greek Way.* New York: Norton, 1930.

Eric A. Havelock, *The Liberal Temper in Greek Politics.* New Haven: Yale University Press, 1957.

B.W. Henderson, *The Great War between Athens and Sparta.* London: Macmillan, 1927.

Knox C. Hill, *Interpreting Literature* [ch. 5 and Appendix II discuss the Funeral Oration]. Chicago: The University of Chicago Press, 1966.

Richard C. Jebb, *The Attic Orators from Antiphon to Isaeos.* 2 vols., London: Macmillan, 1876.

————, *The Rhetoric of Aristotle.* Edited by J.E. Sandys. Cambridge: Cambridge University Press, 1909.

Donald Kagan, *The Great Dialogue. History of Greek Political Thought from Homer to Polybius.* New York: The Free Press, 1965.

————, *The Outbreak of the Peloponnesian War.* Ithaca: Cornell University Press, 1969.

George Kennedy, *The Art of Persuasion in Greece.* London: Routledge and Kegan Paul, 1963. Princeton: Princeton University Press, 1963.

H.D.F. Kitto, *The Greeks.* Baltimore: Penguin Books, 1963.

————, *Poiesis: Structure and Thought.* Berkeley and Los Angeles: University of California Press, 1966.

Helen North, *Sophrosyne: Self Knowledge and Self Restraint in Greek Literature.* Ithaca: Cornell University Press, 1966.

Lynn and Gray Poole, *The Magnificent Traitor. A Novel of Alcibiades and the Golden Age of Pericles.* New York: Dodd, Mead and Co., 1968.

W. Rhys Roberts, *Greek Rhetoric and Literary Criticism.* New York: Longmans Green, 1928.

C.A. Robinson, Jr., *Athens in the Age of Pericles.* Norman: University of Oklahoma Press, 1959.

Jacqueline de Romilly, *Thucydides and Athenian Imperialism.* Translated by Philip Thody. Oxford: Blackwell, 1963.

Arnold J. Toynbee, *Greek Civilization and Character.* New York: New American Library, 1953.

F.W. Walbank, *Speeches in Greek Historians* (the third J.L. Myres Lecture). Oxford: Blackwell, 1966.

Rex Warner, *Men of Athens.* New York: Viking Press, 1972.

H. D. Westlake, *Individuals in Thucydides.* Cambridge: Cambridge University Press, 1968.

Henry Musgrave Wilkins, *Speeches from Thucydides* (translated into English). London: Longmans, Green and Co., 1873.

A. Geoffrey Woodhead, *Thucydides on the Nature of Power.* Cambridge: Harvard University Press, 1970.

The World of Classical Athens. Edited by Giulio Giannelli, translated by Walter Darwell. New York: G.P. Putnam's Sons, 1970.

Sir Alfred Zimmern, *The Greek Commonwealth.* New York: Galaxy Books, 1962.

Articles

A. Andrewes, "The Mytelene Debate." *Phoenix* 1962, 64-85.

————, "Thucydides on the Causes of the War." *Classical Quarterly* n.s. 9 (1959), 223-39.

F.H. Colson, "Some Considerations as to the Influence of Rhetoric on History." *Proceedings of the Classical Association*, vol. XIV (Jan. 1917), 149-173.

Richard C. Jebb, "The Speeches of Thucydides," in *Essays and Addresses.* Cambridge, 1907. Also in E. Abbott, *Hellenica.* London: Longmans, 2nd ed., 1898.

R.W. Macan, "Herodotus and Thucydides," *Cambridge Ancient History*, vol. V, 398-419. Cambridge, 1937.

Paul Shorey, "Implicit Ethics and Psychology of Thucydides," *Transactions of American Philological Association*, 1893, 66-88.

W.P. Wallace, "Thucydides," *Phoenix* 1964, 251-61.

A. Zimmern, "Thucydides, the Imperialist," in *Solon and Croesus.* Oxford, 1928.

Appendix E
Maps

I
The Greek World, 431 B.C.

II
Greece

III
Athens and the Piraeus

IV
Pylos and Sphacteria

V
Syracuse, 415-413 B.C.

The Greek World, 431 B.C.

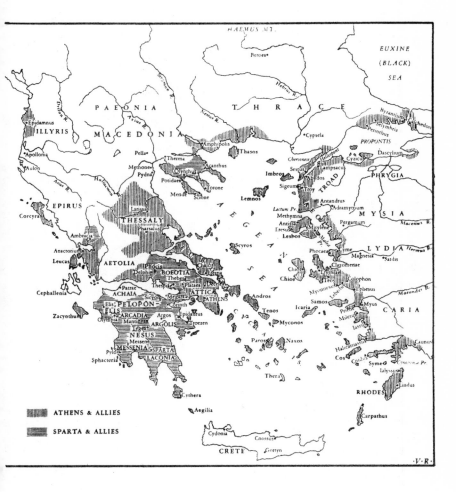

ATHENS & ALLIES

SPARTA & ALLIES

Greece

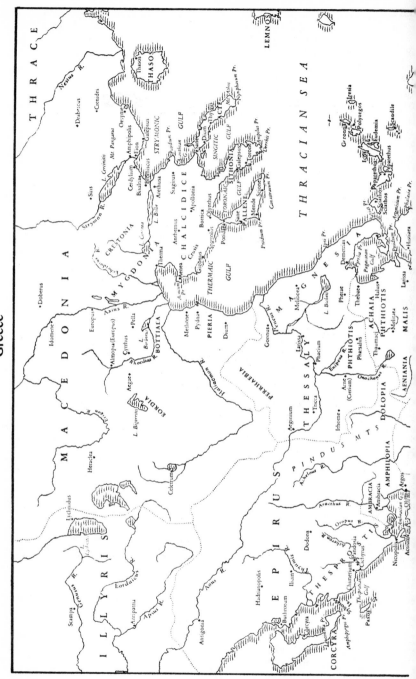

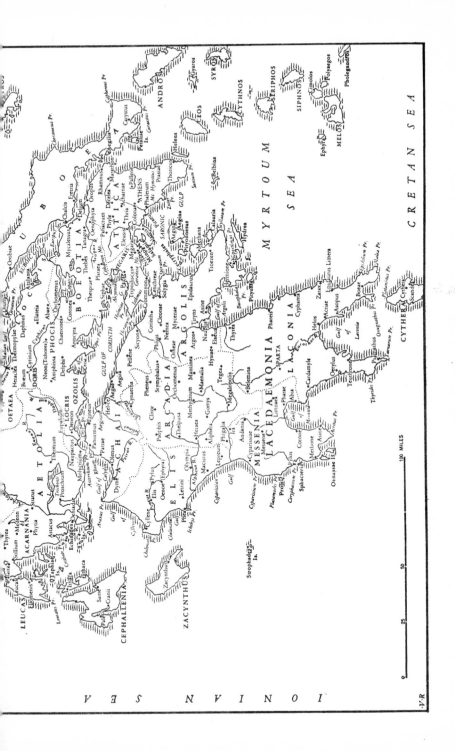

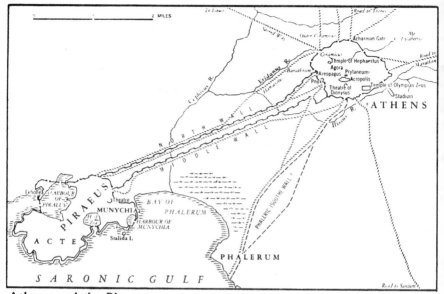

Athens and the Piraeus

Pylos and Sphacteria

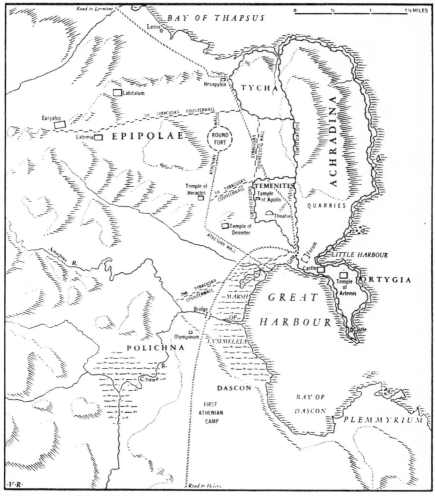

Syracuse, 415-413 B.C.

Index

The sequence of the speeches with dates is to be found in the Table of Contents. This index provides references to the Introduction, the headnotes to the speeches, the speeches themselves, the editor's essay on the speeches of Pericles, the essay on the military harangues, the Appendices: (A) The Speeeches of Thucydides by Sir Richard C. Jebb, (B) Intellectual Background by John H. Finley, Jr., (C) A Chronology of Principal Events, (D) A List of References, (E) Maps. The essays by Jebb and Finley are further commentaries on the speeches. The references are for those who wish to pursue special studies.

DATE DUE

7/13			
FEB 8	1979		
MAR 2	7 1979		
GAYLORD			PRINTED IN U.S.A.